THE IMPORTANCE OF LEARNING STYLES

Recent Titles in
Contributions to the Study of Education

The Vision of the Public Junior College, 1900–1940: Professional Goals and Popular Aspirations
John H. Frye

Adult Education for Community Development
Edwin Hamilton

Archetypal Forms in Teaching
William A. Reinsmith

Labor Relations in Education: An International Perspective
Bruce S. Cooper, editor

The Emerging Worldwide Electronic University
Parker Rossman

A New History of Educational Philosophy
James S. Kaminsky

Does College Make a Difference?: Long-Term Changes in Activities and Attitudes
William E. Knox, Paul Lindsay, and Mary N. Kolb

Assessing What Professors Do: An Introduction to Academic Performance Appraisal in Higher Education
David A. Dilts, Lawrence J. Haber, and Donna Bialik

Encounters with Difference: Student Perceptions of the Role of Out-of-Class Experiences in Education Abroad
Michael R. Laubscher

Public School Reform in Puerto Rico: Sustaining Colonial Models of Development
José Solís

Diversifying Historically Black Colleges: A New Higher Education Paradigm
Serbrenia J. Sims

Socialization and Education: Essays in Conceptual Criticism
Wolfgang Brezinka

THE IMPORTANCE OF LEARNING STYLES

Understanding the Implications for Learning, Course Design, and Education

Edited by Ronald R. Sims
and Serbrenia J. Sims

Contributions to the Study of Education,
Number 64

Greenwood Press
Westport, Connecticut • London

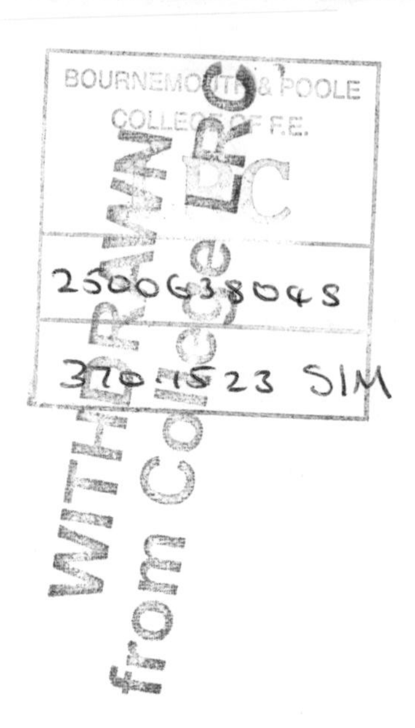

Library of Congress Cataloging-in-Publication Data

The importance of learning styles : understanding the implications for learning, course design, and education / edited by Ronald R. Sims and Serbrenia J. Sims.
p. cm. — (Contributions to the study of education, ISSN 0196–707X ; no. 64)
Includes bibliographical references and index.
ISBN 0–313–29278–7 (alk. paper)
1. Learning, Psychology of. 2. Education, Higher. 3. Cognitive styles. I. Sims, Ronald R. II. Sims, Serbrenia J. III. Series.
LB1060.I46 1995
370.15'23—dc20 94–41665

British Library Cataloguing in Publication Data is available.

Library of Congress Catalog Card Number: 94–41665
ISBN: 0–313–29278–7
ISSN: 0196–707X

First published in 1995

Greenwood Press, 88 Post Road West, Westport, CT 06881
An imprint of Greenwood Publishing Group, Inc.

Printed in the United States of America

The paper used in this book complies with the Permanent Paper Standard issued by the National Information Standards Organization (Z39.48–1984).

10 9 8 7 6 5 4 3 2

To Ronald, Jr., Marchet, Vellice, Nandi, Dangaia, and Sieya

Contents

Illustrations

FIGURES

TABLES

Preface

Perhaps at no other time has there been more discussion, thinking, and tension about issues in higher education than there is now. Of major concern is the question of how to teach to the motivational and learning characteristics of students who make up an increasingly diverse student body. Thus, one of the most significant challenges that higher education instructors and trainers face is to be tolerant and perceptive enough to recognize learning differences among their students and trainees.

While much has been written about learning styles, many higher education instructors and trainers still do not realize that students vary in the way that they process and understand information or attempt to respond to those differences in their pedagogical efforts. The notion that all cognitive skills are identical at the collegiate level or in different training programs smacks of arrogance and elitism by either sanctioning one group's style of learning while discrediting the styles of others or ignoring individual differences altogether.

Effective teaching and training cannot be limited to the delivery of information; rather, it needs to be based on a model of minds at work. Effective instructors are those who understand the importance of involving all of their students in learning how to learn. Effective learning occurs when instructors affirm the presence and validity of diverse learning styles and maximize the climate or conditions for learning in and out of the classroom through the deliberate use of instructional design principles that take account of learning differences and increase the possibilities of success for all learners.

Although individuals learn continually, they do have preferences about how they learn. Thus, everyone has a learning style. However, there exists a confusing array of definitions of learning style, a term often used interchangeably with cognitive style or learning ability. Prior to the mid-1970s, researchers experimented with cognitive style; their definitions were different, but all were concerned with how the mind actually processed information or was affected by individual perceptions. After the early 1970s other writers and researchers developed varied definitions, models, instruments, and techniques for assessing individual learning characteristics. In some ways those models differed, but many revealed essential similarities and were mutually supportive.

How a person learns is the focus of the concept of learning style. Learning styles can be defined as characteristic cognitive, affective, and physiological behaviors that serve as relatively stable indicators of how learners perceive, interact with, and respond to the learning environment. Because there have been and will continue to be studies aimed at improving learning, instructors and their institutions, trainers and organizations will need to increase their understanding of how people learn and be aware of the wide array of individual learning styles, instrumentation, and implications of individual learning styles to learning success.

The extensive work on learning styles has increased in importance to the higher education and training community. Yet, despite the significant amount of research on learning styles that has appeared over the years in scholarly journals and practitioner-oriented articles, there is not presently a book that takes a comprehensive look at the concept of learning styles and its implications for enhancing individual learning, instructor effectiveness, and course design and education. This book is intended to fill the void by providing a look at the important relationship between identifying an individual's learning style and how providing appropriate instruction and training in response to that style can contribute to more effective learning. The book relies on experts in the field of learning and learning style research and examines how learning styles can enhance learning in light of the challenges confronting today's private, public, and not-for-profit organizations and institutions of higher education. These organizations are addressing challenges to established teaching modes brought about by the increasing social and cultural diversity of students and call for greater accountability and increased assessment of the quality of their instruction.

The contributing authors discuss the advantages and disadvantages of different learning style models, instruments, and techniques for assessing individual learning characteristics. In addition, the authors share their views on the future of learning style research and its implications for enhancing learning in higher education institutions and other organizations.

Chapter 1, "Learning Enhancement in Higher Education," discusses the concepts of learning, accepted principles of learning, and the importance of understanding individual learning differences in higher education while highlighting the components of an instructional system within an experiential learning model. Chapter 2, "Learning Styles: A Survey of Adult Learning Style Inventory Models," offers a review of several major North American, European, and Australian learning styles or cognitive style inventories, presents some learning style research on various ethnic populations, and discusses the relevance of inventory information in reference to the assessment of the quality of instruction and training. Chapter 3, "Increasing the Effectiveness of University and College Instruction: Integrating the Results of Learning Style Research into Course Design and Delivery," reviews relevant learning style research and presents the argument that the concept of learning styles is an important element in the design of effective instructional practices and delivery.

Chapter 4, "Toward a Framework for Matching Teaching and Learning Styles for Diverse Populations," argues that a thorough understanding of learning styles becomes more critical when applied to diverse populations and their success and failure in learning environments and suggests that a deductive model can be used to approach the development of a learning style–teaching style paradigm for diverse populations. Chapter 5, "Learning Styles and the Changing Face of Community Colleges," reviews the range of literature directly relating learning style inquiry with both the area of adult learning and the community and discusses findings from a recent study that suggest an institutional bias toward one major style over another, raising doubts about community colleges' current ability to address the national educational challenge. In Chapter 6, "The Importance of Learning Styles in Total Quality Management-Oriented College and University Courses," illustrates the role of learning styles in an Organizational Behavior course delivered under a Total Quality Management approach and offers useful suggestions for others interested in developing similar courses.

Chapter 7, "Adapting Faculty and Student Learning Styles: Implications for Accounting Education," discusses the importance of managing the learning process in accounting programs by adapting teaching methods to particular learning styles. Chapter 8, "Using Experiential Learning Theory and Learning Styles in Diversity Education," applies the experiential learning theories of David Kolb and Paulo Freire to formulate ideas about delivering effective diversity education. Chapter 9, "Experiential Learning: Preparing Students to Move from the Classroom to the Work Environment," offers some suggestions on how to correct the problem of the link between classroom learning and the work environment by emphasizing the need for the student to be a proactive participant within her or his education.

Chapter 10, "The Nature of Adult Learning and Effective Training Guidelines," presents a model and approach to training adult learners in adult human service practice training settings to do individual interviewing and assessment of social problems. Chapter 11, "The Learning Model for Managers, A Tool to Facilitate Learning," discusses how this tool can be used to identify managers' learning styles in a variety of settings and facilitate team building, training program design, employee development, and multicultural understanding. Chapter 12, "Learning and Learning Styles: A Review and Look to the Future," provides a review of key points highlighted throughout the book and discusses other ideas that can increase our effectiveness in understanding, assessing, and using learning styles to enhance individual's learning.

Acknowledgments

A special thanks to Herrington Bryce of the College of William and Mary, who is both an appreciated friend and mentor. The administrative support of the College of William and Mary is also acknowedged. A special thanks to Phyllis Viandis and Terry Trojack. And finally, Ronald, Jr., Marchet, Vellice, Nandi, Dangaia, and Sieya continue to inspire our efforts to share our views with others.

THE IMPORTANCE OF LEARNING STYLES

1

Learning Enhancement in Higher Education

Ronald R. Sims and Serbrenia J. Sims

Institutions of higher education are always looking for ways to make their educational initiatives more effective. Higher education administrators and instructors at all levels are constantly under pressure to provide more effective and efficient services. In colleges and universities, teaching serves as an important vehicle for achieving institutional goals of increased effectiveness, efficiency, and the enhancement of student learning. As a result, today's highly successful colleges and universities are distinguished by the ability to have their faculties continue to improve their efforts to advance student learning. For many of today's and tomorrow's students, success in a changing world will require an ability to explore new opportunities and learn from past successes and failures. These ideas are neither new nor controversial. Yet it is surprising that understanding how people learn, which is so widely regarded as important, receives little ongoing and explicit attention by educators and their institutions. Too often there is a kind of fatalism about learning; one either learns or one does not. The inability to consciously control and manage the learning process in higher education in general, and various classes in particular, lies in a lack of understanding about the learning process itself and can serve as a substantial impediment to student learning and faculty teaching.

Educators must have more knowledge and understanding of the learning process, particularly how individuals learn. This will help them immensely in both the design and implementation of teaching that enhances learning. If educators relied upon models of how individuals learn, they would be better able to enhance their students' ability to learn. For example, Sims, Veres, and Heninger (1989) offered

Kolb's (1984) experiential learning model (ELM) as a framework for understanding ways in which the learning process and individual learning styles can affect learning. Thus, the effective management of the learning process by faculties in institutions of higher education requires that they create environments that facilitate a productive learning climate.

This chapter builds on this recent work by discussing the concept of learning, accepted principles of learning, and the importance of understanding individual learning differences in higher education. The chapter draws attention to what actually constitutes learning (that is, the learning process) and provides a brief discussion on adult learning theory and principles of learning. The chapter also discusses the importance of understanding how people learn and examines a model of experiential learning and thinking and learning styles. In addition, the chapter highlights components of an instructional system that enhances teaching and learning within the ELM. Finally, the chapter provides a discussion on teaching modes and learning enhancement.

LEARNING AND ADULT LEARNING THEORY

Learning has always been a major area of attention for many researchers interested in understanding the process of learning and its implications for educators and more recently trainers in selecting appropriate pedagogical methods in order to improve classroom instruction. Learning is one of the most important individual processes that occurs in organizations, higher education, and training programs. For purposes of this book, learning is defined as a relatively permanent change in an attitude or behavior that occurs as a result of repeated experience (Kimble & Garmezy, 1963).

Whether learning takes place in an institution of higher education or in a private, public, or not-for-profit organization, participants (that is, students or trainees) are expected to learn and apply their learning. Instructors and trainers can benefit from understanding and applying certain principles of learning when designing and implementing their learning or training programs. Because neglect or misapplication of principles of learning could easily result in educational endeavors that fail to achieve results, it is important that instructors and trainers become familiar with principles of learning and the basics of adult learning theory.

Knowles (1984) says that adults will learn "no matter what." Learning is as natural as rest or play. With or without books, visual aids, inspiring trainers, or classrooms, adults will manage to learn. Human resource management specialists can, however, make a difference in what people learn and in how well they learn it. If adults (and, many believe, children as well) know why they are learning, and if the reason fits their needs as they perceive them (the "so what?"), they will learn quickly and deeply.

Adult Learning Theory

Among the major theories of learning, behaviorism is fairly well defined, and most instructors and trainers in the United States associate the term and the theory with its leading contemporary proponent, B.F. Skinner. This is not the case in adult learning theory. There have been many adult learning theorists, researchers, and practitioners, each contributing an element to its development (see for example, Tough, 1979, 1982; Kidd, 1973; Houle, 1961). Malcolm Knowles's theory on adult learning has been used effectively in training in business and industry. Knowles (1980b; Knowles & Associates, 1984) has postulated his adult learning principles and practices under the banner of andragogy. A brief discussion of Knowles's adult learning theory will help the reader understand its usefulness in teaching or training efforts.

As commonly understood in the world of teaching and training, adherence to adult learning theory calls for the design of learning activities to be based on the learners' needs and interests so as to create opportunities for the learners to analyze their experience and its application to their work and life situations. The role of the instructor or trainer is to assist in a process of inquiry, analysis, and decision making with learners, rather than to transmit knowledge.

In the context of adult learning practices, the learner exercises greater autonomy in matching his or her preferred modes of learning to the specified learning objectives and also has more say about what the outcomes of the learning process are intended to be. The emphasis on methods that encourage insight and discovery makes it a familiar approach, close to the unstructured way many people have acquired new knowledge or developed new skills since reaching maturity.

Knowles says he originally defined andragogy as "the art and science of helping adults learn, in contrast to pedagogy as the art and science of teaching children" (1980, p. 43). Later he came to see andragogy as "simply another model of assumptions used alongside the pedagogical model . . . most useful when seen not as dichotomous but rather as two ends of a spectrum" (p. 43).

The principles and practices that fall under the umbrella of andragogy are based on several crucial assumptions about how adult learners are different from children. Margolis and Bell (1984) give us a useful summary of those assumptions, distilled from Knowles's major works (1980; Knowles & Associates, 1984):

1. Adults are motivated to learn as they develop needs and interests that learning will satisfy. Therefore, learners' needs and interests are the

appropriate starting points for organizing adult learning activities.

2. Adult orientation to learning is life- or work-centered. Therefore, the appropriate frameworks for organizing adult learning are life- or work-related situations, not academic or theoretical subjects.
3. Experience is the richest resource for adult learning. Therefore, the core methodology for adult learning programs involves active participation in a planned series of experiences, the analysis of those experiences, and their application to work and life situations.
4. Adults have a deep need to be self-directing. Therefore, the role of the HRM specialist is to engage in a process of inquiry, analysis, and decision making with learners.
5. Individual differences among adult learners increase with age and experience. Therefore, adult learning programs must make optimum provision for differences in style, time, place, and pace of learning. (p. 17)

There is growing evidence that use of the andragogical framework could make a difference in the way adult learning programs were organized and operated as well as in the way trainers and human resources managers saw their role in helping adults learn (Knowles & Associates, 1984).

Learning and Principles of Learning

In recent years there has been a significant shift in the focus of education in general, and adult learning in particular. Sheal (1989) notes that the emphasis has moved from the teacher, the transmission of information, and how best this can be improved, to a focus on the learner and how best to promote learning. With this in mind, a key question that must be answered by any higher education administrator or instructor interested in enhancing learning is What is learning and how does it occur?

Theories of learning have evolved over the last century as a result of numerous experiments that have been conducted, often with animals. Different schools of psychological thinking have made their various contributions to the pool of knowledge. No single theory has obtained complete agreement among psychologists about the details of the learning process, but many accept the basic premise that learning occurs whenever one adopts new or modifies existing behavior patterns in a way that has some influence on future performance or attitudes.

There are a variety of definitions of learning, each one of them highlighting one or more aspects of learning activity. Sheal (1989) notes that theorists tend to agree, however, that learning involves:

An active rather than a passive process. Few people now think of learning as receiving instruction. Instead learning is increasingly defined as an activity in which learners participate and are directly involved.

A relatively permanent change in behavior. Robert Gagne (1985) writes, "The change may be, and often is, an increased capability for some kind of performance. It may also be an altered disposition of the sort called attitude or interest or value" (p. 2).

The acquisition of additional information, skills, or attitudes. Learning then may be simply an addition to what you know or can do already — your present knowledge and skills + X. The additional element, the X factor, produces change. Kidd (1973) writes: "Learning results in certain kinds of changes, the most common being the committing to memory of facts, the acquiring or improvement of a skill or process, the development of a changed attitude" (p. 24). Learning, however, may also be a subtraction such as unlearning a bad or ineffective habit. It may be a modification where old knowledge, skills, and abilities or attitudes are adjusted to cope with new circumstances.

Harris and Scwahn (1961) point out that learning is essentially change due to experience, but then go on to distinguish between learning as a product, which explains the end result or outcome of the learning experience; learning as a process, which emphasizes what happens during the course of the learning experience in attaining a given learning product or outcome; and learning as a function, which emphasizes certain critical aspects of learning, such as motivation, retention, and transfer, and which makes behavioral changes in human learning possible.

Whether teaching takes place in or out of the classroom, students are expected to learn. Because teaching is intended to result in learning, higher education instructors can benefit from understanding and applying certain principles of learning when designing and implementing their teaching initiatives. Also, because neglect or misapplication of principles of learning could easily result in teaching that fails to achieve results, it is important that instructors become familiar with the underlying principles of learning.

According to Sims (1993), learning may not take place if the teaching is not structured to facilitate learning, even when the teaching mode is appropriate. Learning factors (principles) that will affect the learning of students and the success of teaching efforts are: setting the stage — providing clear instructions and modeling appropriate behavior when emphasizing particular skills or competencies; increasing learning during teaching — providing active participation, increasing self-efficacy, matching teaching techniques to students' self-efficacy, providing opportunities for inactive mastery, ensuring specific, timely, diagnostic, and practical feedback, and providing opportunities for students to practice new behaviors; and maintaining basic knowledge in particular areas — developing learning points to assist in knowledge retention, setting specific goals, identifying appropriate reinforcers, teaching students how to reinforce their learning, and teaching students how to take responsibility for their own learning. These factors indicate that the instructor must ensure that the environment is made ready for learning.

Although incorporating these principles of learning is desirable, many courses do not have them or are designed without consideration of individual learning differences and motivation. Nevertheless, application of these principles can increase the learning that occurs during teaching. Another powerful link to successful teaching is an increased appreciation and understanding of what is known about the types of learning and how individuals learn (differences in learning strategies).

TOWARD A BETTER UNDERSTANDING OF HOW PEOPLE LEARN

The learner is the primary focus of the instructional system. Understanding how students learn is an important part of selecting appropriate teaching strategies (Bentz, 1974). Research into how people learn has advanced along two major schools. The first is the stimulus-response school, best exemplified by Pavlov's classical conditioning research and by Skinner's work in operant conditioning. This view focuses on reinforcement of step-by-step mastery of content and skills.

The second school is the cognitive approach, which focuses on the cognitive processes as the source of learning. This school is exemplified by the early work of the Gestaltists and by Piaget's work in developing a continuum of cognitive development. Cognitive learning means knowledge learning. It not only includes the knowledge per se, but also what to do with it or how to apply it. Thus the investigative process and the principles of problem solving and decision making are part of this group. Much learning of this nature is imparted by the lecture method (this and other teaching or learning methods will be discussed in more detail later in this chapter), but can be reinforced by a variety of learning methods such as private study, role plays, and case studies. The cognitive view has dominated most contemporary research on how humans learn.

A recent extension of the cognitive view is the ELM. This model describes the four-stage learning cycle that individuals move through in order to effectively learn and apply concepts. The model has its roots in the psychological literature and has recently been advanced by Kolb (1984). This learning theory states that individuals have two major competing dimensions of learning: the concrete/abstract and the active/reflective. The concrete/abstract dimension indicates how a human processes experience and information. Over time, most individuals develop preferences for a specific dimension by selecting one of the two competing dimensions of the learning cycle: concrete versus abstract and active versus reflective. These preferences are a result of personal experiences, personality differences, and environmental and prior educational factors. One preference is not necessarily better or worse than another; the important fact is that these differences exist and must be recognized by an educator.

The four stages of the ELM are the polar points of the two learning dimensions. The four stages are: concrete experience, reflective observation, abstract conceptualization, and active experimentation. Kolb has assigned titles to the learning styles in each group. For example, divergers prefer concrete reflective learning situations. Convergers do best in abstract active learning situations, and so on with the assimilators and accommodators. Prior research has associated the learning styles with psychological attributes, choices of academic majors, preferences for certain types of instructional styles, and choices of vocations (Baker, Simon & Bazeli, 1987; Baldwin & Reckers, 1984; Freedman & Stumpf, 1978; and Sadler, Plovnick & Snope, 1978).

Kolb (1985) has developed an instrument, the Learning Style Inventory, which is an update from an earlier instrument, to measure the learning styles of individuals. Prior research by Kolb and others has shown an association between the states of the learning cycle and the type of instructional strategy that is most effective in that state (Kolb, 1984).

The basis of learning research must be the individual learner, because that is the learning unit. However, most teaching efforts today are made at the classroom level with a relatively large group of students. Thus, while the teaching approaches are at the class (macro) level, learning must take place at the individual student (micro) level. The challenge to the teacher is to attempt to bridge this gap. Unfortunately, there are too many instances in which instructors fail to bridge the gap and some students in colleges and universities experience something of a culture shock.

Fresh from a world of courses where there are right and wrong answers or concrete-specific problems that they must solve, they may be suddenly immersed in a strange world of generalities where the elegant solution to course problems is sought even when the supposed right solutions have been found. This culture shock is compounded because many instructors still are not aware of what actually constitutes learning for diverse students in their courses. Unfortunately, teaching goes on in the same old way, completely disregarding how individual students process information — their learning style.

Is this kind of teaching successful? It is if the teaching is auditory and the student's learning modality is auditory, if the teaching is visual and the student is visual, if the teaching is tactile-kinesthetic and the student is tactile-kinesthetic. It is if the teaching matches the student's learning preference — affective, perceptive, symbolic, or behavioral — or if the student has a happy combination of all of these learning styles. If not, the odds against success increase dramatically. In fact, higher education administrators and instructors responsible for the success of their teaching efforts can no longer afford to assume that all students will learn through whichever strategy the teacher prefers to use. Why gamble with the potential success of a teaching effort? For the student who has been unsuccessful with previous teaching styles, learning is a misery, and there is little chance that in the next course or class the student will suddenly adjust his or her learning style or even be capable of adjusting.

Higher education administrators and instructors need to decide whether they want students to adjust or to learn. If learning is the objective, then new mind-capturing techniques must be developed and applied for teaching efforts to be successful. The needs of students are different and changing, and this problem must be continually addressed in teaching efforts. More importantly, how students learn must be given top priority, or instructors may never be fully successful in capturing their attention and minds. In reality, it may be more important for instructors to have an understanding of the learning process and skill in facilitating individual and group learning than subject matter skill.

In discussing how students learn, one cannot ignore the question of how learning takes place. Hence, an evaluation procedure is necessary. If rote memorization is not the objective or even an indication that something has been learned, then other methods must be used. Most instructors would insist that the student demonstrate an ability to use the concepts emphasized in the course and an understanding of the evidence that supports the concepts — the structure of the concept.

What is happening in the mind of the student while in a class solving a problem? An answer to this question, how people learn, would help an instructor discover what can be done to help a student learn. There are those experts that maintain that the current issue regarding learning theory is whether the acquisition of knowledge is something that happens to the student or something that a student does or achieves. Whether it is something that happens or something a student achieves, the question still boils down to what is happening in the mind of the student when this is taking place.

John Dewey's (1938) description of how people learn generally included the following elements in some form: "Thinking is initiated only when a person perceives a problem, the person then tries to clarify the exact nature of the problem in order to determine possible solutions" (p. 39). In this endeavor, a person seeks to find relevant solutions and tries to use prior knowledge to understand the problem. The next step is to formulate a hypothesis that might solve the problem. Once tested, the hypothesis may solve the problem. If the problem is solved, Dewey maintains, learning has taken place.

In the teaching environment, students can be given information by their instructor, but unless those students are actively engaged in analyzing an issue, that is, using the information in problem solving and action, it is sterile. "Information severed from thoughtful action is dead, a mindcrushing load" (Dewey, 1938, p. 186). According to Dewey, thinking and learning evolved because they are vital for survival in humans as well as animals. If in nature "thinking was stimulated by problems that the learner was vitally interested in solving, the learner was both physically and mentally active and alert and engaged" (Dewey, 1938, p. 186). The same should be true in the higher education setting.

As noted earlier, work by others (Sims & Sims, 1991; Sims, Veres, & Heninger, 1989) has shown that Kolb's (1984) ELM and accompanying learning styles (1985) can assist those interested in better understanding individual learning differences. Like Kolb's work on learning styles, the work of Sperry, Gazzaniga and Bogen (1969) on brain hemisphericity and thinking styles can also prove beneficial to the higher education instructors in better understanding learning differences and their effect on learning and the learning process.

Brain Hemisphericity and Thinking Styles

Research on right and left brain functions began with Roger Sperry during the 1950s (Sperry, 1973; McCarthy, 1980). In the early 1960s, Sperry and his colleagues (Sperry, Gazzaniga, & Bogen, 1969) established that the human brain actually functions in many ways as two brains and that the way in which we experience the world and experience teaching is fundamentally affected by which hemisphere of our brain is dominant.

It had been known that the functions of the two hemispheres were different. Each hemisphere of the brain has its own critical function and value to life. While the right hemisphere is the initial receiver of all incoming information, the left side is called the dominant hemisphere because it is where language and speech are produced (Sperry, 1973; McCarthy, 1980).

In processing information and stimuli, the left brain does a lineal, rational, sequential type of processing, while the right brain uses a global process in which data is perceived, absorbed, and processed even while it is in the process of changing. Experiments have shown that people who tend, or have been trained, to use one side of the brain more than the other (accountants and engineers versus artists and musicians) find it difficult to switch when necessary. However, when the weaker side of the brain is stimulated and encouraged to cooperate with the stronger side, there is a great increase in ability and effectiveness.

Just as people are right- or left-handed, studies have shown that most individuals favor the thinking style of one side of the brain or the other, although there are those who use each hemisphere equally. Statistics show that approximately 30 percent or more of all adults are right-brained (Hodgetts, 1991). For years, society has nurtured only individuals with an analytical left brain. In fact, Albert Einstein, a great genius, was removed from grade school because he was thought to be dumb. However, in reality, Einstein may have been totally right-brained.

The thinking styles of individuals can be observed in their behaviors. Left-brain-dominant individuals are highly structured, more logical, and organized (Hines, 1987; Lynch, 1986). They utilize their motor skills with ease and tend to down-play visual methods of thinking. They prefer a more analytical approach to problem solving. In addition, they tend to be good in day-to-day implementation of programs, in seeing that plans and procedures are followed, at following through with reports and paperwork, and at getting people down to the basics. They are unemotional, logical, and rational in working with crises. Some liabilities associated with a left-brain preference are: they have problems seeing the total picture (want simple answers to complex problems), are not creative in planning and organization (stick to rules only), are not creative in program design, are inflexible in decision making, and upset others due to an unemotional approach to human relations. They fight against change and want the status quo (Piatt, 1983). Right-brain-dominant individuals prefer to think more holistically, are artistic in nature, quiet, less reliant on words and logic, and are generally less organized (Taggart & Robey, 1981; Robey & Taggart, 1981). They are more spatially oriented and creative in problem solving, planning, and decision making. In addition, they are good in brainstorming sessions, initial program design, interpersonal relations and people-centered positions, and people motivation. Some of the liabilities associated with a right brain processing preference are: they do not follow through with the details of the tasks; allow subordinates too much freedom without adequate follow-up; complete tasks in ways which may not be compatible with directives, procedures, etc.; alter the original designs and programs to fit their way of doing them; and use emotions instead of logic (Piatt, 1983).

Higher education instructors can enhance learning in their teaching initiatives by understanding that like learning styles, each thinking style has its own strengths and weaknesses and students can benefit by knowing and consciously using the side of their brain that is best equipped for certain kinds of tasks. What does all this mean to the higher education instructor?

Applications of Learning and Thinking Styles to Teaching

With increased calls for accountability and assessment in higher education and calls for a greater acceptance and appreciation of individual differences, higher education instructors cannot afford not to increase their understanding of learning and individual learning differences. By using such information, the instructors will be better able to design and use teaching as a vehicle for leveraging student learning (for example, by identifying individual learning strategies and, where appropriate, matching them to teaching modes). That is not to say that students should not be periodically exposed to contextual demands that do not precisely match their styles. But, as for the future, instructors need to do more in utilizing accepted learning theories, principles, and teaching technology that will enhance learning and assist students in developing themselves to their full potentials.

There are several applications of the concept of learning and the learning theories discussed in this chapter to higher education's efforts to enhance learning. These applications are as follows:

1. Knowledge about one's own brain hemisphericity and learning style can aid instructors in identifying strengths and weaknesses in their teaching methods. The task for the instructors is to understand that both sides of the brain are active in the teaching and learning process. Instructors must identify and accept the fact that all individuals prefer to learn in one way or another or to use one side of the brain over the other to solve problems, interact with peers, and meet the challenges of daily life. This acceptance must be shown by students, even though the style may differ from their preferred style.

2. The faculty can improve teaching effectiveness and learner productivity by taking note of their own thinking styles and sharing this information with each other and students. With this information, instructors can better understand what inhibits, frustrates, or promotes learning. Knowledge of learning styles or whole-brain thinking can assist individuals in becoming more flexible and effective in teaching, both in and out of the classroom.

3. Identification of learning preferences will better enable the instructor to identify and accept his or her own preferences in teaching. Identification and acceptance of specific learning or thinking styles are essential in the teaching process of all individuals. For example, left-brain-dominant instructors and students prefer outlines, rigid didactic environments, straight lecture, and long reading assignments (for example, case studies). Rarely do they discuss or wish to discuss the assigned outlines during teaching. Right-brain-dominant teachers prefer the use of stories, experiential problem solving, and visual transparencies. They become frustrated with long reading assignments, time restrictions on assignments, and outlines that left-brain-dominant teachers like to use. Right-brain-dominant students also enjoy unstructured experiential learning sessions instead of straight lecture periods.

4. To meet the learning needs of students, instructors must consider their own teaching methods. Teachers must develop and use teaching methodologies that will effectively teach to all four learning styles and both right and left brain modes. Right-brained students may need to have more outlines and more structure in their teaching or learning experiences. Left-brained students may need to have more

unstructured teaching experiences (for example, experiential discussion periods).

5. Instructors should improve the learning climate of courses and classes by predicting learning difficulties. For example, they should anticipate who will respond most positively to different teaching methods or activities. Predictions like these are useful because they enable the instructor to handle the design of a particular teaching environment more appropriately from the start, rather than feeling his or her way for a period as students' learning tendencies gradually reveal themselves.

Higher education instructors must take stock of their own and students' learning skills and, if abilities in any one of the learning styles or on either side of the brain are lacking, seek to develop them to reach their fullest potential and assist students to do so as well. Students should also increase their understanding of the available learning or teaching methods.

In addition to understanding how individuals learn, we believe that it is important for instructors to understand some accepted assumptions about instructional design in conjunction with their decisions to select instructional strategy from among the many that are available (Baker, Simon, & Bazeli, 1987). Such an understanding should increase the likelihood of students' learning and the effectiveness of the teaching endeavor.

ENHANCING LEARNING: THE ROLE OF INSTRUCTIONAL DESIGN

Instruction is a function of the interrelationships between such factors as the organization of the body of knowledge of a discipline, the instructional objectives of a course, the modes of instruction employed by the instructor within the instructional system, and student-based factors such as learning styles, intellectual development, previous learning, and motivation.

Instructional design is the process of selecting a series of events to facilitate learning. This process requires the instructor to operate within an instructional system and select those specific aspects of the system that he or she determines will result in the desired learning. How is instruction to be designed? Some basic assumptions are necessary to guide the instructor's decision-making process. A widely known model of instructional design has been developed by Gagne and Briggs (1979, pp. 4–5), and has the following basic characteristics:

Instructional design must be aimed at aiding the learning of the individual, not a group or class of individuals. Learning must occur within each member of the group.

Instructional design has phases that are both immediate and long-range. Immediate concerns are the day-to-day decisions that are often made while the instructor is preparing for that day's class. Long-range concerns are centered on the design of a course or sequence of courses. Thus, instructional design involves curricular design at the program-wide level as well as at the level of what should be in the daily content of a specific course.

Systematically designed instruction can greatly affect individual human development. The instruction should be designed so that all students have opportunities to develop their talents to the fullest degree.

Instructional design should be conducted by means of a systematic approach beginning with an analysis of objectives and ending with an evaluated system of instruction to determine if the selected design meets the objectives.

Designed instruction must be based on knowledge of how human beings learn, because the learning experience must take place within the student, not the instructor.

Often, instructors develop an instructional design without considering the objectives and needs of the class. Many instructors follow the selected textbook and provide lectures and discussion on the material because that is the method with which they are most comfortable. Again, for many instructors, the concerns of instructional design are first met as faculty sit on departmental curriculum committees. We believe that learning can be enhanced if each instructor is aware of the dynamics of instructional design and periodically reevaluates the design to determine if it continues to meet the goals and needs of the specific courses taught.

The Instructional System

The instructor is the manager or, more appropriately, the facilitator of the instructional system, and the classroom is a dynamic and complex mix of variables. Kozma, Belle, and Williams (1978) depict the instructional system within the communication theory model (Baker, Simon, & Bazeli, 1987). The system has five components, all acting together to accomplish the learning objectives. The instructor is the source of the educational message. The subject matter is the message, the media is the vehicle to communicate the message, and the learner is the receiver of the message. Evaluations of both the source (instructor) and the receiver (student) are periodically made to assess the efficiency and effectiveness of the system. Surrounding this system is the necessary environmental support supplied by the institution. These environmental variables include administrative, secretarial, and physical resources support. Viewing the instructional system in this manner provides additional insight into the interrelated nature of all the components and the necessity for each one to function adequately for the system to fulfill its objective of student learning. However, each component has many aspects that provide for a virtually unlimited number of permutations and combinations.

The subject matter is more than the content of the course; in a broader sense, it includes the skills and capabilities that students obtain. Beyond learning the concepts and principles of the course, the instructor desires that students understand the importance of the concepts and principles and become able to transfer them to applications in real-life situations. Subject matter must be based on the objectives of each course.

The most widely known taxonomy of instructional objectives was developed by a committee of educators chaired by Benjamin Bloom (1956). Bloom's taxonomy was an attempt to develop more specific objectives than simply stating, for example, "The student should understand accrual accounting." Simplified, Bloom's taxonomy has the following objectives:

knowledge: familiarity with basic information and generalizations;

comprehension: ability to interpret material and understand facts;

application: ability to apply concepts and principles to new applications;

analysis: ability to derive the distinguishing features of principles and theories and recognize logical errors when analyzing them;

synthesis: ability to make use of combinations of concepts and generalizations to solve major problems and to generate new strategies; and

evaluation: ability to judge the value or usefulness of a system or strategy.

The ultimate goal is to have students obtain life skills objectives so they may apply their collegiate learning experiences in their professional careers. These life skills must be relevant for today, tomorrow, and into the twenty-first century.

A countering view to the content objectives of the educational process is offered by Wyer (1984), who argues that goals of education should be phrased in terms of desired intellectual and ethical growth, not just content acquisition. Wyer feels the conceptual-procedural model is only an interim step in the definition and discovery of larger goals of education.

Objectives must be operationalized; that is, the instructor must determine what types of behavior he or she wants to induce in the students. We can motivate behaviors that result directly in the attainment of the objectives, not the other way around. To state simply that the student must know or understand a concept is not sufficient specificity. More specific responses are: design, list, evaluate, assess, explain, identify, construct, or solve. The subject matter indicates what the student should be able to design, list, and so forth.

The media available to instructors in an instructional system model include the devices used to transmit the message: lecture, books, film or video, audio, models, figures and charts, discussion, role play, simulation, laboratory experiences, and more recently, computer-assisted instruction. The purpose of the media is to provide a message-stimulus and evoke a response, hopefully learning. The lecture is one of the most widely used media because it is efficient and the instructor controls all aspects of the message being sent. However, recent research indicates that the lecture is one of the most complex media and may not accomplish the intended objectives. Lectures do not provide for active student involvement in the communication process and many students "phase out" during the lecture (Davis, 1976, p. 57). The instructor should select a variety of media. These media should be related to the instructional objectives, appropriate for the subject content, aimed at the specific types of learners in the class, and integrated with the specific teaching style of the instructor. Again, the instructional system involves a wide array of combinations.

Teaching Modes

The instructor, as the manager or facilitator of the instructional system, selects the instructional strategies to be used within the system (Sims, 1993; Baker, Simon, & Bazeli, 1987). A variety of teaching modes have been developed from the alternative views of the instructional system and learning theories. A mode is the specific stimulus pattern presented to the student. Each mode captures the basic view of the learner and the selection of appropriate teaching strategies. A mode may incorporate many specific teaching techniques. Techniques are the behaviors or procedures used to accomplish the selected teaching strategy.

The six modes presented in the next few paragraphs (lecture and discussion; programmed instruction; mastery learning; problem-centered seminar, laboratory, workshop; experiential learning; and systems analysis) represent views of the teaching and learning process as shown in a wide body of educational research literature (Baker, Simon, & Bazeli, 1987; Bigge & Hunt, 1968; Gage & Berliner, 1975; Hill, 1963; Joyce & Weil, 1986; Kolb, 1984; Milton, 1978; and NSSE, 1976).

The order of the modes represents increasing opportunities for students to explore applications to real world problems. For example, the lecture and discussion mode is used when a large amount of information transmission is required. Students come away from the learning experience with a knowledge base but have not had the opportunity to apply their knowledge to actual applications. Students tend to be passive learners in this "chalk and talk" mode (Gage & Berliner, 1975).

Programmed instruction includes systematic information transmission and lower-level skill learning. An example of this mode might be found in any beginning or introductory class (that is, accounting, computer languages, etc.).

Mastery learning is objective-controlled study. While some objectives are of a higher order of skills, this mode does not include much synthesis and transfer to actual situations. In addition, this learning environment requires the flexibility necessary for instructors to work individually with each student. Most colleges and universities do not have that level of resource capability (Gage & Berliner, 1975).

The next level, problem-centered seminar, lab, or workshop, begins to include learning experiences in which the student applies the concepts to problems in the real world. The student transfers what he or she has learned to specific applications. The case approach is a cornerstone of this mode. A significant shortcoming of using this approach in introductory accounting is that cases tend to require a large amount of class time and eliminate time that could be used to acquire basic knowledge items (Rowntree, 1974; Baker, Simon, & Bazeli, 1987).

The next mode is experiential learning. In this mode, the instructional system is a four stage cycle that ends with applications to real world situations (Kolb, 1984). The cyclical approach takes the learner through a sequence of learning stages in which each stage has specific objectives and builds upon the knowledge, skills, and abilities learned in the previous stage(s). For each major concept covered within a course, the cycle begins with concrete learning experiences, moves to reflective experiences, is followed by abstract experiences, and ends with active experimentation experiences. The final objective of the learning experience is the ability to apply the concepts to the real world experiences the students will face upon graduation. Thus, the student is gaining experiential knowledge of the world he or she will be participating in and acquiring the necessary life skills to be successful within that world (Kolb, 1984).

The final mode is systems analysis. This mode is most appropriate for obtaining a high level of understanding in which the learner must be able to integrate portions of other concepts and academic areas. This mode is most applicable in Masters of Business Administration courses and for continuing professional education seminars for practicing accountants (Joyce & Weil, 1986).

The six modes presented indicate the variety of theoretical views that have developed and show the alternatives presently available to each instructor. Within each mode instructors must understand that the student not only obtains specific types of learning skills, but also the values and attitudes necessary for success in the discipline (Baker, Simon, & Bazeli, 1987). The instructor is often the role model for these values and must be aware that the instructional environment involves the initiation of student beliefs about personal values and attitudes of practitioners of the discipline (Fuhrmann & Grasha, 1983).

Instructional Strategies to Enhance Learning

The ELM model states that effective learning is promoted if the learner goes through all four stages of learning. The instructor must identify the major concepts to be covered within each course and then design the instructional strategy for these major concepts to ensure that each of the four states of learning are completed. As a preliminary step, an instructor could use the chapter-by-chapter breakdown in the course textbook as an indication of the major concepts to be covered. Thus, the instructor should develop the four stage cycle for the concept covered within each chapter. In our experience, we have found that as a first step the instructor should spend an equal amount of time in each stage. Over time, the instructor can begin to modify the extent of coverage and the time spent in each stage of the cycle as he or she becomes more familiar with the objectives of the concept, the learning styles of the class, the prior experiences of the class, and the alternative resources available at the instructor's university to accomplish each learning stage. For example, some universities have excellent library resources, computer-based learning systems, high levels of graduate teaching support for individual student consultations and grading, high quality audio-visual equipment, strong contacts with local practicing professionals, and other environmental supports that can be used within the instructional design.

It is important to note that different students will be more comfortable in different stages of the learning process. Some students will become bored and impatient when the instructor is utilizing a teaching strategy other than the one most congruent for their learning stage. This is one reason why instructors who use just one teaching strategy in a course will have students who do not understand the material. These students may give the instructor very low teaching evaluations when the instructor feels he or she taught at an outstanding level. Also, when higher education institutions use graduate teaching assistants in various courses, it is essential that the course coordinator work with the graduate assistants to help them develop an understanding of the experiential learning model and its application within the course.

Each student must structure new knowledge in his or her own cognitive domain in order to be able to utilize that domain later in life. All too often, college or university instructors may assume that a great lecture is the best method for students to learn the material. Many students, however, find it difficult to sit quietly in a lecture room and concentrate on an instructor building the conceptual framework of a field. Virtually all learning and teaching research indicates that a range of learning situations must be available to the students, including the opportunity to apply the concepts being learned to real world situations through either cases, interviews, or other grounded experiences (Baker, Simon, & Bazeli, 1987).

In order to fully utilize experiential learning principles, large classes need to be subdivided into study groups of five to eight students. Formation of groups can provide support for individual students who are having difficulty with a specific learning stage. In addition, group activities mirror the real world team approach to problem solving. Subdivision of the class may be based on random selection, acquaintance selection, common interests, or background. Instructors should exercise some judgment in organizing the groups in order to promote cohesiveness. Study groups are utilized differently during each stage of the experiential learning cycle (Sims & Lindholm, 1993).

Concrete Experience Stage

During the concrete experience stage of the instructional cycle, the purpose is to present students with samples of objects, artifacts, behaviors, processes, or phenomena found in practice. These items demonstrate the concepts, principles, or generalizations the instructor wishes to introduce. Samples may be obtained from direct experience in practice, simulated situation, case studies, talks by experts, field trips, film episodes, or examination of original, or facsimiles of, documents, materials, or workproducts. The instructor has the responsibility of guiding the study groups concerning the kinds of data to collect and the method of organization and examination they should make of the raw data found in the samples. At the end of this stage, the instructor leads a discussion about the properties and uses of the samples, making sure that students are able to relate the samples to the concept or generalizations being discussed. The instructor then gives additional examples that exemplify the concept.

Reflective Observation Stage

The activities carried on in the concrete experience stage lead into those of the reflective observation stage. After students have observed samples of the concepts or generalizations, the concepts are proved deductively, expanded, and added to related concepts and generalizations. This period of reflection and expansion focuses on building a structured understanding of the discipline. The instructional method in this stage is usually the deductive lecture or discussion. The instructor provides the appropriate concepts and principles in the knowledge hierarchy, gradually increasing the detail and specificity of the concepts and information subsumed by the generalization. This provides anchoring for the acquisition of new knowledge and its relationship within the logic hierarchy. New material should be integrated with previously learned material that makes the study of new material easier and more meaningful. Group activities during this stage could include reviewing reading assignments selected by the instructor on the basis that the readings provide a perspective on the theory or principle. Each group's spokesperson should then present and defend the findings of the group's analysis of their readings.

Abstract Conceptualization Stage

At this point students are ready to enter the theory-building and problem-solving stage of the learning cycle. The concrete experience and reflective observation stages are primarily information-giving from the instructor to the students. The abstract conceptualization and reflective observation stages require the student to become more active in the learning process (for example, through individual and group homework assignments or cases). The focus of the in-class discussion should be on the group activities, because these are an important part of the instructional design of experiential learning. Individual student activities should complement the students' learning processes. The case approach is very effective during this stage as study groups must isolate the relevant variables and hypothesized causal relationships. The groups then have the opportunity to test their hypothesized cause-effect relationships during class discussions. It is important that instructors spend some time discussing expert solutions to the cases and any differences between the study group's solutions and those of the experts.

Active Experimentation Stage

The learning process in this stage leads to the application of what has been learned to the real life or practical problems as they would be encountered in work or other settings. This stage is the synthesis part of the learning cycle. Students learn to function as they would in work settings. We have found that simulation gaming is an excellent teaching method for this stage. Students play assigned roles, confront problems drawn from real work situations, make decisions based on their understanding of the course material or principles studied in the first three stages of the learning cycle, and adjust their behavior as a result of the consequences of their decisions.

Evaluation instruments such as quizzes, tests, case analysis write-ups, and personal application assignments are part of the feedback mechanism that the instructor uses to inform the students of their progress in the learning environment. The evaluative instruments should include a variety of questions from each of the four steps as well as integrative questions involving all four stages.

Over the years we have found that many instructors have some initial difficulties implementing the four stage learning model in their classes. This is especially the case for instructors who traditionally rely on the lecture and discussion mode. Also, some students have difficulty with several of the stages, and the instructor must recognize that this is normal. An additional consequence of adopting the experiential learning mode is that changes in instructional strategy require instructors to spend additional time designing the course. However, after some experience, instructors will be able to select the optimal strategy and teaching techniques for their instructional system. In our experience the rewards (that is, enhancing learning), both present and future, make the effort worthwhile.

Selecting a Teaching Method

A knowledge of principles of learning, how people learn, and the methods of teaching available, including their advantages and disadvantages, provides the instructor with information needed to select the most appropriate teaching modes to enhance learning for a specific agency. Woolridge (1988) notes that the contingency approach to instruction design can be useful in developing learning experiences. This approach suggests that the specific design and delivery of learning experience, the instructor, the choice of instructional strategy, and class exercises should all be contingent on the specific learning objectives to be achieved and the anticipated learning styles of the audience (Woolridge, 1978).

Within the past few years, some excellent work in adult training that can be generalized to teaching in higher education has related the effectiveness of various teaching methods (for example, lectures, films, case studies, role playing) to specific learning objectives. McClearly and McIntyre (1972) assessed the effectiveness of 15 methods of instruction. They measured the extent to which the methods tended to be practical and effective in reaching the objective (which could be technical, conceptual, or human relational) at a specific level of learning (familiarity, understanding, or application). Newstrom (1980), Olivas and Newstrom (1981), and Carroll, Paine, and Ivancevich (1972) have reported similar relationships.

This literature can provide higher education instructors with some general guidelines that can help to select a teaching methodology that will be suited to achieving certain broad categories of learning objectives. As Newstrom (1980, p. 12) points out,

> Tradition often locks educators into suboptimal behavior patterns. . . . Whenever training/teaching techniques are selected on the basis of illogical or irrelevant criteria, we have committed an injustice to our trainees/students. . . .Why might trainers/teachers knowingly use methods that are either inadequate or inappropriate for the objectives they hope to accomplish? Some possible reasons include . . . lack of knowledge about the competitive effectiveness of various approaches or even the perception that the trainees/students like a certain method best.

One can take the teaching method objective one step further. Many teaching strategies confront students with the risk of failure and the possibility of revealing things about themselves to others that they would prefer to leave unknown. Moreover, the teaching methods that are selected must be sequenced properly in order to achieve the aims of the overall teaching experience. Thus, the question college and university instructors should ask is, Have the teaching methods to be used proved effective in achieving the learning objectives that have been identified? If so, have the strategies been sequenced so as to have a positive effect on learning?

Unfortunately, selection of the appropriate teaching method or methodologies does not ensure the enhancement of student learning. Success also depends on an understanding of learning theories, effective use of learning principles (such as reinforcement and feedback), provisions for positive transfer of learning, effective instructors, and systematic and supportive institutional policies (that is, incentives for enhancing student learning) for the teaching of students. Even then, the success of teaching and learning cannot be assumed until the effectiveness of teaching has been assessed.

SUMMARY

Researchers have struggled for years to define what constitutes learning and to better understand how people learn. Because there has and will continue to be studies aimed at improving learning in higher education, instructors and their institutions have a responsibility to be open-minded to concepts or ideas that may indeed improve our understanding of how people learn and what makes some teaching more successful than other teaching.

Learning in college and universities is what teaching is all about, and instructors have a responsibility to their institutions and students to be familiar with and participate in research on learning and the development of theories on learning styles, brain dominance, or any other variables that are part of the teaching equation. Instructors must move away from the mentality of wanting to just teach and not actively participate in the inquiry process on ways to improve learning and teaching in general.

It is vital for instructors to be aware of the wide variety of learning styles. The instructor must be cognizant of the implications of individual learning styles and integrate appropriate responses into the teaching or instructional design and environment. In light of the importance of learning styles to learning, it is natural to ask if the teaching, design, delivery, and facilities take the variety of learning styles of the anticipated audience in account.

Armed with a better understanding of learning principles, instructors are in a better position to select sound teaching methods. There is no one best way to teach students, because teaching effectiveness depends in part on the skills and knowledge to be learned and the level at which they need to be learned. In conclusion, college and university instructors must understand that seeking an answer to the question of how people learn is difficult. In reality no one knows for sure, but in the end an increased knowledge of how learning occurs and individual learning strategies, as well as one's own learning style, can help enhance learning in educational endeavors.

As suggested earlier in this chapter, the prime objective of any teaching endeavor is to help students learn, and to achieve this objective it is necessary for college and university faculty to understand some basic assumptions of instructional design to adopt the appropriate method. A variety of factors can affect the choice. These include the nature of the information or skill to be learned; the learning resources available, including time; the size of the class; and the instructors' strengths or preferences as a teacher.

There are a variety of learning methods available to help participants. However, the instructor who chooses a method he or she is uncomfortable with will probably give a below-par performance, resulting in a negative effect on the learning of students. In reality, no one method or combination of methods can be applied with equal success in all circumstances. The instructor will often have to experiment with several different approaches to find the right one for a particular course and class.

Several concluding recommendations seem important to the enhancement of learning in institutions of higher education.

First, understanding how individuals learn and the learning process should be an explicit objective that is pursued as consciously and deliberately as productivity. Higher education instructors should budget time to allow themselves and students to learn from their experiences as they progress through classes, courses, and individualized programs. This leads to the second recommendation. The nature of learning in the educational process is such that opposing perspectives, action and reflection, concrete involvement and analytical detachment, and right- and left-brain functioning are all essential for optimal learning. Students must be provided with learning experiences that not only reinforce their learning strengths but also teach them to learn more effectively in their less dominant areas.

For example, one can provide teaching to students on becoming other brained. That is, left-brain thinkers could be encouraged to develop their right brain by engaging in unstructured activities such as creative daydreaming. Right-brained thinkers could be encouraged to develop their left brain by outlining things, solving mathematical problems, and engaging in analytical thinking. For higher education faculty, this means balancing the curriculum to encompass the complete range of learning styles and brain functions. When one perspective comes to dominate others, the effectiveness of learning in education is reduced. From this, one can conclude that the most effective teaching systems are those that enhance learning and can tolerate differences in perspective.

REFERENCES

Baker, R. E., Simon, J. R., & Bazeli, F. P. 1987. Selecting instructional design for introductory accounting based on the experiential learning model. *Journal of Accounting Education*, *5*, 207–226.

Baldwin, B. A., & Reckers, P. 1984. Exploring the role of learning style research in accounting education policy. *Journal of Accounting Education*, *2*(2), 63–76.

Bentz, W. F. 1974. Using learning theory to teach accounting more efficiently. In J. D. Edwards (Ed.), *Accounting education: Problems and prospects* (pp. 213–230). New York: American Accounting Association.

Bigge, M. L., & Hunt, M. 1968. *Psychological foundations of education*. New York: Harper and Row.

Bloom, G. (Ed.). 1956. *Taxonomy of educational objectives. Book I: Cognitive domain.* New York: Longman.

Carroll, S. J., Paine, F. T., & Ivancevich, J. J. 1972. Relative effectiveness of training methods: Expert opinion and research. *Personnel Psychology*, *25*, 495–509.

Davis, J. R. 1976. *Teaching strategies for the college classroom*. Boulder, CO: Westview Press.

Dewey, J. 1938. *Democracy and education*. New York: The MacMillan Company.

Freedman, R. D., & Stumpf, S. A. 1978. What can one learn from the Learning Style Inventory. *Academy of Management Journal*, *21*, 275–282.

Fuhrmann, B. S., & Grasha, A. F. 1983. *A practical handbook for college teachers*. Boston: Little, Brown, and Co.

Gage, N. L., & Berliner, D. 1975. *Educational psychology*. Chicago: Rand McNally.

Gagne, R. M. 1985. *The conditions of learning*. New York: Holt, Rinehart and Winston.

Gagne, R. M., & Briggs, L. J. 1979. *Principles of instructional design*. New York: Holt, Rinehart and Winston.

Harris, T. L., & Scwahn, W. E. 1961. *Selected readings on the learning process*. New York: Oxford University Press.

Hines, T. 1987. Left brain/right brain mythology and implications for management and training. *Academy of Management Review*, *12*(4), 600–606.

Hodgetts, R. M. 1991. *Organizational behavior: Theory and practice*. New York: Macmillan Publishing Co.

Houle, C. 1961. *The inquiring mind*. Madison: University of Wisconsin Press.

Joyce, B., & Weil, M. 1986. *Modes of teaching* (3rd ed.). Englewood Cliffs, NJ: Prentice-Hall.

Kidd, J. R. 1973. *How adults learn*. London: Cambridge Publishers.

Kimble, G. A., & Garmezy, N. 1963. *Principles of general psychology*. New York: Ronald.

Knowles, M. S. 1980. *The modern practice of adult education: From pedagogy to andragogy* (rev. ed.). New York: Cambridge.

Knowles, M. S., & Associates. 1984. *Andragogy in action: Applying modern principles of adult learning*. San Francisco: Jossey-Bass.

Kolb, D. A. 1985. *The learning style inventory*. Boston: McBer & Company.

Kolb, D. A. 1984. *Experiential learning: Experience as a source of learning and development*. Englewood Cliffs, NJ: Prentice-Hall.

Kozma, R. B., Belle, L. W., & Williams, G. W. 1978. *Instructional techniques in higher education*. Englewood Cliffs, NJ: Educational Technology Publications.

Lynch, D. 1986, February. Is the brain stuff still the right (or left) stuff?, *Training and Development Journal*, *40*(2), 23–26.

McCarthy, B. 1980. *The 4MAT system: Teaching to learning styles with right/left mode techniques*. Arlington Hgts, IL.: Excel Inc.

McCleary, L. E., & McIntyre, K. E. 1972. Competency development and university methodology. *National Association of Secondary School Principles Bulletin, 56*(332), 53–68.

Margolis, F. H., & Bell, C. R. 1984. *Managing the learning process: Effective techniques for the adult classroom*. Minneapolis: Lakewood.

Milton, O. (Ed.). 1978. *On college teaching*. San Francisco: Jossey-Bass.

National Society for the Study of Education (NSSE). 1976. *Seventy-fifth year book, Psychology of teaching methods*. University of Chicago Press.

Newstrom, J. W. 1980. Selecting training methodologies. *Training and Development Journal, 29*(9), 55–80.

Olivas, L., and Newstrom, J. W. 1981. Learning through the use of simulation games. *Training and Development Journal, 35*(9), 63–66.

Piatt, J. G. 1983, December. Brain processing preferences: Key to an organization's success. *NASSP Bulletin*, pp. 64–69.

Robey, D. and Taggart, W. 1981, July. Measuring managers' minds: The assessment of style in human information processing. *Academy of Management Review, 6*(3), 382.

Rowntree, D. 1974. *Educational technology in curriculum development*. New York: Harper & Row.

Sadler, B. R., Plovnick, M., & Snope, F.C. 1978. Learning styles and teaching implications. *Journal of Medical Education, 53*, 847–849.

Sheal, P. 1989. *How to develop and present staff training courses*. London: Kogen Page.

Sims, R. R. 1993. *Training enhancement in government organizations*. Westport, CT: Quorum.

Sims, R. R. & Lindholm, J. 1993. Kolb's experiential learning model: A first step in learning how to learn from experience. *Journal of Management Education, 17*(1), 95–98.

Sims, R. R. and Sims, S. J. 1991. Improving training in the public sector. *Public Personnel Management, 20*(1), 71–82.

Sims, R. R., Veres, J. G., & Heninger, S. 1989. Training for competence. *Public Personnel Management, 18*(1), 101–107.

Sperry, R. W. 1973. Lateral specialization of cerebral function in the surgically separated hemispheres. In F. J. McGuigan and R. A. Schonover (Eds.)., *The psychophysiology of thinking* (p. 23). New York: Academic Press.

Sperry, R. W., Gazzaniga, M. S., & Bogen, J. E. 1969. Interhemispheric relationships: The neocortical commissures; Syndromes of hemispheric disconnections. In P. J. Vinken and G. W. Bruyn (Eds.)., *Handbook of clinical neurology* (pp. 273–289). Amsterdam: North Holland Publishing Co.

Taggart, W. and Robey, D. 1981, April. Minds and managers: On the dual nature of human information processing and management. *Academy of Management*, p. 190.

Tough, A. 1979. *The adult's learning projects: A fresh approach to theory and practice in adult learning* (2nd ed.). Austin, TX: Learning Concepts.

Tough, A. 1982. *Intentional changes: A fresh approach to helping people change*. New York: Cambridge Book Company.

Woolridge, B. 1978, Spring. New training directions: Learning styles can determine success. *Network News*, p. 1.

Woolridge, B. 1988. Increasing the productivity of public-sector training. *Public Productivity Review, 12*(2), 205–217.

Wyer, J. C. 1984. Procedural v. conceptual: A developmental view. *Journal of Accounting Education, 2*(1), 5–18.

2

Learning Styles: A Survey of Adult Learning Style Inventory Models

Leslie K. Hickcox

This chapter will offer a review of several major learning style inventories. The majority of the survey will focus on the North American adult populations throughout the late 1970s, 1980s and mid-1990s with regard to learning styles. "Adult" will refer to those 18 and older. Learning preferences and learning styles will also be used interchangeably. A description and comparison among North American, European, and Australian research and learning style inventories will be presented. Two concluding sections will present some learning style research on various ethnic populations and the relevance of inventory information in reference to the assessment of the quality of instruction and training.

As an adult educator it is important to understand criteria for selecting appropriate inventories for the student or client population. The basic characteristics that indicate better quality inventories will be presented. This will be followed by discussions on the comparison among learning style models and the strengths and weaknesses of learning style research. The chapter will offer a description of inventories within three major learning style categories: (1) instructional and environmental learning preferences, (2) information processing learning preferences, and (3) personality related learning preferences. These three categories were initially discussed by Curry (1987). Learning style studies that focus on various ethnic populations will also be described. The chapter will conclude with a discussion on the relevance of learning style inventory information with regard to assessment of the quality of instruction and training.

DETERMINING THE QUALITY OF LEARNING STYLE INVENTORIES

Major North American and Australian learning style inventories and theories are presented in this chapter. The inventories and theories reviewed emerged during the 1960s through 1980s. The inventories are discussed in reference to Curry's learning style topology developed in the mid-1980s.

As you review the inventories described consider the following three key criteria in determining the overall quality of a learning style instrument: (1) what are the extent and results of the reliability and validity testing? (that is, sample sizes of test groups; numbers less than 30 tend to be questionable); (2) Has the instrument been revised since its origination? Relevance of language and issues tested for change with time (for example, an instrument created in 1975 may use gender-biased language in 1995); (3) Is the instrument designed to be administered to your adult population? If you are working with primarily traditional age and non-traditional age student groups from Caucasian backgrounds, several of the instruments are relevant. If not, you may question the use of the instrument. It should be noted that most instruments developed between the 1950s and the 1980s were not ethnically described in terms of the reliability and validity test samples. Thus, the author has made the assumption that the majority of instruments were developed based on Caucasian college-educated test samples. You can determine if the instrument is age appropriate by the reliability or validity test sample age specification; (4) What type of inventory do you want to use? This will be determined by the descriptive self-knowledge about the students that will best serve the student's and the teacher's needs.

The instructional and environmental preference inventories assist the student with regard to study or work setting needs. This type of inventory can also assist the teacher or trainer with regard to arrangement of the learning environment. The information processing inventories give the student vital in-class learning mode preferences as well as cues for being aware of possible teacher learning style preferences. The teacher or trainer may use the learning style information for better curriculum and process planning, making class sessions more inclusive.

The personality related learning style inventories offer the student excellent information for personal self-knowledge and how it may relate to learning settings. The Myers-Briggs Type Indicator is an example of this type of inventory. These inventories are also useful for teacher advising sessions in which important personality preferences may assist a teacher or advisor in guiding a student with regard to college major or career issues.

A Comparison among North American, Australian, and European Learning Style Models

Research on learning or cognitive styles evolved from the psychological research on individual differences (Curry, 1987). Individual difference research was widespread in psychology during the late 1960s and early 1970s. During this time a number of learning style concepts were proposed for consideration and application.

There is a distinct difference between North American learning style research and Australian and European learning style research. The North American researchers have developed learning style concepts from their backgrounds in psychology and cognitive psychology and emphasized psychometric considerations from the beginning. European and Australian researchers developed concepts based on the European approach to learning style research. This approach began with detailed observations of learning behaviors of small numbers of learners (Curry, 1987). Examples of the two approaches are: North American — Friedman and Stritter (1976), Kolb (1976), and Yando and Kagan (1970); European and Australian — Curry (1983) and Biggs (1979).

Differences in these research approaches continue to make it difficult to resolve issues, such as an acceptable definition of learning style inventory validity. Since the late 1980s, North American researchers have written about behaviors used by learners in learning situations. Three examples are: Levin (1986), "Four cognitive principles of learning-strategy instruction;" Thomas and Rohwer (1986), "Academic studying: The role of learning strategies;" and Kolb (1989), "From learning styles to learning strategies: The Executive Skills Profile." These researchers have focused on behaviors that are thought of as strategies (by North American researchers) and are relatively easy to change. In contrast, the European researchers consider such learning behaviors directly analogous to deeper style concepts (Curry, 1987).

Learning Style Literature Trends: Strengths and Weaknesses of Learning Style Research

Most of the literature on learning styles has focused on improving the immediate and long-term results of teaching and learning episodes. The following papers exhibit this emphasis: Andrews (1981), "Teaching format and student style: Their interactive effects on learning;" Biggs (1979), "Individual differences in study process and the quality of learning outcomes;" and Papalia (1978), "Assessing students' learning styles and teaching for individual differences."

Another focus of learning style research has been in the area of professional education. Investigators have applied learning style concepts to a number of issues of specific importance in their professional area. For example, medical school admissions, training programs, scholarly achievement, willingness to practice in small communities, and choice of specialty and professional competence have all been researched by correlational studies in reference to one or several of the learning style conceptualizations (Curry, 1987). The investigators' rationale for such studies was that the quality of the learning style used by students is likely to determine the quality of what is learned, and this can act as an outcome to compare various curricular approaches (Coles, 1985; Newble & Clarke, 1986).

The majority of the learning style research has continued in the face of significant difficulties in regard to the adequacy of learning style conceptualizations. A key difficulty is the confusion of definitions surrounding learning style concepts and the resulting wide variation in scale or scope of behavior claimed to be predicted by various models. For example, some conceptualizations claim only to predict an individual's choice between a lecture-style and a small group-style course (Friedman & Stritter, 1976); others attempt to predict an habitual response over all learning acts in which a student might engage (Yando & Kagan, 1970).

Curry (1987) pointed out that the evidence, gathered to support the various conceptualizations, varies radically in terms of psychometric standards for reliability and validity. Curry has presented a paper that reviewed the major learning style theories and inventories in North America, Europe, and Australia in order to critically present the reliability and validity of the various learning style instruments. Her review was a key reference for this overview of the North American, Australian, and European learning style literature.

Shipman and Shipman (1985) reviewed a wide variety of learning style conceptualizations and observed a variation in regard to psychometric considerations. Their review presented an updated version of the Messick (1976) listing of learning style dimensions. They concluded that "there is a considerable variety among the processes indexed by the various cognitive styles, . . . that styles have been defined at different levels of discourse and as operating at different levels of generality" (Shipman & Shipman, 1985). They also concluded that there was enough educational utility in both the long and short terms to pursue learning style research and applications (Shipman & Shipman, 1985).

Curry (1987) conducted a psychometric survey of 21 learning style conceptualizations and instruments from North America, Europe, and Australia over a five year period. She found, based on psychometric evidence and written documentation, that it was possible to reorganize thematically the 21 learning style instruments into a three-layer system.

Curry's system has three layers like an onion. The first layer (or core) presents learning behavior as controlled at a fundamental level by the central personality dimension. The middle layer centers around a theme of information processing dimensions. The outer layer, influenced by the interaction with the environment, is based on the theme of instructional preferences. The outermost layer of the model, and the most observable, is the instructional preference learning style conceptual approach. The three-layer connection between the personality layer and the outermost instructional preference layer, she claimed, is analogous to the trait and state concepts of personality theory.

A study by Marshall (1987) corroborates the validity of Curry's learning style topology. Marshall conducted a study to examine the construct validity of Curry's learning styles onion model, with a focus on the information processing level (topology), and then determined whether or not the model translated into the instructional preference topology. He concluded: "This study does provide evidence that the topology has promise as a tool in learning style research and application. As a starting point, the topology can be used for classifying learning style models and instruments into a meaningful structure. It can provide a framework for the re-examination of much of the earlier research and for conducting future research" (pp. 426–427).

The following three sections focus on each layer of the topology. Eighteen of the 21 learning style inventories and their conceptualizations are reviewed according to the layer they are classified within (see Table 2.1). This discussion focuses on the North American and Australian learning style conceptualizations. Sixteen North American learning style inventories fall within all three layers. Two Australian learning style inventories fit within the information processing layer.

Learning Style as Instructional and Environmental Preferences

As stated previously, the outermost layer, which is the most observable, is entitled Instructional Preference. Eight of the learning style research groups concerned themselves with the instructional preference or the individual's choice of environment in which to learn. Because this layer interacts most directly with learning environments, learner expectations, teacher expectations, and other external features, it is expected that instructional preference is the least stable across time and the most easily influenced level of measurement in the learning environment (Curry, 1987).

The Canfield and Lafferty Learning Styles Inventory was designed with 120 self-report rank ordered items to investigate 20 scales grouped into four areas: conditions of learning, content of learning, mode of learning, and expectations for learning. The purpose of this inventory was to "identify learner preferences for instruction" (Canfield, 1980). The investigators' reliability testing involved 1,397 students with no ages specified in development of the instrument. The overall psychometric ratings of the inventory by Curry were poor reliability evidence and poor validity evidence.

The second inventory presented was the Dunn, Dunn, and Price Learning Style Inventory. Several versions of this inventory were

TABLE 2.1
Review of Learning Styles Inventories

Level of Curry's Model	*Author(s)*	*Inventory Title*
1. Instructional and Environmental Preference	Canfield & Laffert	Learning Styles Inventory
	Dunn, Dunn, & Price	Learning Style Inventory
	Friedman & Stritter	Instructional Preference Questionnaire
	Goldberg	Oregon Instructional Preference Inventory
	Grasha & Riechmann	Student Learning Interest Scales
	Hill	Cognitive Style Interest Inventory
	Renzulli & Smith	Learning Style Inventory
	Rezler & Rezmovic	Learning Preference Inventory
2. Information Processing Preference	Biggs	Study Process Questionnaire
	Entwistle & Ramsden	Approaches to Studying
	Hunt	Paragraph Completion Method
	Kolb	Learning Style Inventory
	Reinert	Edmonds Learning Style Identification Exercise
	Schmeck, Ribich, & Ramanaih	Inventory of Learning Process
	Schroeder	Paragraph Completion Test
3. Personality Related Preference	Kagan	Matching Familiar Figures Test
	Myers	Myers-Briggs Type Indicator
	Witkin	Embedded Figures Test

defined and rated, as well as a presentation of the overall conception of the inventory. It is composed of 100 self-report true or false items in order to investigate 24 scales grouped into five categories considered likely to affect learning: environmental elements, emotional elements, physical elements, sociological elements, and psychological elements. The authors proposed that "this instrument analyzes the condition under which students in grades three through twelve prefer to learn" (Dunn, 1983, p. 496). In their reliability testing they studied 930 students in grades one to three, 163 students in grades three to five, and 1,046 students in grades six to twelve. The number of adults tested was not specified.

It was explained that analogous instruments have been developed for use with adults (Dunn, Dunn, & Price, 1986) and for grades one and two (Perrin, 1982). The Dunn, Dunn, and Price inventory and its theory were placed in the instructional preference layer because the majority of the theory (17 of the 20 scales) describes features of the situations in which learning occurs. The three scales titled Psychological Elements describe a kind of information processing typically exhibited. These scales fit well into the second layer of Curry's onion topology. The Dunn, Dunn, and Price inventories were psychometrically rated overall as good reliability evidence and good validity evidence.

The Friedman and Stritter Instructional Preference Questionnaire (1976) contains 40 self-report items with Likert-type six point scales used to describe student preferences for pacing, influence over learning, media, active role in learning, and feedback in learning. The authors created this questionnaire in an "attempt to assess student preferences according to empirically defined instructional characteristics" (Friedman & Stritter, 1976, p. 85). This questionnaire was psychometrically rated with reliability and validity testing of 252 medical law and business students, 613 medical students, and 109 engineering students. The psychometric rating was fair in relation to reliability and fair in terms of validity.

The Goldberg Oregon Instructional Preference Inventory (1963) consists of 82 items to be completed by an individual in a two alternative, forced choice format. The items are not organized into scales and range across a wide variety of issues considered important to instructional preference by the author. This instrument was developed to indicate "those characteristics of college students which predispose them towards learning more effectively from one, rather than some other particular instructional format" (Goldberg, 1972, p. 153). The reliability and validity testing involved 2,709 college students. The inventory was psychometrically rated fair in terms of reliability and poor as related to validity.

The Grasha and Riechmann Student Learning Style Scales (1974) is a series of self-report, Likert-type five point scale items that describe the learner along three bipolar scale dimensions (independent-dependent, avoidant-participant, and collaborative-competitive). The purpose of these scales was "to develop an instrument that was based on the type of learning styles college students demonstrate in the classroom," which they felt was the appropriate approach "if teachers are to innovate and take student learning needs into consideration" (Riechmann & Grasha, 1974, p. 213). The scales developed center on how students interact with the teacher, other students, and the learning task. The reliability and validity testing involved 940 college students. The scales were rated fair in regard to reliability and fair in terms of validity.

Hill's 1976 Cognitive Style Interest Inventory is composed of 216 items, each of which involves a three point Likert-type scale to be completed by the student. The items are arranged to measure 27 different scales in three areas: symbols and their meanings, cultural determinants, and modalities of inference. The instrument was developed to provide an overall picture of a learner's "mode of behavior in deriving meaning" (Whitley, 1982, p. 25). Although this purpose appears to be an attempt at information processing, according to Curry, the majority of scales describe media preferences and other features of the learning environment. Curry gave the inventory no psychometric rating for reliability or validity. Apparently, no formal testing was conducted for this inventory. The investigator argued that each of the reliability estimation methods is inappropriate for application to style measurements. This being one of the earliest instruments, it offers an interesting perspective that challenges the traditional psychometric view toward inventory measurement.

The Renzulli and Smith (1978) Learning Style Inventory is composed of 65 items, with five point Likert-type scales in which the students self-report. The items are categorized into nine scales: projects, drills and recitation, peer teaching, discussion, teaching games, independent study, programmed instruction, lecture, and simulation. The author's purpose was to provide teachers with information about "how pleased" students feel when participating in the types of learning environments described by the nine scales. This information was "designed to guide teachers in planning learning experiences that take into account the learning style preferences of students within their classrooms." The investigators derived reliability data by testing 700 seventh and eighth grade students. The psychometric ratings for this inventory were poor for reliability and fair for validity (Renzulli & Smith, 1983).

The Rezler and Rezmovic (1974) Learning Preference Inventory is composed of 15 items, of which the student is asked to rank order six choices. The choices are descriptive of three bipolar concepts: abstract versus concrete, individual versus interpersonal, and student structure versus teacher structure. The key purpose of the learning preference inventory was "to identify preferred modes of learning" with preference determined by the "choice of one learning situation or condition over another" (Rezler & Rezmovic, 1981, p. 28). The reliability and validity data were based on testing 262 allied heath workers and students and 95 medical students. The psychometric ratings were good in regard to reliability and fair in terms of validity.

Learning Styles as Information Processing Preferences

This is the second or middle layer of the learning style onion model. Concepts at this level describe the individual's cognitive approach to assimilating information and, in that respect, these concepts can be related to the classic cognitive information processing model (Gage & Berliner, 1979). Information processing is a set of processes that function at the intersection between fundamental personality levels, individual differences, and environmentally based learning format choices.

The Biggs (1979) Study Process Questionnaire represents one of the key Australian learning style theories and inventories. It is composed of 42 Likert-type, five point scale self-report items inquiring about motive-strategy dimensions. These dimensions are as follows:

surface (instructional versus reproducing), deep (intrinsic versus meaning), and achieving (achievement versus organizing). This instrument was designed to measure these three concepts, and the author believes it "offers a parsimonious and theoretically coherent model for conceptualizing the more important ways in which students may feel about, and behave towards their study" (Biggs, 1979, p. 384). This learning style conceptualization, according to Curry, fits less well within the onion model than do others. Biggs focused both on the learner's motives for approaching learning in a particular way, and the strategies used to accomplish that motive. The first emphasis appears to be on instructional preference, and the second emphasis is based on information processing. If the onion model had an intermediary space between the two layers, this would be the place for the Biggs conceptualization and inventory. The reliability data was based on testing both 1,823 fourteen- and sixteen-year-olds and 2,545 university students. The psychometric ratings were good for reliability and fair for validity. This inventory represents one of the two Australian inventories.

The Approaches to Studying Inventory was developed by N. J. Entwistle and Paul Ramsden (1983). This is the other learning style theory and inventory that represents the Australian approach to learning style research. The inventory was designed to operationalize concepts developed by Marton and Saljo (1976) and Pask (1976) based on holistic and serialist learning. Their intent was to define approaches to learning styles in ways that are directly related to the experience of students. To accomplish this the inventory involved 64 self-report, five point Likert scale items. The four scales of the inventory represented the following scores: meaning orientation, reproducing orientation, achieving orientation, and holistic orientation.

The Entwistle and Ramsden conceptualization, like Biggs, has the elements of both instructional preference and information processing. The Approaches to Studying Inventory was developed to incorporate some of Biggs' questions. Ramsden (1983) has developed the most complete documentation on the Approaches to Studying Inventory to date. He suggests that its most pertinent use is for informing teachers about their students' study patterns so that "they will be in a better position to organize their teaching to ensure that students learn effectively" (Ramsden, 1983). Entwistle has compared their inventory with the Inventory of Learning Processes developed by Schmeck (Schmeck, Ribich, & Ramanaiah, 1977). Schmeck's inventory is the most highly rated instrument described in Curry's model. The reliability and validity testing involved 2,777 high school students and 3,457 college students. The psychometric ratings for the Entwistle and Ramsden inventory were good for both reliability and validity.

The Hunt Paragraph Completion Method (Hunt et al., 1971) encompasses the completion of six open-ended sentences by the students, which are scored by trained raters for their level of "conceptual complexity, interpersonal maturity and self-other understanding" (Miller, 1981, p. 33). The sentence stems deal with responses to rules, criticism, parents, being disagreed with, uncertainty, and being told what to do. The investigator reliability and validity tested approximately 311 sixth through eleventh graders in the development of this inventory. The instrument received a fair rating for both reliability and validity.

A similar conceptualization was developed by Schroeder (Schroeder, Driver, & Streufert, 1967). In his Paragraph Completion Test he asked for a completion of five open-ended sentence stems, concerning the following issues: disagreements, doubt, rules, criticism, and confusion. Both Hunt and Schroeder developed their tests as indicators of "the integrative component of cognitive complexity," which they define as the ability to think in multiple conceptual terms (Curry, 1987, p. 12). In this way their orientation was toward the structure of thought. The "This I Believe" test, developed in 1961 by O. J. Harvey in cooperation with Hunt and Schroeder, focused on the levels of influenceability of thought, defined by Schroeder in 1967 as the "developmental potential" (Schroeder, Driver, & Streufert, 1967). Miller (1981) offers a detailed review of these three similar approaches to the definition and manipulation of "conceptual type" (Miller, 1981, p. 51). The reliability testing involved 236 college and university students. Schroeder's inventory was rated good in terms of reliability and fair in regard to validity.

The Kolb (1985) Learning Style Inventory contains 12 sentence stems, each having four sentence completers to be rank ordered. Responses are organized into bipolar concepts: concrete experience versus abstract conceptualization and reflective observation versus active experimentation. The reliability testing involved 982 graduate and undergraduate students for the 1985 version. The earlier 1981 version encompassed the testing of 1,933 adults from 18 to 60 years. Kolb's Learning Style Inventory was psychometrically rated as strong in regard to reliability and fair in terms of validity.

Curry (1987) observed that at least four variations of Kolb's model are in use. Two derivatives have been developed for business applications: McKenney and Keen (1974) and Honey and Mumford (1982). McKenney and Keen presented a model, without acknowledging Kolb, based on two bipolar concepts (information gathering and information evaluation). The instrument was tested in relation to Masters of Business Administration students by 12 standard reference tests for cognitive factors developed by the Educational Testing Service (McKenney & Keen, 1974). Honey and Mumford did credit Kolb for stimulating their model, in which managers were tested to identify four style types (activist, reflector, theorists, and pragmatists), which Honey and Mumford describe in terms that are quite parallel to Kolb's terms. A third variation of Kolb's model is by Marshall and Merritt (1985), who have designed an alternative measure for the Kolb procedure. It is applied in educational settings. A fourth inventory, by Gregorc and Ward (1977), is a Kolb-like bipolar scale (abstract/concrete and sequential/random) derived from observations and interviews with teachers and learners. The inventory was published without reference to Kolb. The Kolb Learning Style Inventory is the only one of these 18 to have stimulated the development of four other learning style inventories.

The Edmonds Learning Style Identification Exercise was designed in 1976 by Harry Reinert (1976). The exercise is based on 50 words read aloud individually to the respondent, who is asked to describe his or her reaction to the words according to a forced choice among four alternatives: visualization, written (spelling), listen (sound), and activity (feeling). These four alternatives describe the four types of learning methods into which the words are grouped. The objective of this exercise for Reinert was "to provide practical help for the classroom teacher interested in providing more effective counseling for his students. The basic pedagogical principle proposed here is that the student's initial contact with new material [should be] by means of his most efficient learning style" (Reinert, 1976, p. 160). The reliability testing involved 763 undergraduates. The overall psychometric ratings for the Edmonds Learning Style Identification Exercise were poor for reliability and no evidence for validity.

The Schmeck, Ribich, and Ramanaiah Inventory of Learning Processes (1977) was created by extrapolating ideas from Craik and Lockhart into the area of everyday study methods. The inventory is composed of 62 written items in a true-false format that are responded to by the student. These items are organized into four scales: synthesis-analysis, study methods, fact retention, and elabortive processing. This inventory was designed to assess "the behavioral and conceptual processes which students engage in while attempting to learn new material" (Ribich & Schmeck, 1979, p. 515). The reliability testing encompassed 957 undergraduate students. The construct and predictive validity testing involved 312 undergraduates. The psychometric ratings for this instrument were strong for both reliability and validity. This was the most highly rated inventory of the 21 instruments rated by Curry.

In regard to collaboration between North America and Australian learning style research, Curry found that Schmeck worked with Entwistle and Ramsden to produce an instrument combining their approaches in 1983. The Inventory of Approaches to Studying (Entwistle & Ramsden), and Inventory of Learning Processes (Schmeck, Ribich, & Ramanaiah) used 75 items to compose the combined scales of Entwistle and Ramsden and of the Schmeck instrument. The strong correlation that resulted supported the thematic relationship between these two instruments (Curry, 1987). The collaborated inventory was not psychometrically rated within Curry's study.

Learning Style as Personality-Related Preferences

The third and central layer of the thematic learning style onion model is cognitive personality style. This concept is defined as an individual's approach to adapting and assimilating information. This adaption does not interact directly with the environment. Rather, these are underlying and relatively permanent personality constructs. These constructs form part of the construct description of personality.

One of the earliest indicators of personality type developed was the Myers-Briggs Type Indicator, which was designed in 1962 (Myers, 1962). This inventory was theoretically based on Jung's theory of psychological types. The Myers-Briggs Type Indicator contains 143 forced-choice items, each with four alternatives. Each choice is oriented toward one of four bipolar concepts: extroversion versus introversion, sensing versus intuition, thinking versus feeling, and judging versus perceiving. This instrument was designed to measure the constructs in Jung's theory of psychological types, although the last two polarities (judging and perceiving) were proposed by Myers and Briggs. The pattern of results generated by the four bipolar concepts is interpreted in terms of Jungian theory. This in turn is used to predict attitudes and behavior. The reliability test sample involved 91 medical students and 56 undergraduate students. The predictive validity testing took place over 12 years involving 5,355 medical students. The overall psychometric ratings were good for reliability and strong for validity.

The work of Jerome Kagan (1964) resulted in the development of the Matching Familiar Figures Test. This test is based on 12 visual items, each involving meaningful line drawings and requiring a match to an available target. Each item is timed for accuracy of the match. The scoring places each respondent on a bipolar scale purporting to measure conceptual tempo or the tendency to venture answers with a cursory or careful approach (Curry, 1987). Kagan's labels for this style difference are impulsivity or reflectivity, respectively. The underlying concept of the test was to demonstrate the degree to which people tend to reflect on the validity of hypothesized solutions for problems that contain response uncertainty. The reliability testing involved over 120 second grade students. The psychometric ratings were fair for both reliability and validity.

The Witkin Embedded Figures Test was developed in 1969. It is composed of 18 pictorial items, each involving identification of non-meaningful geometric target shapes hidden within larger non-meaningful geometric shapes. The items are scored for time and accuracy. The scores place respondents on a bipolar scale which measure the degree of field dependence or independence. The measure was designed to reveal a respondent's "general tendency to function at a more differentiated or less differentiated" level (Witkin et al., 1971).

Another form of the Embedded Figures Test was also developed to be administered in groups. The Group Embedded Figures Test was made available in 1971. More current work by Shade (1984) supports the proposal that Witkin's tests are measuring individual variation in perceptual preference patterns rather than behavioral tendencies. The reliability testing encompassed 793 college students, 53 older students, 347 high school students, and 27 specified as general students. The psychometric ratings overall for Witkin's tests were strong for reliability and good for validity.

Ethnicity as Related to Learning Style Research and Inventories

As an educator or trainer begins to survey the learning style research, he or she realizes the breadth and depth of the several hundred learning style inventories available in North America alone. Thus, a framework composed of three key inventory categories was presented previously. This framework may be used in order to better discriminate among learning style inventories that will meet specific learning setting needs.

In the introduction of this chapter it was stated that a majority of the instruments were developed based on college educated Caucasian reliability and validity test samples. This was the inventory development trend from the 1950s through the 1980s. With the diversity issue raised on college campuses throughout the United States since the 1980s, much of the learning style research may be questioned with regard to the relationships between ethnicity and learning style.

As an educator or trainer, it is important to scrutinize the validity and reliability of the test samples the inventories are based on, as this will determine the relevance of the inventory to a specific student group. If one works with a majority of Caucasian college-educated students or clients using any of the previously described instruments, with the exception of those designed for children and adolescents, the instrument(s) will be appropriate. If one works with a multi-cultural cross-section of students or any one ethnic group, it is suggested that one further scrutinize the inventories available and relevant to the student group.

Three approaches have been taken in regard to the ethnic learning style research. One approach was to develop an inventory for a particular ethnic group. Another approach was to conduct research on various ethnic groups using existing learning style instruments. A third approach involved direct interviews or observations of students. The second approach may be questioned as to the appropriateness of the research method. The research approach of administering an instrument that is based on a college-educated Caucasian sample may need to be addressed when investigating learning styles of a particular ethnic group.

Learning style inventories specific to ethnic groups began in the 1980s. An inventory developed by Ramirez and Castaneda (1974) focused on the Mexican American student. Other research topics on Mexican Americans and learning styles are as follows: learning styles of Mexican American and Anglo-American elementary students, Mexican American language learning and learning style, and perceptual learning style differences among Mexican American high school and university students.

Another ethnic group studied in regard to learning style research was the Native American. This research often involved the administration of existing inventories to various Native American subgroups. Research topics studied on Native Americans and learning style were as follows: Native Americans and higher education, drama education and Native Americans, and cognitive styles hemispheric functions and Native American students.

A third major ethnic group that has been studied in regard to learning style has been the African American ethnic group. A study by McKenney, Guild, and Fouts (1990) considered the learning style preferences of 1,000 elementary students in the Seattle area. The investigators used the Witkin Embedded Figures Test. The two styles defined by Witkin are field independent (analytic), and field dependent (global). The study results elaborated on the learning styles of the white and African American students. It was found that the learning style differences between white students and African American students were quite small. Previous research indicates there are more learning style differences among members of any ethnic group than between ethnic groups. It was also found that when the sample was separated into high achievers and low achievers, based on the California Achievement Test scores, the high achievers tended to be field independent and low achievers tended to be field dependent.

These results should not be interpreted to say that most high achievers are field independent learners and most low achievers are field dependent, as the Witkin inventory is not an intelligence test. This is only one elementary learning style study. It was recognized that this research may demonstrate that the California Achievement Test may promote educational programs with a field independent or analytic learning style bias, in terms of test achievement.

A fourth major ethnic group studied, with several subgroups, is Asian Americans. Some of the learning style topics research with regard to Asian Americans were the following: Asian immigrant children, the Hmong and field dependence/independence and problem solving, and cognitive assessment of Asian Americans.

In summary, it is found that much of the ethnic based learning style literature focused on the Mexican American, Native American, African

American, and Asian American ethnic groups. When selecting an inventory for a specific ethnic student group it is critical to study the validity and reliability test samples the inventory is based on. One problem with this scrutiny is that many inventory explanations (data and statistics) do not specify the test sample ethnic group representation. A rule of thumb may be if the inventory description does not include or focus on an ethnic group, most likely it is based on a white educated sample or an unknown multi-cultural test sample. The most critical issue that needs to be studied is to consider what is valued in each culture. With this understanding, an investigator would look at how these values relate to ways of learning within each ethnic group.

LEARNING STYLE INFORMATION AND ASSESSMENT FOR THE QUALITY OF INSTRUCTION AND TRAINING

Throughout the past 30 years, as the issue of learning style has been raised, researched, and applied it appears that educators in elementary, secondary, and higher education have found a plethora of uses, as well as some misuses, for learning style inventories.

The use of learning style instruments has been quite widespread in the private sector as well. Trainers have found them most useful within human resource development seminars, particularly those focused on communication skills, team building, conflict resolution, and intercultural communication.

This discussion will suggest uses with regard to assessment within higher education, adult education, and training settings. Some key questions that need to be addressed in relation to learning style assessment would be: Why do we assess learning style in a teaching or training setting? When is it best to assess style? Who should assess for learning style? and What are the various methods to assess for learning style?

In response to why we assess for learning style in adult teaching and training settings, two major concepts address this issue. The first reason is that researchers often propose that teachers need to broaden their awareness of learner preferences in order to more effectively stimulate student learning. Learning style instruments often refer to access of results for teacher application in the classroom. Methods and curriculum are the two key aspects for teacher or trainer learning style application. Models such as the Dunn Learning Style Inventory or the Kolb Learning Style Inventory and Learning Cycle are typically applied for methods and curriculum development.

A second key reason for learning style assessment is to increase student self-knowledge. If an inventory is administered to a class or training group, the instructor needs to explain how the students can use the learning style knowledge for themselves. Some researchers emphasize that learning style awareness is primarily for student knowledge and that it is their responsibility to use the knowledge as they navigate through learning throughout life. The administrator of an inventory should also explain that learner preferences can change with a shift in learning environments (for example, the movement from a long-term job to a graduate school setting). Other learning style assessment uses would involve the following adult learning settings: supervision and evaluation (in school or work setting), counseling, and interpersonal and group communication.

Considering all the various purposes for learning style assessment, the when question will be answered in relation to three key learning settings: the classroom or training setting, counseling, and a supervision environment. When beginning a college course or adult education course or training, it is suggested that the teacher or trainer introduce the learning style inventory first. An explanation of its purpose (teacher and student knowledge and self responsibility) is important, as well as the inventory uses. Results should be shared and the teacher should allow one course session for class or small group discussion. Students may want to meet with the teacher to discuss the results and application to the course setting.

In the counseling setting, inventories are most helpful when a student is having difficulties with a course or the learning environment. If a counselor receives inventory results prior to meeting with the student or client, then the session can be spent problem solving with regard to the person's learning strengths, weaknesses, and strategies. Often learning strategies can be created collaboratively by the end of the session.

It is important to note that the learning style instrument needs to be used only for learning style problem solving. If the student has a learning disability, he or she needs to be referred to a developmental learning specialist.

The use of learning style instruments is very valuable for both the supervisor and the supervisee. It is suggested that as a new staff person joins a department that an inventory be administered. The purposes should be explained (for example, to ensure good communication, to better meet the needs in this department) before it is administered. The new staff person should know that the information would not be used in reference to hiring or firing practices. In recent years inventories have been misused with regard to personnel practices. After the results are received, time should be taken to review the meaning and results of the inventory. The staff member should be encouraged to develop communication strategies or work environment strategies with the information.

In response to who should administer learning style inventories, three responses will be made with respect to the teaching or training settings, the counseling setting, and the supervisory setting.

In most classroom and training settings, the instructor or trainer is responsible for administering the inventory. If in particular settings the instructor has access to a learning style specialist, this person may be the appropriate person to administer the instrument. In the case of the instructor or trainer administering the inventory, it is critical that the instructor clearly understands the purpose of the inventory, can explain the inventory directions and self scoring procedures (if it is self-scoreable), and can assist the students with interpretation of the results. This may involve additional information and explanation.

In the case of a counselor or supervisor administering an inventory, the criteria for administration of an inventory would directly correlate with the three criteria stated for the instructor or trainer. Special personality-based inventories may require additional training before an individual may administer such an inventory. The Myers-Briggs Type Indicator is an example of required training background prior to administration of inventories.

The following discussion will explain the five major methods of learning style assessment. These five methods are as follows: inventories, tests, interviews, observations, and analysis of products of learning (Guild & Garger, 1985, p. 82).

The inventory self-report approach is one of the most common learning style assessment methods. People give direct information about themselves by responding to various questions or preferences and often feel quite comfortable with them. The cognitive process inventories are all examples of the self-report type. One of the weaknesses of this approach is that people may reflect wishful thinking or mood rather than reality. It was Carl Jung who questioned a person's self-knowledge ability: "In respect to one's own personality, one's judgement is as a rule extraordinarily clouded" (1971, p. 3).

The second assessment type is a test of a particular skill or task. Witkin's Embedded Figures Test is an example of this type of skill test. A specific task has been shown to correlate with style characteristics, and the degree of success with the task indicates the style. This type of inventory has the advantage of being more objective. It is limited to measurement of a specific skill and all extensions are inferred.

The third approach to assess style is to ask a person directly. An interview may use self-report inventory questions or may involve open-ended questions. The interviewer and interviewee need to be aware that both are affected by their own styles and bring their own perspectives to the conversation.

A fourth approach is to observe a person involved in a task or learning situation. Several researchers encourage teachers to observe students and have developed observational checklists to systematize the process. Researchers who offer such observational checklists are Lawrence (1982) and Barbe and Swassing (1979). It is also important to keep in mind that the observation of another person will be colored by the observer's perception, and this interaction needs to be acknowledged (Guild & Garger, 1985).

The fifth method of assessment is to consider the products of a person's behavior. Activities that are consistently successful for an individual will give the assessor indications of that person's pattern or learning preference. It may also be observed that tasks or situations that are consistently difficult will give information about learning dislikes or weaknesses. One example is that of a teacher using a miscue-analysis (observing results of reading) approach to assess the reading style of several students. The results tend to correlate strongly with several characteristics of style (Guild & Garger, 1985).

The authors of learning style instruments often point out that no instrument is 100 percent valid for every person. Thus, researchers suggest assessment of styles through the use of more than one instrument. Curry has suggested that students should experience one instrument from each of the three inventory types (instructional preference, information processing, and personality-based).

In the case of teachers or trainers responsible for a large number of adult students, the assessment of each person's style implies having plans to accommodate the individual learning preferences. Instructors, counselors, or supervisors in this situation must be clear about the purpose of their efforts. It is suggested that caution should be used in the widespread assessment of style, or it might result in unrealistic expectations and frustrations on the part of the student and instructors. It is important to explain the purpose and use of the results prior to or as the results are discussed.

Assessment of learning style is often a necessary first step in application of style concepts. At the same time, many accommodations to style can be made by a genuine acceptance of diversity without specifically labeling the characteristics of each person. Instructors and trainers can consciously accommodate for style through a variety of instructional methods and curricula that demonstrate benefit for many learners. The inventory administration process has been found particularly helpful to broaden adult students' self-knowledge, empower them to develop their own learning strategies, and, in the long term, take responsibility for learning throughout their life.

SUMMARY AND CONCLUSIONS ON LEARNING STYLE CONCEPTS AND INSTRUMENTS

According to Curry (1987), learning style researchers "have not yet unequivocally established the reality, utility, reliability or validity of their concepts" (p. 16). On one hand, learning styles may not exist other than as unsubstantial artifacts of the interaction between people and the learning environment. On the other hand, learning styles can be real and stable enough to be useful to educational planners, specifically those who are concerned about individualized educational programs.

Based on the literature Curry (1987) reviewed, she drew no clear conclusions. Her emphasis was on the psychometric qualifications of the instruments. With the variation in results among the 21 instruments, it was difficult to offer clear conclusions. Kolb (1984) proposed that if one understands learning style as a state as opposed to a trait, due to the interdependence of the learning modes, then one realizes the very low expectancy of any individual in a given sample to be a pure learning style over time. These factors reduce the reliability of the learning styles inventory (Geller, 1979). In this way the issue of learning style inventory psychometric reliability results becomes less relevant.

Curry (1987) suggested that more research should be conducted to improve the learning style inventory psychometrics. She stated that people responsible for educational program design and delivery may find the benefit in experimental program application of these learning style instruments in an effort to individualize education. This may be done by assuming responsibility to help clients develop self-knowledge about their own learning style and then to understand the implications for their style in learning settings. This type of understanding will help educators plan and select educational experiences more appropriately and utilize their habitual styles more effectively. They should seek to match the primary mode of educational delivery to the best learning style information available, and in turn apply the information most appropriately to the intended audience (Curry, 1987).

Another recommendation is that educators and planners should consider offering a cross-section of courses in order that critical course material is offered with a diversity of teaching methods corresponding with a variety of learning styles. "The point is to offer planned variation in teaching approaches that will reinforce or reinterpret course content from didactic, discussion, or practice perspectives" (Curry, 1987, p. 16). In this way learning styles are acknowledged, and students are challenged to adapt to other ways of learning. Over time, adult learners become more complete learners.

Given the rudimentary and varying psychometric support for the majority of these learning style concepts, Curry recommended not to choose randomly among the 21 inventories. Curry suggested that it would be unwise to utilize any one instrument as the one true indicator of learning style. It is recommended that educators administer at least three evaluations, each representing the three layers of her model. Curry made these recommendations in light of the lack of a unitary concept of learning style. From the psychometric view of the need for standardization in order to find meaning, one may judge learning style constructs as unacceptable. Yet, from the educational philosophy that values context and that states that people must be viewed as individuals with unique experiential backgrounds, it is difficult to describe one singular construct for learning style. This philosophy is grounded in Dewey's (1938) educational constructs and Kolb's views, specifically in reference to their viewpoints on experience and education. In summary, many learning style constructs are needed in order to define learning style because humans are unique, although patterns may be observed among the diversity.

With the psychometric and individuality perspectives in mind, one recommendation may be suggested. Using only one measure assumes that one inventory is more correct than others. At this time that assumption cannot be made. It may be assumed that, with human individuality, multiple descriptions of learning style are necessary. This does not support the one inventory approach. Thus, it is recommended by Curry (1987) that "when making descriptions of individuals, to triangulate upon the concepts of interest by utilizing at least three measures with reasonable psychometric standards at each level of learning style," according to the model (pp. 17–28). These three levels represent instructional and environmental learning style preferences, information processing preferences, and personality-related preferences.

If an investigator wants to use a learning style construct, he or she is well advised to carefully consider the most appropriate level of learning style for application. For example, it would be unwise to use an instrument that is measuring constructs at one level if the purpose is to predict behavior governed by another level of the model.

It is concluded that the heuristic value of the onion model seems reasonably established, particularly in reference to the Marshall study findings. Learning style concepts appear to be grouped based on two key organizing principles: (1) similarities in the type of behavior measured and predicted, and (2) similarities in the duration of the effect measured (test-retest reliability) (Curry, 1987, p. 19).

In summary, the Australian learning style instruments reviewed (Biggs, 1979; Entwistle & Ramsden, 1983) approach learning style as a deeper or broader holistic concept, compared to the majority of North American learning style conceptualizations. The North American learning style conceptualizations tend to propose learning style as a variable inner cognitive process, behavioral, or an instructional/environmental preference concept.

With these learning style conceptual issues considered, as well as ethnicity and assessment issues outlined, it is suggested that the various learning style inventory selection and use guidelines be applied. This chapter has offered a descriptive framework that defines criteria upon which more discriminating learning style inventory decisions can be made. As a teacher or trainer realizes the importance of individual development in adult learning settings, the purpose and use of learning style inventories in adult education will continue to make an important contribution.

REFERENCES

Andrews, J. D. W. 1981. Teaching format and student style: Their interactive effects on learning. *Research in Higher Education, 14*(2), 161–178.

Barbe, W. B. & Swassing, R. H. 1979. *Teaching through modality strengths: Concepts and practices.* Columbus, OH: Zaner-Bloser, Inc.

Biggs, J. 1979. Individual differences in study process and the quality of learning outcomes. *Higher Education, 18*, 384–394.

Canfield, A. A. 1980. *Learning styles inventory manual.* Ann Arbor, MI: Humanics Media.

Coles, C. R. 1985. Differences between conventional and problem-based curricula in their student's approaches to studying. *Medical Education, 19*, 308–309.

Curry, L. 1983. Individualized CME: The potential and the problem. *The Royal College of Physicians and Surgeons of Canada Annuals, 16*(6), 521–526.

Curry, L. 1987. *Integrating concepts of cognitive or learning style: A review with attention to psychometric standards.* Ottawa, Ontario, Canada: Canadian College of Health Service Executives.

Dewey, J. 1938. *Experience and education.* New York: Collier MacMillan.

Dunn, R. 1983. Learning style and its relation to exceptionality at both ends of the spectrum. *Exceptional Children, 4*(6), 496–506.

Dunn, R., Dunn, K., & Price, G.E. 1986. *Productivity environmental preference survey.* Lawrence, KS: Price Systems.

Entwistle, N., & Ramsden, K. 1983. *Understanding student learning.* London, England: Croom Helm.

Friedman, C. P., & Stritter, F. T. 1976. An empirical inventory comparing instructional preferences of medical and other professional students. *Research in Medical Education Processing.* 15th Annual Conference. November, San Francisco, pp. 85–90.

Gage, N. L., & Berliner, D. C. 1979. *Educational psychology.* Rand McNally, Chicago.

Geller, L. M. 1979. Reliability of the Learning Style Inventory. *Psychological Reports, 44*, 555–561.

Goldberg, L. R. 1979. Student personality characteristics and optimal college learning conditions: An extensive search for trait-by-treatment interaction effects. *Instructional Science, 1*, 153–210.

Goldberg, L. R. 1972. Student personality characteristics and optimal college learning conditions: An extensive search for trait-by-trait treatment interaction effects. *Instructional Science, 1*, 153–210.

Goldberg, L. R. 1963. Test-retest item statistics for the Oregon instructional preference inventory. *Oregon Research Institute Monograph 3*(4): 153–210.

Gregorc, A. R., & Ward, H. B. 1977. Implications for teaching and learning: A new definition for individual. *National Association of Secondary School Principals. NASSP Bulletin, 61*, 20–26.

Guild, P.B., & Garger, S. 1985. *Marching to different drummers.* Alexandria, VA: Association for Supervision and Curriculum Development.

Honey, P. & Mumford, A. 1982. *The manual of learning styles.* Maidenhead, Berkshire: Peter Honey.

Hunt, D. E., Butler, L. F., Noy, J. E., & Rosser, M. E. 1978. *Assessing conceptual level by the paragraph completion method.* Informal Series 13. Toronto, Ontario Institute for Studies in Education.

Jung, C. G. 1971. *Psychological types.* Princeton, NJ: Princeton University Press. (Original work published 1921).

Kagan, J. 1964. *Matching familiar figures test.* Cambridge, MA: Harvard University.

Kolb, D. A. 1989. *The executive skills profile.* Boston: McBer & Company.

Kolb, D. A. 1985. *Technical specifications manual learning style inventory.* Boston:

McBer and Company.

Kolb, D. A. 1984. *Experiential learning: Experience as the source of learning and development.* Englewood Cliffs, NJ: Prentice-Hall.

Kolb, D. A. 1976. *Learning style inventory: Technical manual.* Boston: McBer and Company.

Lawrence, G. 1982. *People types and tiger stripes: A practical guide to learning styles.* Gainesville, FL: Center for Applications of Psychological Types.

Levin, J. R. 1986. Four cognitive principles of learning-strategy instruction. *Educational Psychologist, 21*(1 & 2), 3–17.

Marshall, J. C. 1987. The examination of a learning style topology. *Research in Higher Education, 26*(4), 417–429.

Marshall, J. C., & Merritt, S. L. 1985. Reliability and construct validity of alternate forms of the learning style inventory. *Educational and Psychological Measurement, 45,* 931–937.

Marton, K., & Saljo, R. 1976. *On qualitative differences in learning: Outcome and processing employed by medical students.* Unpublished doctoral dissertation, Hebrew University of Jerusalem.

McKenney, J. L., & Keen, P. G. W. 1974. How managers' minds work. *Harvard Business Review, 52,* 79–90.

McKenney, J. L., Guild, P. B., & Fouts, J. 1990. *A study of the learning styles of elementary students: Low achievers, average achievers and high achievers.* Seattle: Academic Achievement Programs, Seattle Public Schools.

Messick, S. 1976. *Individuality in learning: Implications of cognitive styles and creativity for human development.* San Francisco: Jossey Bass.

Miller, A. 1981. Conceptual matching models and interactional research in education. *Review of Educational Research, 51*(1), 33–84.

Myers, I. B. 1962. *The Myers-Briggs type indicator.* Palo Alto, CA: Consulting Psychologists Press.

Newble, D. I., & Clarke, M. 1986, July. The approaches to learning of students in a traditional and in an innovative problem-based medical school. *Medical Education, 20*(4), 267–273.

Papalia, A. 1978, May. Assessing students' learning styles and teaching for individual differences. *Hispania, 61,* 318–322.

Pask, G. 1976. Styles and strategies of learning. *British Journal of Educational Psychology, 46,* 128–148.

Perrin, J. 1982. *Learning style inventory: Primary version.* Learning Styles Network. St. John's University.

Ramirez, M., & Castaneda, A. 1974. *Cultural democracy, by cognitive development and education.* New York: Academic Press.

Ramsden, P. 1983. *The Lancaster approaches to studying and course perceptions questionnaire: Lecturer's handbook.* Oxford: Oxford Polytechnic.

Riechmann, S. W., & Grasha, A. F. 1974. A rational approach to developing and assessing the construct validity of a student learning style scales instrument. *Journal of Psychology, 87,* 213–223.

Reinert, H. 1976. One picture is worth a thousand words? Not necessarily! *The Modern Language Journal, 60*(4), 160–168.

Renzulli, J. S., & Smith, L. H. 1978. *Learning styles inventory: A measure of student preference for instructional techniques.* Mansfield Centre, CT: Creative Learning Press.

Rezler, A. G., & Rezmovic, V. 1974. The learning preference inventory. *Journal of Allied Health, 19*(1), 28–34.

Ribich, F. D., & Schmeck, R. R. 1979. Multivariate relationships between measures of learning style and memory. *Journal of Research in Personality, 13,* 515–529.

Schmeck, R. R., Ribich, F. D., & Ramanaiah, N. 1977. Development of a self-report inventory for assessing individual differences in learning processes. *Applied Psychological Measurement*, *1*(3), 413–431.

Schroder, H. M., Driver, M. J., & Streufert, S. 1967. *Human information processing*. New York. Holt, Rinehart and Winston.

Shade, B. J. 1984. Field dependency: Cognitive style or perceptual skill? *Perceptual and Motor Skills*, *58*, 991–995.

Shipman, S., & Shipman, V. C. 1985. Cognitive styles: Some conceptual methodological and applied issues. In E. W. Gordon (Ed.). *Review of Research in Education*. Vol. 12. Washington, DC: American Educational Research Association.

Thomas, J. W., & Rohwer, W. D. 1986. Academic studying: The role of learning strategies. *Educational Psychologist*, *21*(1 & 2), 19–41.

Whitley, J. 1982, May. Cognitive style mapping: Rationale for merging old and new technologies. *Educational Technology*, pp. 25–26.

Witkin, H. A., Oltman, P. K., Raskin, E., & Karp, S. A. 1971. *A manual for the embedded figures tests*. Palo Alto, CA: Consulting Psychologists Press.

Yando, R. M., & Kagan, J. 1970. The effect of task complexity on reflection, impulsivity. *Cognitive Psychological Journal*, *1*, 192–200.

3

Increasing the Effectiveness of University/College Instruction: Integrating the Results of Learning Style Research into Course Design and Delivery

Blue Wooldridge

"It is a sad but indisputable fact that much of the teaching that goes on in our colleges and universities is of very poor quality. Indeed, virtually any college student can relate stories about the incredible tribulations he suffered at the hands of incompetent instructors" (Cahn, 1978, p. ix). Yet, as the report entitled *Faculty Development in a Time of Retrenchment* points out, a curious thing about teaching is that, although it is the most central business in the university and college world, it is the least talked about. One rarely hears an intelligent discussion of it (Group for Human Development in Higher Education, 1974). Cahn goes on to suggest that "the crisis in college teaching . . . results . . . from a failure to recognize the crucial principle that intellectual competence and pedagogical competence are two very different qualities. One cannot be an outstanding teacher without thorough knowledge of subject matter, but to possess that knowledge does not guarantee the ability to communicate it to a student" (1978, p. ix).

The lack of pedagogical training for faculty is well documented. In the past, the Ph.D., with its emphasis on specialized study in the discipline and its predominant orientation to research, was considered the necessary credential for teaching. Today, with an increasingly diverse student body and research that clearly identifies the elements of effective college teaching, a greater realization exists that faculty preparation should include other areas of knowledge as well (Claxton & Murrell, 1987, p.78).

Traditional doctoral programs, which form the core of the training of university faculty, do not concern themselves with teaching future faculty about the teaching and learning process. Theories of how people learn and the consequences of different educational strategies are not addressed in a systematic way by most doctoral programs. In fact, concern with educational issues such as appropriate teaching strategies, important characteristics of students, and effective pedagogical strategies are sometimes viewed disdainfully by faculty in traditional academic programs (Wooldridge & Janhna, 1990).

Malcolm Knowles (1973), among others, points out that understanding how a person learns is a major requisite for a successful educational program. The question of how a person learns is the focus of the concept of learning style (Pigg, Busch, & Lacy, 1980). Learning styles can be defined as characteristic cognitive, affective, and psychological behaviors that serve as relatively stable indicators of how learners perceive, interact with, and respond to the learning environment (Keefe, 1979).

Cognitive styles are information processing habits of representing the learner's typical mode of perceiving, thinking, problem solving, and remembering. Affective styles refer to those motivational processes viewed as the learner's typical mode of arousing, directing, and sustaining behavior. Physiological styles are biologically-based modes of response that are founded on sex-related differences, personal nutrition and health, and accustomed reactions to the physical environment (Keefe, 1979, pp. 4, 8, 11 & 15).

Some researchers believe that the concept of learning style "is the most important concept to demand attention in education in many years and is the core of what it means to be a person" (Guild & Garger, 1985, p. viii). Studies have shown that identifying a student's learning style and providing appropriate instruction in response to that style can contribute to more effective learning (Claxton & Murrell, 1987). Information about certain of these characteristics can also help faculty become more sensitive to the differences that students bring to the classroom. As Doyle and Rutherford (1984) point out, "the wide popularity of proposals and programs for matching learning styles would seem to have two sources. First, the logic underlying the approach is compelling. Learners differ in a wide variety of ways and these differences are likely to influence how they respond to and benefit from a given instructional method or program. . . . Second, the approach seems to offer an intelligent and practical framework for the organizational problems of dealing with diversity among students" (p. 20). However, "except for some relatively isolated situations and work of particular individuals, . . . it is fair to say that learning style has not significantly affected educational practices in higher education" (Claxton & Murrell, 1987, p. 1).

A major obstacle to improving instructional effectiveness through an understanding of learning styles is the lack of consensus as to definitions of important concepts in this field. In this chapter, a variety of learning styles that have been identified as having specific relevance to the improvement of the learning process will be discussed. A brief description of each of these dimensions will be presented, with a description of learning style instruments that instructors can use to measure specific learning styles and take responsive action.

LEARNING STYLE DIMENSIONS IMPORTANT FOR IMPROVING THE LEARNING PROCESS

Keefe (1979) has identified several dimensions of learning styles that appear to have the most relevance to the improvement of the learning process. They are field independence versus dependence (Witkin et al., 1971); perceptual modality preferences (Price, Dunn, & Dunn, 1978); conceptual tempo (Kagan, 1966); leveling versus sharpening (Holzman & Klein, 1954); conceptual level (Hunt, 1977; Hunt et al., 1978; Price, Dunn, & Dunn, 1978); locus of control (Rotter, 1971); achievement motivation (McClelland, 1971); social motivation (Hill & Nunnery, 1973); and masculine-feminine behavior (MacCoby & Jacklin, 1974). Each of these dimensions will be described and discussed below.

Field Independence versus Dependence

This dimension of cognitive learning styles measures whether the learner uses an "analytical as opposed to a global way of experiencing the [subject matter] environment" (Keefe, 1979, p. 9). In the same book, he suggests that field independence versus dependence seems to have a great implication for improving the learning process.

The concept of field independence versus dependence is the most researched of all of the learning styles dimensions. Its founder, Herman A. Witkin, was listed among the 100 authors most cited in the *Social Science Citation* index (Goodenough, 1986), and as early as September 1981 there were almost 4,000 manuscripts related to this concept (Cox & Gall, 1981). Claxton and Murrell (1987) state, "the extensive body of research on field dependence and independence, however, has not significantly affected college teaching. . . . At the same time, however, these two dimensions may be the most fundamental ones" (p. 13).

In a field dependent mode of perceiving, perception is dominated by the overall organization of the surrounding field, and parts of the field are experienced as fused. In a field independent mode of perceiving, parts of the field are experienced as discrete from the organized ground. Persons who are labelled field dependent/global learners rely upon the environment of the learning situation for structure. Field dependent learners are sensitive to social cues without being alerted to them. They are interpersonally oriented and rely heavily on external stimuli. This motivates them to look toward others for reinforcement of opinions and attitudes.

The field dependent/global learner has a short attention span, is easily distracted, and likes informal learning situations. People with this type of learning style view the teacher as just another individual. They respond best to a learning environment that evokes their feelings and experiences. They are less achievement-oriented and competitive than the analytic learner. For them learning is a social experience.

The field independent/analytical learner does not rely on the learning environment for referents. Field independent learners have an internal structure that enables them to analyze information and solve problems without outside assistance. In addition, field independent learners appear to be more active, autonomous, self-motivated, and task-oriented in their approaches to life. These individuals have the ability to analyze information from the learning situation and solve problems independently. The analytical-oriented learners resist distractions that would adversely affect their educational experience and have a longer attention span and greater reflectivity than global learners. They tend to be more sedentary and prefer formal learning situations, viewing the instructor merely as a source of information. They are competitive, achievement-oriented, and impersonal (Witkin et al., 1971; Witkin et al., 1977; Witkin & Goodenough, 1981).

There is one common theme running through the literature on field independence versus dependence research. Field dependent participants require more structure than do field independent participants to achieve the same level of learning. Whether this structure is manifested through a presentation of objectives and planned activities in human relation training (Mezoff, 1982), through structured lecture outlines (Frank, 1984; Ward & Clark, 1987), or in the inherent organization of the task material itself (Davis & Frank, 1979), its existence appears to remove any difference between the amount of material learned. This finding is ironic because, as the literature reviewed indicated, the field dependent learner prefers less structured learning environments such as discussion or discovery.

Field independence versus dependence is usually measured by such instruments as the Body Adjustment Test, Rod and Frame Test, or various embedded figures tests (Witkin & Goodenough, 1981). One frequently used instrument is the Group Embedded Figures Test (GEFT). The GEFT consists of a test booklet that presents 25 complex test figures plus two sample figures. Eight simple forms are printed on the back cover of the booklet; each is identified with a capital letter. The task presented is to find a simple figure located in a more complex design. This simple figure is to be outlined in pencil. The first part of the GEFT is a practice set consisting of seven items that are not scored. This practice set is intended to test comprehension of the test. Sections two and three consist of 18 figures. The test booklet is scored by visually comparing the traced simple figures with those provided in a special scoring key. Scores on the GEFT range from 0 to 18. Lower scores indicate a field dependent/global learner; higher scores reflect a tendency toward field independence/analytical learning. MacNeil (1980) reviewed much of the relevant research on this topic and concluded that the cut-off point between field independent and field dependent learners is somewhere between 12 and 13 on the GEFT.

Perceptual Modality Preferences

This cognitive learning style dimension measures a learner's "preferred reliance on one of the sensor modes of understanding experience. The modes are kinesthetic or psychomotor, visual or spatial, and auditory or verbal" (Keefe, 1979, p. 9). A brief elaboration of each of the elements that make up this learning style dimension, taken from Price and Griggs's (1985) *Counseling College Students Through Their Individual Learning Styles* is provided below.

Auditory Preferences

This perceptual area describes people who can learn best when initially listening to a verbal instruction such as a lecture, discussion, or recording.

Visual Preferences

Learners whose primary perceptual preference is visual can recall what has been read or observed. When asked for information from printed or diagrammatic material, they often can close their eyes and visually recall what they have read or seen earlier.

Tactile Preferences

Students with tactile perceptual preferences need to underline as they read, take notes when they listen, and keep their hands busy, particularly if they have low auditory preferences.

Kinesthetic Preferences

Learners with kinesthetic preferences require whole body movement and real life experiences to absorb and retain material to be learned. These people learn most easily when they are totally involved. Acting, puppetry, and drama are excellent examples of kinesthetic learning; others include building, designing, visiting, interviewing, and playing.

Productivity Environmental Preference Survey

A useful learning style instrument for measuring this dimension is the Productivity Environmental Preference Survey (PEPS) developed by Price, Dunn, and Dunn (1978). This instrument claims to be the first comprehensive approach to the diagnosis of an adult's individual productivity and learning style. Further, the instrument aids in prescribing the type of environment, working conditions, activities, and motivating factors that would maximize individual output. PEPS does not claim to measure underlying psychological motivation, value systems, or the quality of attitudes. Rather, it is said "to yield information concerned with the patterns through which the highest levels of productivity tend to occur. It therefore reveals *how* an employee prefers to produce or learn best, not why" (Price, Dunn, & Dunn, 1978, p. 2). The PEPS analyzes an individual adult's personal preferences for each of 21 different elements. These include, in addition to the four elements of perceptual modality preferences described above, noise level — quiet or sound, light — low or bright, temperature — cool or warm, design — informal or formal, unmotivated or motivated, non-persistent or persistent, irresponsible or responsible, structure — needs or does not need, learning alone or peer-oriented learner, authority figures present, learning in several ways, requires intake, functions best in evening or morning, functions best in late morning, functions best in afternoon, and mobility.

As can be seen from the brief description of PEPS provided above, this instrument also measures certain affective and physiological learning styles, which Keefe considers to have less implication for improving the learning process. These include the affective dimension of persistence or perseverance that Keefe characterizes as: "variations in learner's willingness to labor beyond the required time, to withstand discomfort and to face the prospect of failure. High persistence is characterized by the disposition to work at a task until it is completed, seeking whatever kinds of help is necessary to persevere. A low persistence style results in short attention span and the inability to work on a task for any length of time" (Keefe, 1979, p. 12).

Physiological learning styles that are measured by the PEPS include: health-related behavior, which is "individual response differences resulting from the physical imbalance of malnutrition, hunger, and disease. Dunn and Dunn refer to an aspect of this style as *intake*" (Keefe, 1979, p. 15); time rhythms or "individual variations in optimum learning patterns depending on the time of day" (p. 15); need for mobility, defined as "differences in learner need for change in posture and location" (p. 15); and environmental elements, which are "individual preferences for, or response to, varying levels of light, sound, and temperature" (p. 15). Although Keefe suggests that these physiological learning styles might have less implications for improving the learning process, this author thinks that investigation into learning variations has much potential for classroom research as suggested by Cross (1990).

Conceptual Tempo

Another important cognitive learning style that Keefe thinks has major importance for improving the learning process is conceptual tempo. Individuals differ in the speed and adequacy of hypothesis formulation and information processing on a continuum of reflection versus impulsivity. Impulsives tend to give the first answer they can think of even though it is frequently incorrect. Reflectives prefer to consider alternative solutions before deciding and to give more reasoned responses (Keefe, 1979, p. 10).

Claxton and Murrell (1987) identify the instruments used to measure this tendency as the matching figures test and the identical picture test. In the identical picture test, for example, the subject is to study a picture of an object (the standard), such as a geometric design, a house, or a car, and then is shown several similar stimuli, only one of which is identical to the standard. The subject's task is to select the picture that is the same as the standard in a limited time. Impulsive subjects respond to this factor of conceptual tempo by glancing quickly at the sample and selecting the answer that appears most nearly correct. Reflective persons carefully examine each alternative before finally selecting what they believe is the correct one (p. 17).

This learning style dimension has important implications for university instruction. "Heavy reliance on multiple-choice examinations may not give an accurate picture of how much a student actually knows" (Claxton & Murrell, 1987, p. 17). Under pressure to achieve a certain grade, the impulsive person is unable to become more reflective, and the reflective learner might be unable to carry out sufficient deliberations in the time allowed.

Leveling versus Sharpening

The purpose of this cognitive learning style is to "isolate principals of organization in cognitive behavior, termed *cognitive system-principals*, that will account for or predict a person's typical modes of perceiving, remembering, thinking" (Holzman & Klein, 1954, p. 105).

This dimension measures individual variations in memory processing. Levelers tend to blur similar memories and to merge new percepts readily with previous assimilated experiences; they tend to overgeneralize. Sharpeners are inclined to magnify small differences and to separate memory of prior experiences more easily from current data; they tend to overdiscriminate (Keefe, 1979, p. 10).

Selection of levelers and sharpeners can be defined using a situation termed "schematizing" in which subjects are called upon to judge in inches the size of squares:

> (Fourteen) squares varying from slightly more than 1" on a side to 14" were projected singly from a film strip on to the screen. Each square appeared for three seconds after which S had five seconds to record on a record sheet his absolute judgement of the size of the squares. At first only the first five smallest squares were shown, each three times and in fixed random order. Then, without warning and without interrupting the procedure, the smallest square of this series of five was removed and a square larger than any seen

thus far was added to the series. Each square in this new series of five squares was again presented three times. *In this way a square gradually shifted from being largest in one series of five to the smallest in another.*

Levelers were those who not only were inaccurate in detecting the position of the squares with a series throughout the test, but also showed a high percentage loss of accuracy when squares moved from the salient end position (i.e. largest or smallest of the series) to the middle position in any one series. They tended to judge all squares that occupied middle positions as similar in size. *Sharpeners* were those who effectively differentiated the squares in the middle position of each series and were also highly accurate throughout. (Holzman & Klein, 1954, p. 108–109)

Research has shown that levelers tend to seek a maximum simplicity of the cognitive field, whereas the sharpeners seek maximum complexity and differentiation (Holzman & Klein, 1954).

AFFECTIVE LEARNING STYLES

Affective learning styles are those dimensions of personality that have to do with attention, emotion, and valuing (Keefe, 1979, p. 11). The first of these learning style dimensions that Keefe thinks has implications for the improvement of the learning process is that of conceptual level.

Conceptual Level

Conceptual level is described as "a broad development trait characterizing how much structure a student requires in order to learn best. . . . Closely related to it are responsibility, the capacity of students to follow through on a task without direct or frequent supervision, and need for structure, the amount and kind of structure required by different individuals" (Keefe, 1979, p. 12).

Certain elements of this learning style, responsibility and the need for structure, are measured by PEPS.

It has been suggested that conceptual level may serve as the basis for "optimizing the teaching/learning process" (Hunt, 1977, p. 78). Hunt goes on to suggest that several characteristics of conceptual level theory contribute to its potential value for education.

It identifies present information-processing skills.

It indicates the specific process goals to be developed.

It specifies the training environment most likely to facilitate such development.

It applies both to students and to teachers.

It permits a reciprocal analysis of the teaching and learning process.

Hunt (1971; Hunt et al., 1978) reviews research that identifies some of the distinguishing characteristics of students varying in conceptual level. Studies have found, for example, that students with low conceptual level are more likely to choose one of their numbers to direct them, while high conceptual level students are more likely to work without a leader; when two kinds of information are presented, low conceptual level students are more affected by what they experienced first. High conceptual level students have shown greater accuracy in person perception than low conceptual level students.

Differences have also been shown in teacher trainees varying in conceptual level and their initial teaching styles. For example, high conceptual level trainees were higher in reflective index scores than low conceptual level trainees. High conceptual level teacher trainees preferred to teach using the example rule (or inductive) approach, where low conceptual level trainees were more likely to use a rule-exempt approach, thus matching the preferences of students having similar conceptual level styles. Conceptual level is frequently measured by the Paragraph Completion Method (Hunt et al., 1977).

Locus of Control

This learning style concept is interested in variations in individual perceptions of causality in behavioral outcomes on a continuum on internality versus externality (I-E). The internal person thinks of himself as responsible for his own behavior, as deserving praise for successes and blame for failures. The external person sees circumstances beyond his control, luck, or others as being responsible for his behavior (Keefe, 1979, p. 13).

This I-E phenomena is frequently measured using Rotter's forced-choice 29 item scale for measuring an individual's degree of internal and external control. Using this scale, a subject reads a pair of sentences and then indicates with which of the two statements he more strongly agrees. Subject scores on the I-E can range from zero (the consistent belief that individuals can influence the environment — that rewards come from internal forces) to 23 (the belief that all rewards come from external forces) (Rotter, 1971).

I-E findings show that people differ in the tendency to attribute satisfactions and failures to themselves rather than to external causes and these differences are relatively stable (Rotter, 1971). Several studies that are relevant to the instructional processes include findings that lower economic children tend to be more external than children from richer, better educated families; among disadvantaged children in the sixth, ninth, and twelfth grades, the students with high scores on an achievement test were more internal-orientated than children with low achievement scores; internal students were more successful in getting other students to change their attitudes than were external students; and, interesting enough, in today's public policy environment, nonsmokers have been shown to be significantly more internal than smokers (Rotter, 1971).

Achievement Motivation

David C. McClelland has suggested a theory of motivation closely associated with learning concepts (Gibson, Ivancevich, & Donnelly, 1994). His concept of achievement motivation is interested in individual differences in patterns of planning and striving for some internalized standard of excellence. Individuals with high achievement motivation are interested in excellence for its own sake rather than for any rewards it may bring. They set their goals carefully after calculating the success probability of a variety of alternatives. This style is also called need for achievement. This is probably the most thoroughly researched affective style (Keefe, 1979, p. 13).

McClelland proposes measuring need for achievement, not by asking an individual or by assuming that those who are observed working hard have a need for achievement, but rather, "study his fantasies and dreams. If you do this over a period of time, you will discover the themes to which his mind returns again and again" (McClelland, 1971). To measure an individual's relative need for achievement, affiliation, or power, McClelland uses the Thematic Apperception Test. "A person is shown pictures and asked to write a story about what he sees portrayed in them" (Gibson, Ivancevich, & Donnelly, 1994, p. 157). This mode of measurement is predicated on the assumption that people tend to write stories that reflect their dominant needs.

McClelland's proposed strategies for developing individuals with high need for achievement where there is no fear of success are reported in Gibson, Ivancevich, and Donnelly (1994)

> Arrange job tasks so that employees receive periodic feedback on performance, providing information that enables them to make modifications or corrections.
>
> Point out to employees models of achievement. Identify and publicize the accomplishments of achievement heroes, the successful people, the winners, and use them as models.
>
> Work with employees to improve their self-image. High in n-Ach [need for achievement] people like themselves and seek moderate challenges and responsibilities.
>
> Introduce realism into all work-related topics; promotions, rewards, transfers, development opportunities, and team membership opportunities. Employees should think in realistic terms and think positively about how they can accomplish goals. (Gibson, Ivancevich, & Donnelly, 1994, p. 160)

Social Motivation

This learning style dimension measures differences in value-based behavior based on variations in social and ethnic world view. Learners not only vary in socio-economic background, in cultural determinants and value codes, and in peer-group conformity but also are variously affected by the standards and expectations of these groups. "Differences in social motivation may derive from one of a combination of determinants" (Keefe, 1979, p. 14).

The major developments in this learning style dimension result from the work of Joseph Hill at the Oakland Community College in Michigan. In a book by Hill and Nunnery (1973), the principles of the educational sciences are described. These seven sciences are:

symbols and their meanings, which are based on the belief that people use theoretical and qualitative symbols basic to the acquisition of knowledge and meaning;

cultural determinants of the meaning of symbols, which are concerned with the cultural influences that affect what the symbols mean to particular individuals;

modalities of influence, which are the elements that show how a person makes inferences;

biochemical and electrophysiological aspects of memory-concern;

cognitive style, which is the product of the first four sciences;

teaching, counseling, and administrative style; and

systematic analysis decision making. (Claxton & Murrell, 1987, p. 47)

These sciences are captured in a model of cognitive style mapping. Using the results of this mapping can lead to the design of more effective learning experiences. Terrell (1976) tested community college students to measure their level of anxiety and cognitive style. Students whose cognitive style matched the instructional mode tended to achieve higher grades and experienced greater reduction in anxiety (Claxton & Murrell, 1987).

Masculine-Feminine Behavior

Research, as well as conventional wisdom, reports that there are variations in typical brain-behavior responses of males and females. Researchers agree that males generally are more aggressive, and sensitive to spatial (visual) relations and perhaps to mathematical processes. Females are more verbal and excel in fine muscular control (Keefe, 1979).

MacCoby and Jacklin (1974) reviewed over 2,000 books and articles on the sex differences in motivation, social behavior, and intellectual ability to determine "which benefits about sex differences are supported by evidence, which beliefs have no support, and which are still inadequately tested" (p. 109). Eight myths that MacCoby and Jacklin suggest are not supported by evidence are: girls are more social than boys; girls are more suggestible than boys; girls have lower self-esteem than boys; girls lack motivation to achieve; girls are better at role learning and simple repetitive tasks, boys are better at high-level tasks that require them to inhibit previously learned responses; boys are more analytic than girls; girls are more affected by heredity, boys by environment; and girls are auditory, boys visual.

There were four differences that did appear to be supported by evidence available at that time: boys are more aggressive than girls, girls have greater verbal ability than boys, boys excel in visual spatial ability, and boys excel in mathematical ability.

Finally, MacCoby and Jacklin found eight areas that are still questions, where more research needs to be conducted. Are there differences in tactile sensitivity? Are there differences in fear, timidity, and anxiety? Is one sex more active than the other? Is one sex more competitive than the other? Is one sex more dominant than the other? Is one sex more compliant than the other? Are nurturance and maternal behavior more typical of one sex? Is one sex more passive than the other? The authors summarize their findings by saying, "We must conclude from our survey of all the data, that many popular beliefs about the psychological characteristics of the two sexes have little or no basis. . . . The explanation may be that people's attention is selective" (MacCoby & Jacklin, 1974, p. 112).

IMPLICATIONS FOR UNIVERSITY AND COLLEGE ACTION

University academic departments must become interested in making learning style research an important part of the teaching and learning process. Manifestations of such interest can take the form of integrating the results of learning style research into the design and delivery of courses — faculty development activities, promotion of classroom-based research, orientations for students on their individual learning styles and how to develop strategies for adapting them effectively (including candidate understanding of student differences, including learning styles, when hiring new faculty), and conducting more research, relevant to the specific academic curriculum, on learning styles (many of these action items were first suggested by Claxton and Murrell, 1987). Each of these recommendations is discussed more fully.

Faculty Development

Faculty development activities, such as workshops, seminars, and similar activities, can be useful in helping faculty better understand the concepts behind learning styles and how an understanding of these concepts can lead to an improvement in student learning.

This insight is important for more than understanding how to modify course design and delivery as suggested in the previous section. Research has indicated that teachers are more likely to use instructional methods that are congruent with their cognitive learning style. Wu (1968, as quoted in Bertini, 1980) found that field dependent student teachers in social studies ranked discussion as more important to the practice of good teaching than lecture, which was favored by more field independent instructors. "A discussion approach, it should be noted, not only emphasizes social interaction, but also gives the student more of a role in structuring the classroom situation" (Bertini, 1980, p. 95). After summarizing the relevant literature reviewing research on the relationship between instructors' cognitive styles and their preferred instructional methods, Bertini concluded: "On the whole, the evidence gathered suggests that field-dependent and field-independent teachers have different teaching preferences syntonic with their own personal styles, and that, based on these differences, they may conduct their classes differently thereby showing different patterns of actual teaching behavior in the classroom" (1980, p. 96).

This natural tendency might have special significance for university and college faculty. Research findings indicate that subjects with undergraduate preparation in the social professions were significantly more field dependent than students with other undergraduate preparation (Wooldridge, 1994b). One could infer a significant number of university and college faculty are field dependent. Combining this hypothesis with the findings that instructors have teaching styles that are congruent with their own personal styles, it could be concluded that there might be a large number of classroom situations where field dependent instructors are using low or non-structured teaching methods with field dependent students. The research findings described earlier, however, suggest that such teaching methods and student characteristics combinations place the field independent student at a disadvantage.

In addition to increasing the sensitivity of the field dependent faculty member to the possible dysfunctional consequences of the congruent instructional style on field independent students, both field independent and field dependent faculty need to be made aware of how teacher to student matching or mismatching of learning styles can lead to bias in assessment. DiStefano (1970, as described in Bertini, 1980) found when teachers and students have similar cognitive styles they tended to describe each other in positive terms, not only in personal but intellectual characteristics as well. "Teachers often believe that students whose cognitive styles match theirs are smarter than those whose styles are different from theirs. They say that the former are more intelligent, more logical, and more successful as students" (Bertini, 1980, p. 97).

These findings should also be of interest to field independent faculty members having their instructional effectiveness assessed by a class with a high percentage of field-dependent students.

Classroom Research

In October 1990, an article in the *Chronicle of Higher Education* stated that, "for teaching to gain prestige in higher education, faculty members must make pedagogy a subject of scholarly debate" (Watkins, 1990, p. A11). This article goes on to quote Lee S. Shulman, a professor of education at Stanford University, as saying, "teaching will be considered a scholarly activity only when professors develop a conception of pedagogy that is very tightly coupled to scholarship in the disciplines themselves" (p. A11). Commanding a professional base of knowledge of subject matter with knowledge of how to teach it effectively to others is the primary purpose of classroom research (Cross, 1990). "Classroom research is the careful, systematic, and patient study of students in the process of learning" (Cross, 1990, p. 2). Its goal is making teaching more professional based on understanding, insights, knowledge, and skill. This goal is congruent with Ernest L. Boyer's observation that "the time has come for us to inquire much more carefully into the nature of pedagogy. It's the most difficult and perhaps most essential work in developing future scholars" (Watkins, 1990, p. A12). The concept of different learning styles is an ideal topic for classroom research. Instructors can identify the various learning style profiles of the participants in each class and, using the Cronbach and Snow's (1969) concept of Aptitude-Treatment Interaction, design effective learning strategies.

Cronbach and Snow state: "The educator continually devises and applies new instructional treatments, hoping for improved results. He seeks the best methods of instruction for a given purpose. Since learners differ, the search for generally superior methods should be supplemented by a search for ways to fit the instruction to each kind of learner. One can expect interaction between learner characteristics and instructional method. Where these exist, the instructional approach that is best on the average is not best for all persons" (1969, p 1).

Student Orientations

Orientation activities should be designed for students that will make them aware of their own learning styles, preferences, strengths, and weaknesses. Based on such insight, students can select courses and instructors that would lead to the most effective learning conditions for them (perhaps in contrast to those that the students would prefer or feel more comfortable in). "Attention should also be given to helping students develop strategies for succeeding in courses taught in ways that are incongruent with their primary learning abilities" (Claxton & Murrell, 1987, p. 78).

Hiring New Faculty

It has been estimated that, during the next 20 years, more than half the faculty of any given university will probably retire. Colleges and universities will have to hire thousands of new faculty members to replace those that leave higher education. "Today, with an increasingly diverse student body and research that clearly identifies the elements of effective college teaching . . . a greater realization exists that faculty preparation should include other areas of knowledge as well" (Claxton & Murrell, 1987, p. 78). Departments and selection committees should include the candidate's knowledge of pedagogy, including the implications of different learning styles, as a selection criteria.

FUTURE RESEARCH

It is ironic that in spite of all of the research that was conducted in the area of learning styles (Claxton & Murrell, 1987; Keefe, 1979) there still remains so much left to be done. Learning style research is critically needed in the following areas: learning styles of minorities, women, and international students; differences in learning styles of the part-time, non-traditional students; implication of learning styles for the use of technology in delivery of higher education; and the implication of individual learning style differences for the selection of the most effective instructional instrument for different types of learning objectives. Each of these areas will be discussed below.

First, attention should be paid to the study of learning styles as they relate to minorities, women, and international students. Forecasts of the increased diversity of the work force by the year 2000 are plentiful (Johnston & Packer, 1987; Wooldridge & Maddox, 1994). This diversity will also be reflected in the academic community. In the coming decades, "there will be a new army of Hispanic students, one as large as that of the blacks. And there will be a much larger number of Asians. America's colleges and universities . . . have also become increasingly attractive to the better foreign students" (Keller, 1983, p. 13). Research is finding that there are different learning style profiles related to individuals with gender and racial differences. Further research directed at more precisely identifying these differences and their implications for the design and delivery of college level education is needed.

In addition to the change in ethnic, racial, and national backgrounds of students, a second major change in emphasis for learning style research should focus on non-traditional students. By 1990, the student population increased 45 percent over the 1970s, from 8.6 million to 12.5 million, but the proportion described as traditional had fallen by more than one-fifth, to 57 percent. The rest of the students are older, commute, or study part-time. What is more, the "graying" of the campus so much in evidence today promises to persist indefinitely, as the national population continues to age (Green, 1989, p. 79).

Additional research needs to be conducted to determine the relationship between the different learning style dimensions that have important implications for improving the learning process, and such independent demographic variables as age or full versus part-time student status.

Third, emphasis should be placed on learning styles and their use in higher education technology. A major reason given for the decline in productivity in higher education is that college and university budgets are highly labor-intensive (Massy, 1989; Levin, 1989).

"Capital can be substituted for professional labor. . . . Now information technology is producing a 'second industrial revolution' and this one holds great promise for the knowledge industry including colleges and universities. Investment in computers, communication systems, and other kinds of intelligent machines can leverage faculty time" (Massy, 1989, p. 5).

However, research findings indicate a large number of the students enrolled in universities are field dependent. The literature suggests that field dependent individuals are interpersonally oriented and rely heavily on external stimuli. This motivates them to look toward others for reinforcement of opinions and attitudes. Field dependent people like to be with other people, show an interest in them, and are sociable. They appear to prefer to be physically close to people and emotionally open. For them, learning is a social experience.

In light of these characteristics of field dependent students, and in view of the assumption that a large percentage of university and college students are field dependent, research must be conducted to determine the effectiveness of using technology in the delivery of higher education course offerings (Wooldridge, 1994a).

Finally, the relationship of individual learning styles, types of learning objectives, and effective instructional methodology should receive additional attention. Within the past few years, some excellent work has been carried out that relates the effectiveness of different instructional methods (for example, lectures, films, case studies, role playing, etc.) to specific learning objectives (McCleary & McIntyre, 1972; Newstrom, 1980; Olivas & Newstrom, 1981; and Carroll, Payne & Ivancevich, 1972). Research needs to be conducted to test the "Contingency Approach to Instructional Design" (Wooldridge, 1978), which suggests the effectiveness of an instructional method is contingent on both the learning objective to be achieved and the learning style of the participant. University and college education would be enhanced by an understanding of how the relative effectiveness of different teaching methods, optimal for a specified set of learning objectives, needs to be modified to take into account differences in learning styles of individual students (Wooldridge, 1978).

CONCLUSION

Higher education is operating in an environment that calls for greater accountability, including increased assessment of the quality of its instruction. Anything an academic department can do to improve its teaching process will respond to this legitimate demand from the clients of university and college education. Evidence has been presented in this study that suggests the concept of learning styles is an important element in the design of effective instructional design and delivery. Truly, "style is the most important concept to demand attention in education in many years [and] is the core of what it means to be a person" (Guild & Garger, 1985, viii). This study indicates there is sufficient diversity among the learning styles of university and college students to warrant increased attention to this concept by faculty members. Significant contributions to the enhancement of learning can be made by the integration of the findings of learning style research into course design and delivery. The higher education community would be negligent if it fails to take advantage of this opportunity to improve university and college education.

REFERENCES

Bertini, M. 1980. Some implications of field dependence for education. In M. Bertini, L. Pizzamiglio, and S. Wapner (Eds.), *Field dependence in psychological theory, research, and applications: Two symposia in memory of Herman Witkin.* Hillsdale, NJ: Lawrence Erlbaum Associates.

Cahn, S. M. 1978. *Scholars who teach: The art of college teaching.* Chicago, IL: Nelson-Hall.

Carroll, S. J., Paine, F. T., & Ivancevich, J. J. 1972. Relative effectiveness of training methods — expert opinion and research. *Personnel Psychology, 25,* 495–509.

Claxton, C. S., & Murrell, P. H. 1987. *Learning styles: Implications for improving educational practices.* (ASHE - ERIC Higher Education Reports, No. 4). Washington, DC: Association for the Study of Higher Education.

Cox, P. W., & Gall, B. E. 1981. *Field dependence-independence and psychological differentiation.* Research Report: Supplement No. 5. Princeton, NJ: Educational Testing Service.

Cronbach, J. J., & Snow, R. E. 1969. *Individual differences in learning ability as a function of instruction variables: Final report.* Stanford, CA: Stanford University School of Education.

Cross, K. P. 1990. *The current status of classroom learning.* Paper presented at the meeting of the National Conference on College Teaching and Learning, Jacksonville.

Davis, J. K., & Frank, B. M. 1979. Learning and memory of field independent-dependent individuals. *Journal of Research in Personality, 13,* 469–479.

Doyle, W., & Rutherford, S. 1984. Classroom research on matching learning and teaching styles. *Theory Into Practice, 23,* 20–25.

Frank, B. M. 1984. Effect of field independence-dependence and study technique on learning from a lecture. *American Educational Research Journal, 21,* 669–678.

Gibson, J. L., Ivancevich, J. M., & Donnelly, J. H., Jr. 1994. *Organizations: Behavior, structure, processes.* Burr Ridge, IL: Richard D. Irwin.

Goodenough, D. R. 1986. History of the field dependence construct. In M. Bertini, L. Pizzamiglio, and S. Wapner (Eds.), *Field dependence in psychological theory, research, and applications: Two symposia in memory of Herman Witkin.* Hillsdale, NJ: Lawrence Erlbaum Associates.

Green, M. F. (Ed.). 1989. *Minorities on campus: A handbook for enhancing diversity.* Washington, DC: American Council on Education.

Group for Human Development in Higher Education. 1974. *Faculty development in a time of retrenchment.* New Rochelle, NY: Change Magazine Press.

Guild, P. B., & Garger, S. 1985. *Marching to different drummers.* Alexandria, VA.: Association for Supervision and Curriculum Development.

Hill, J. E. & Nunnery, D. N. 1973. *The educational sciences.* Bloomfield Hills, MI: Oakland Community College Press.

Holzman, P. S., & Klein, G. S. 1954. Cognitive system — principles of leveling and sharpening: Individual differences in assimilation effects in visual time error. *Journal of Psychology, 37,* 105–122.

Hunt, D. E. 1977. Conceptual level theory and research as guides to educational practices. *Interchange, 8*(4), 78–90.

Hunt, D. E. 1971. *Matching models in education: The coordination of teaching methods with student characteristics.* Monograph series No. 10. Ontario Institute of Technology.

Hunt, D. E., Butler, L. F., Noy, J. E., & Rosser, M. E. 1978. *Assessing conceptual level by the paragraph completion method.* Informal Series 13. Toronto: Ontario Institute for Studies in Education.

Johnston, W. B., & Packer, A. H. 1987. *Workforce 2000: Work and workers for the 21st century.* Indianapolis: Hudson Institute.

Kagan, J. 1966. Reflection-impulsivity: The generality and dynamics of conceptual tempo. *Journal of Abnormal Psychology, 71,* 17–24.

Keefe, J. W. 1979. Learning style: An overview. In J. W. Keefe (Ed.) *Student learning styles: Diagnosing and prescribing programs.* Reston, VA: National Association of Secondary School Principals.

Keller, G. 1983, March. A change in plans: The view from four colleges. *Change, 15*(2), 34–43.

Knowles, M. 1973. *The adult learner: A neglected species.* Houston, TX: Gulf Publishing.

Levin, H. M. 1989. Reaching productivity in higher education. Paper presented for the Higher Education Research Program and the Pew Memorial Trust. Philadelphia, PA: The Trustees of the University of Pennsylvania.

Massy, E. F. 1989. A strategy for productivity improvement in college and university academic departments. Paper presented at the Forum for Postsecondary Governance, Santa Fe.

MacNeil, R. 1980. The relationship of cognitive style and instructional style to the learning performance of undergraduate students. *Journal of Educational Research, 73,* 354–59.

MacCoby, E., & Jacklin, C. N. 1974, December. What we know and don't know about sex differences. *Psychology Today,* pp. 109–112.

McCleary, L. E., & McIntyre, K. E. 1972. Competency development and university methodology. *The National Association of Secondary School Principals Bulletin.*

McClelland, D. C. 1971. *Motivational trends in society*. Morristown, NJ: General Learning Press.

Mezoff, B. 1982. Cognitive style and interpersonal behavior: A review with implications for human relations training. *Group and Organization Studies*, *7*(1), 13–34.

Newstrom, J. W. 1980. Evaluating the effectiveness of training methods. *The Personnel Administrator*, *25*, 12–16.

Olivas, L., & Newstrom, J. W. 1981. Learning through the use of simulation games. *Training and Development Journal*, *35*, 63–66.

Pigg, K. E., Busch, L., & Lacy, W. B. 1980. Learning styles in adult education: A study of county extension agents. *Adult Education*, *30*, 233–244.

Price, G. E., Dunn, R., & Dunn, K. 1978. *Productivity environmental preference survey*. Lawrence, KS: Price Systems, Inc.

Price, G. E., & Griggs, S. A. 1985. *Counseling college students through their individual learning*. Ann Arbor, MI: ERIC Counseling and Personnel Services Clearinghouse.

Rotter, J. B. 1971, June. External control and internal control. *Psychology Today*, *5*, 1–28.

Terrell, W. R. 1976, October/December. Anxiety level modification by cognitive style matching. *Community/Junior College Research Quarterly*, *1*, 13–24.

Ward, T. J., & Clark, H. T., III. 1987. The effect of field dependence and outline condition on learning high- and low-structure information from a lecture. *Research in Higher Education*, *27*(3), 259–272.

Watkins, B. T. 1990, October 31. To enhance prestige of teaching, faculty members urged to make pedagogy focus of scholarly debate. *The Chronicle of Higher Education*, pp. A11–A12.

Witkin, H. A., & Goodenough, D. R. 1981. *Cognitive styles: Essence and origin*. New York: International University Press.

Witkin, H. A., Moore, C. A., Goodenough, D. R., & Cox, P. W. 1977. Field dependent and field independent cognitive styles and their educational implications. *Review of Educational Research*, *47*, 1–64.

Witkin, H. A., Oltmann, P. K., Raskin, E., & Karp, S. A. 1971. *A manual for the embedded figures tests*. Palo Alto, CA: Consulting Psychologists Press.

Wooldridge, B. 1994a, June. Changing demographics in the work force: Implications for the use of technology in public organizations. *Public Productivity and Management Review*, *17*(4), 371–386.

Wooldridge, B. 1994b. A strategy for improving education for management: Integrating the results of selected learning style research into management course design and delivery. Unpublished manuscript.

Wooldridge, B. 1978. New training directions: Learning styles can determine success. *Network News*. Washington, DC: National Training and Development Service.

Wooldridge, B., & Janha, D. 1990. Enhancing the instructional capabilities of public administration faculty. Paper presented at the 13th National Conference on Teaching Public Administration, Tempe, Arizona.

Wooldridge, B., & Maddox, B. 1994. Demographics changes and diversity in personnel; Implications for public administrators. In J. Rabin., et al. (Eds.) *Handbook of public personnel administration and labor relations*, 2nd ed.

4

Toward a Framework for Matching Teaching and Learning Styles for Diverse Populations

James A. Anderson

Several frameworks exist that have been utilized to discuss and classify human styles of learning. Some are very generic and speak to a broad range of learning behaviors and dimensions. Other frameworks are more focused and highlight certain dimensions. A model proposed by Curry (1983) suggests that learning styles is a generic term under which three general levels of learning behavior are subsumed. These levels are as follows:

cognitive personality style: the individual's approach to adapting and assimilating information;

information processing style: the intellectual procedures used by individuals in assimilating information; and

instructional preference: the individual's preference for learning environments and activities.

A more specific model is proposed by Kolb (1984) and focuses primarily on how persons receive and process information. In particular, learning style activity is described in terms of the dimensions of perception, input, organization, processing, and understanding.

Many of the seminal discussions about learning styles could fit under the umbrella of one of the two aforementioned approaches. What moved the discussion away from the general platform was the assertion by several authors that the existing models and frameworks did not account for the learning strengths and assets of populations that were diverse by race and culture. Later, the issue of gender differences also became prominent in this discussion.

CULTURAL AND RACIAL STYLES

Several authors have speculated extensively on the notion that different cultural and racial groups have preferred learning styles that are indigenous in origin (Anderson, 1988; Decker, 1983; Hilliard, 1989). Although the current research in this area is limited, a strong case has been made by certain groups, and new models are emerging. For example, Willis (1989) suggests that the observations, theories, and research about black children's learning style can be grouped into four groupings of characteristics:

social/affective: people-oriented, emphasis on affective domain, social interaction is crucial, social learning is common;

harmonious: interdependence and harmonic/communal aspects of people and environment are respected and encouraged, knowledge is sought for practical, utilitarian, and relevant purposes, holistic approaches to experiences, synthesis is sought;

expressive creativity: creative adaptive, variable, novel, stylistic, intuitive, simultaneous stimulation is preferred, verve, oral expression; and

nonverbal: nonverbal communication is important intonation (body language, etc.), movement and rhythm components are vital.

Azibo (1988) takes an approach somewhat similar to Curry in that he suggests formulating and describing cognitive style using African personality traits and constructs.

One of the most significant issues concerning the success or failure of diverse populations involves the inclusion of demographic factors as part of the discussion about the dynamics of the learning environment. In particular, how does the inclusion of the factors of gender, race, culture, and class affect what we know about, or how we think about, teaching and learning and the styles associated with each? Various authors have assigned different degrees of importance to such factors in an educational context.

Asa Hilliard (1994) represents the perspective of those who contend that the inclusion of most demographic or diversity-related factors serves a political function but not an educative one. He feels that neither gender nor socioeconomic status explains issues associated with teaching and learning; thus, they should not be considered. It is the reactions of instructors, professionals, and administrators to aspects of diversity that will tell us about the limitations or facilitation within learning environments. The author does concede, however, that cultural diversity may present professional and pedagogical issues for educators.

A second group of authors (Anderson, 1988; Banks 1994; Longstreet, 1994; Shade, 1982) contends that culture, ethnicity, class, and gender play important roles in shaping the learning preferences and styles of students. These authors refrain from identifying some monolithic dimension of learning style as emanating solely from race or culture, etc. To do so runs the risk of "megagrouping," that is, the tendency to identify as homogeneous the broad, diverse characteristics within a group. It is more important to study the interplay among diverse characteristics and then to examine how such factors affect learning preferences. It is possible, for example, that the cultural values and perspectives of certain groups lend more easily to a collaborative learning environment (as opposed to a competitive one) at the secondary and postsecondary level.

If this is true, and some evidence suggests it is, then other questions and issues clearly follow. How do diversity-related factors affect the cognitive and affective domains? What can we learn from the socialization processes outside the classroom that suggests how we might restructure the traditional classroom? What are the examples of existing educational programs and models that are successful and that incorporate diversity into the teaching and learning process? Is it possible to subsume the teaching and learning process under demographic issues and concerns such that we produce uncritical thinkers who are shaped by culture, politics, egocentrism, other "isms," and social conditioning?

LEARNING STYLES AND PROGRAM STRUCTURE

Many who research learning styles among diverse populations follow the same pattern of study. They utilize an inductive approach in which they identify the characteristic under study, connect it to a specific population, discuss how it can be observed and assessed, and end with suggestions for the teaching and learning environment.

This author would like to suggest that a deductive approach to the study of learning styles might be just as valuable. For example, a review of academic programs at different levels that service diverse populations might show that these programs may be succeeding because they address critical diversity-related factors like learning styles. The critical interaction among teaching styles, learning styles, and classroom environment is fundamental to program structure and process. Why, for example, do certain math and science programs produce success among students of color while others do not?

If one were to examine the characteristics of successful mathematics and science programs for African American, Hispanic, and Native American students at either the precollege level or the freshman year in college, one should expect to find an overlap among the characteristics associated with effective teaching. The characteristics may also mesh with the preferred learning styles and strengths that students bring. Anderson (1994) has identified and summarized these characteristics of effective mathematics and science instruction for students of color as follows:

fosters a sense of community grounded on the shared experience of doing serious work,

utilizes student feedback to periodically assess teaching ability and effectiveness,

individualizes and personalizes classroom presentations when necessary,

introduces relevancy of information to be learned,

provides students with hands-on activities and involvement,

provides appropriate feedback when students experience conceptual difficulty,

acknowledges developmental level of students and teaches to that level,

varies instructional method,

encourages students to express their reasoning process in their own words (especially difficulty and futility),

guides students in learning how to frame new questions,

guides students in the use of alternate learning strategies, and

shows connections between isolated pieces of information.

The aforementioned characteristics could easily be identified as simply characteristics of high quality, effective teaching. However, it is more important to note that the affective dimension of learning is facilitated because of the emphasis upon connecting skill development to factors like motivation, confidence, persistence, verbal facilitation, anxiety reduction, collaborative learning, academic self-esteem, and competence. This is not to suggest that this is the only way to teach certain students. Instead, the suggestion is that if we motivate and teach students to become effective learners, then they will be able to adapt to a variety of instructional styles and learning environments.

Certain authors move beyond the linking of instructional styles to learning styles to a discussion of how teaching and learning can represent social, economic, political, and cultural empowerment. For example, Frankenstein (1994) suggests that critical mathematics educators understand that:

thought develops through interactions in the world and that people come from a variety of ethnic, cultural, and economic backgrounds;

people teach and learn from a varied number of perspectives;

most cases of learning problems in schools can be explained primarily on motivational grounds and in relationship to social, economic, political, and cultural contexts, as opposed to in terms of a lack of aptitude or cognitive deficit; and

the reality of the anxiety that is associated with the learning of math (and science) should be recognized but dealt with in a way that does not blame the victim and that recognizes both the personal psychological aspects and the broader societal causes.

The assertions associated with this model are interesting because, while they acknowledge the interplay between variations in teaching and learning style, they also introduce the impact of macro societal influences.

EXPANDING OUR KNOWLEDGE BASE

How does the expanding knowledge about diverse learning styles affect the general knowledge base that has been developed on that same topic? One thing that has happened is that researchers spend more time discussing the learner in a holistic way. Not only are traditional questions asked — How does the student prefer to process information? — but we now include ones like:

What cognitive, affective, and cultural assets do diverse students bring to learning environments, and how do such assets facilitate or inhibit their performance?

What aspects of information processing are similar or different for diverse groups? How do these differences show up in educational settings?

What new methods of assessment are needed to accurately evaluate and portray the learning styles of groups differentiated by gender, race, culture, and class?

Should the relationship of learning styles research affect the changes in instructional techniques, and, if so, how would this be done?

If one examines the research on learning styles at all educational levels, one finds that much of the focus historically has been on the assessment of styles. This is true for traditional populations as well as diverse ones. At the elementary school level, the study of learning styles is often combined with an examination of cultural style, behavioral style, and communication style. Cognitive processes and activities are generally the source of learning style assessments with college and precollege populations.

Whatever the nature of the assessment, there exist some questions as to the strength of the accumulated evidence for the reliability and validity of measurements. Curry (1990) suggests that problems with reliability, limited data sets, unsubstantiated indications of factor loadings, and overlapping learning style conceptualizations contribute to pervasive assessment problems. These problems are magnified when the factors of gender, race, and culture are introduced. How, for example, does one control for conceptual ambiguity between groups when there is so much variation within each group?

So far in the research literature, little attention has been given to the effect of class or socioeconomic differences upon variations in learning style. It might be that poor and rural African American, Hispanic, and Asian samples (male and female) overlap considerably along certain learning style dimensions (Anderson & Adams, 1992). The question is whether or not the results are due to class status or cultural and behavioral similarity. The fundamental issue seems to be that more attention must be given to the assessment of diverse learning styles and minimization of the confounding influence of demographic factors.

Whereas the assessment of learning styles has occupied the attention of many researchers, considerably less time has been spent upon the possible adaption of findings to educational settings. Few theorists have been able to conjoin the areas of assessment and classroom application when the population under study is diverse by race, culture, and class. Clearly, any adaptive model would have to possess three components: alternative approaches to curricular and instructional methods, careful and effective matching of learning style to these methods, and evaluation designs sensitive enough to distinguish real effects.

DOES LEARNING AND TEACHING STYLE MATCHING WORK FOR DIVERSE POPULATIONS?

One of the reasons that the aforementioned question has been difficult to answer with confidence has been alluded to before: researchers have not examined sufficiently the overlapping characteristics of educational models and programs to identify the preferred type of learning style that was exhibited and whether variations in instructional style produced positive outcomes and enhanced performance. The simple assessment of learning styles alone is not as critical as knowing the most important dimension to examine. For example Anderson (1994, 1992, 1988) and Willis (1989) summarize the research, which suggests that one of the most critical dimensions that affects the performance of diverse students is the interplay between the cognitive and affective dimensions. The general finding and assertion is that for women and people of color many cognitive decisions and processes are influenced by affective considerations that are culturally influenced. The examination of a learning style dimension that is not as prominent in the learning process does not highlight the learning strengths and assets of that population.

Many authors have highlighted the importance of affect and the affective dimension on learning among traditional and adult student populations (Lowman, 1984; Wlodkowski, 1985). Among diverse populations the issue is not as simplistic as to suggest that these are feeling-oriented learners. Instead, the issue is that, as diverse learners process, organize, and assimilate information, they seek to make it meaningful, relevant, familiar, and evaluative within their own cultural parameters in ways different from other learning types.

Curry (1990) suggests that the research is inconclusive as to whether optimal results are achieved when the learning styles of individual learners are matched with comparable teaching styles. An example of a study that is weighted on the assessment end but inconclusive (yet strongly suggestive) on the outcome end was conducted by Claudia Melear (1992) from East Carolina University. Dr. Melear examined learning style preferences and differences among sixth and eleventh grade African American students using the Myers-Briggs Type Indicator. Her results support the notion that the affective dimension is present among the sixth grade populations to a great degree but begins to decline in usage as a decision-making strategy by the eleventh grade among science students but not other students. Eleventh grade students replaced the feeling aspect of the affective dimension with the expressive and sensing aspects.

From this type of broad assessment, the author suggests what might be some instructional variations that match with comparable diverse populations. She suggests that teachers offer options in type, time, and completion date of tasks together with project and assignment options. Instructors need to identify the balance between imposed structure and flexibility. Instructors need to decide which aspects of their instruction need to be culturally sensitive. Finally, students who are similar in style may need to perform some academic tasks together.

This latter notion can be referred to as a "clustering" of styles. It is not just what students do, but can also be an instructional or support strategy that recognizes the advantages of organizing students into academic teams in order to provide a supportive and nurturing environment that will enhance their motivation, performance, and ultimate academic success. The suggestion might be made that if we group students according to styles, skill levels, culture, ethnicity, and gender we will actually limit their ability to engage in independent task completion and thinking and hinder their ability to engage different teaching styles. The evidence from successful programs and models does not support this assertion. It is not the "clustering" that affects learning outcomes but the interactive dynamics among students and with the instructor that enhances confidence and competence and that exposes students to the learning styles and thinking skills of their peers.

INTERACTIVE STYLES MODEL

Most of the research on matching the learning styles of diverse populations with corresponding instructional styles has compared one dimension of the learner with one aspect of instruction. Such a linear format does not really reflect what occurs in programs that work. For example, we might assess a population of diverse students and identify that they exhibit a field sensitive orientation when they process information. This group would be matched with an instructor who exhibits a similar orientation. But how do the two groups match up on other dimensions that are critical if the linear relationship is to work? In other words, besides knowing the visual and information processing component of field sensitivity, do we also need to know something about human-relational style, learning style, communication style, and cultural style? The following identifies the characteristics of human-relational style that many diverse students who are field sensitive expect from instructors.

What Students Expect from Faculty
(Based Upon Preferred Style)

Field-Sensitive Orientation	*Field Independent Orientation*
To give support, show interest, be emotional	To focus on task and objective
To provide guidance modeling and constructive feedback	To provide independence and flexibility
Seek verbal and non-verbal cues to support words	Commands and messages are given directly and articulately
Minimize professional distance	Maximize professional distance
Seek opinions when making decisions and incorporate effective considerations	Make decisions based upon analysis of problem and objective criteria
Identify with values and needs of students	Identify with goals and objectives of task

The contention of this author is that stylistic matching between students and instructors is more functional when it crosses several dimensions. Moreover, outcomes assessment should reflect this matrix of interactions, as should alterations in the classroom environment. It might be that the linear assessment of matching can only partially explain the powerful dynamics of teaching and learning in certain environments. Perhaps a more comprehensive scheme would be as presented in Figure 4.1.

CONCLUSION

The importance of having a thorough understanding of learning styles becomes more critical when applied to diverse populations and their success and failure in learning environments. The notion of matching learning styles with instructional styles has received mixed reviews and remains a promising area of research. The suggestion has been made that a multi-dimensional model of assessment and matching could be more revealing than linear ones that have been historically used.

It is also suggested that a deductive model can be used to approach the development of a learning style–teaching style paradigm for diverse populations. Educational efforts and programs that support diverse populations and that have been successful for quite some time seem to share certain characteristics. These characteristics reflect various aspects of style. The research on teaching effectiveness corroborates the fact that much of the teaching that produces success among varied

FIGURE 4.1
Interactive Styles Model

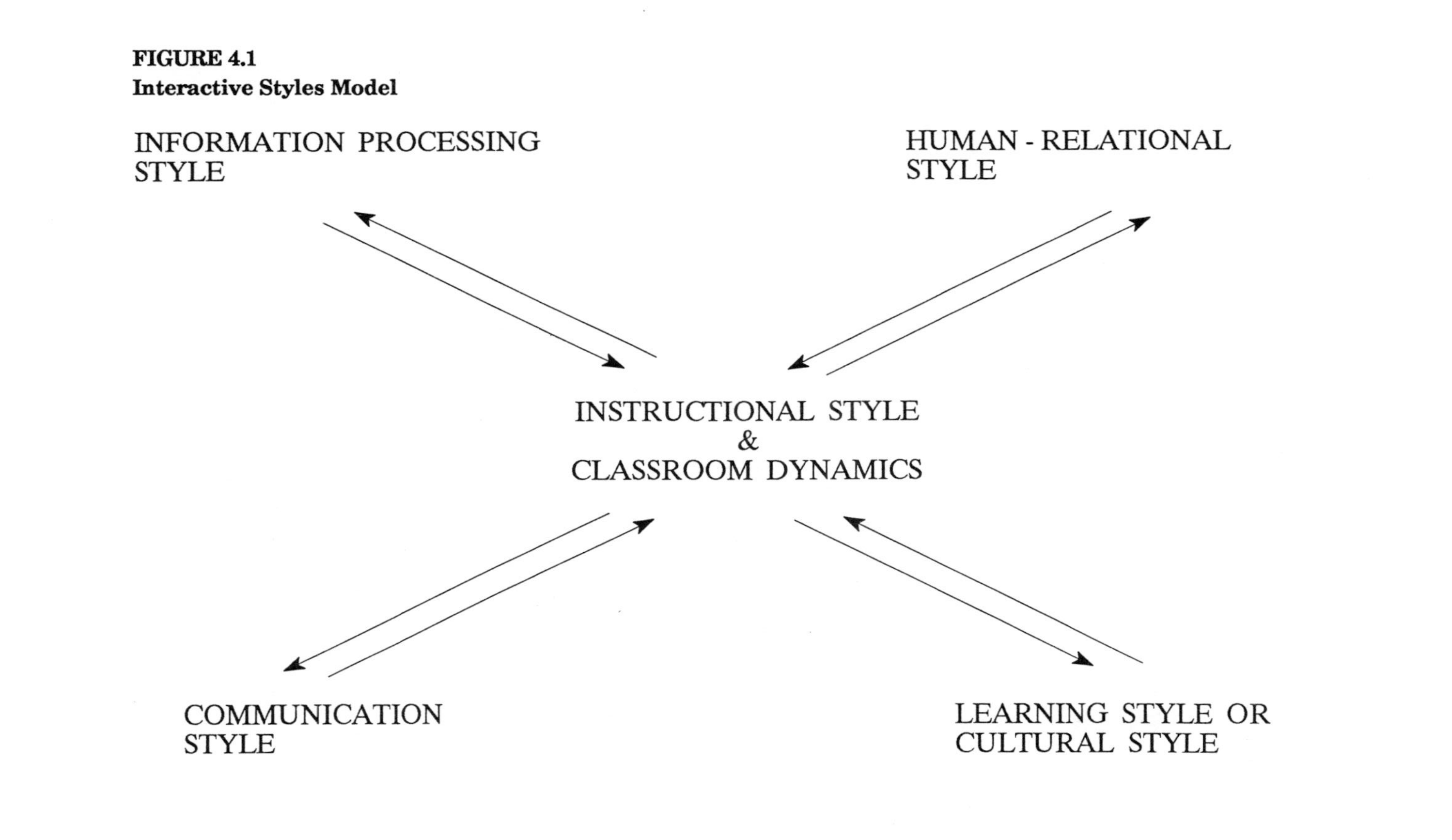

populations would do so for most students.

As student populations become increasingly more diverse, faculty need to recognize the assets and needs of different learners. If they are truly committed to optimal teaching and learning, they will seek to arm themselves with the knowledge, skills, and techniques that will foster success among diverse populations.

REFERENCES

Anderson, J. A. 1994. Examining teaching styles and student learning styles in science and math classrooms. In M. M. Atwater (Ed.), *Multicultural education: Inclusion of all* (pp. 99–100). Athens: University of Georgia Press.

Anderson, J. A. 1988. Cognitive styles and multicultural populations. *Journal of Teacher Education, 39*, 2–9.

Anderson, J. A., & Adams, M. 1992. Acknowledging the learning styles of diverse student populations: Implications for instructional design. In L.L.B. Border & N. V. Chism (Eds.) *Teaching for diversity*. San Francisco: Jossey-Bass, Number 49, Spring, pp. 19–33.

Azibo, D. 1988. Understanding the proper and improper usage of the comparative research framework. *The Journal of Black Psychology, 15*(1), 81–91.

Banks, J. 1994. Dimensions of multicultural education. Insights on Diversity. *Kappa Delta Pi*, pp. 14–15.

Curry, L. 1990, October. A critique of the research on learning styles. *Educational Leadership*, pp. 51–52.

Curry, L. 1983. An organization of learning styles theory and research. Paper presented at the AERA convention, Montreal, Quebec. ERIC No. ED 235 185).

Decker, B. 1983. Cultural diversity: Another element to recognize learning styles. *NASSP Bulletin*, p. 67.

Frankenstein, M. 1994. Critical mathematics education: Bringing multiculturalism to the mathematics classroom. In M. M. Atwater (Ed.), *Multicultural education: Inclusion of all* (pp. 167–169). Athens: University of Georgia Press.

Hilliard, A. 1994. How diversity matters. Insights on Diversity. *Kappa Delta Pi*, p. 6.

Hilliard, A. 1989. Cultural style in teaching and learning. *NEA Today, 7*, 65–69.

Kolb, D. A. 1984. *Experiential learning: Experience as the source of learning and development*. Englewood Cliffs, NJ: Prentice-Hall.

Longstreet, W. 1994. Understanding ethnicity. Insights on Diversity. *Kappa Delta Pi*, pp. 14–15.

Lowman, J. 1984. *Mastering the techniques of teaching*. San Francisco: Jossey-Bass.

Melear, C. T. 1992. Considering relational learning style of African American students in science instruction. Paper presented to the Charlottesville public schools, Charlottesville.

Shade, B. J. 1982. Afro-American cognitive style. A variable in school success? *Review of Educational Research, 52*, 219–244.

Willis, M. G. 1989. Learning styles of African American children: A Review of the literature and interventions. *Journal of Black Psychology, 16*(1), 54.

Wlodkowski, R. J. 1985. *Enhancing adult motivation to learn: A guide to improving instruction and increasing learner achievement*. San Francisco: Jossey-Bass.

5

Learning Styles and the Changing Face of Community Colleges

William Purkiss

A western man saw his Asian friend putting a bowl of rice on his grandfather's grave and asked, "When will your grandfather get to eat the rice?" To which his friend replied, "At the same time that your grandfather gets up to smell the flowers you put on his grave." Different means different, not better than or worse than. (Cuch, 1987, p. 65)

During the past election, candidate Bill Clinton said that, during their lifetimes, current high school seniors will face the probability of seven different professions, six of which have not yet been invented. He has challenged the nation's educators to develop learners who are not only literate, numerate, and prepared for some professional endeavor, but who also are capable of synthesizing developing information structures into evolving competencies for yet undefined tasks in the information-oriented world of the twenty-first century. Building on this theme of the need for increasing learner sophistication is the growing challenge of unskilled manufacturing positions leaving the country for places south and far to the east.

This chapter examines our community colleges, the most appropriate social institution to respond to these issues. Looking first to the role of this unique American educational experience in the current post-secondary milieu and the need for a range of new curricular and pedagogical strategies to meet the emerging challenges, the chapter goes on to review the range of literature directly relating learning style inquiry with both the area of adult learning and the community college. A recently completed study will be explored, providing some startling information about community colleges in what appears to be a clear institutional bias toward one major style over another, raising doubts about community colleges' current ability to address the national educational challenge.

THE COMMUNITY COLLEGES: IN THE EYE OF THE EDUCATIONAL STORM

Because they offer a universally available and affordable opportunity for higher education, community colleges bear a special burden in these revolutionary times. To a population that is becoming increasingly diverse in race, age, disability, and gender consciousness, and hard pressed by the new economic and competency realities, community colleges are the primary opportunity for addressing academic challenges. The major responsibility for these institutions is to orient their teaching and learning environment so that it genuinely supports an increase in the level of success for all students. Community colleges must also develop a curriculum and pedagogy that actively engage a burgeoning concrete/experiential learning style dominant student population with a learning model that encourages the development of effective and synthesis-based competencies for a group that has often been educationally neglected. Acquiring knowledge in an environment of flux, the twenty-first century learner will need to be able to master both the technical and liberal arts disciplines.

The country's evolving demographics show that postsecondary education can expect an increasingly non-uniform, female dominant student population. This emerging student body will require the development of a broad range of academic disciplines and alternative pedagogies designed to provide the more inclusive learning engagement necessary to guarantee all groups meaningful participation in a socially democratic cultural and economic dynamic. Beside the fact that women, a unique learning group, are a clear majority of our national population (Abudu, 1990), people of color are also a growing percentage of the general population: Washington, D.C. — 72 percent non-white population, Hawaii — 68 percent, New Mexico — 49 percent, California – 43 percent, Texas — 39 percent, and nine other states possess approximately 30 percent non-white population (Abudu, 1990, p. 2).

With these newly emerging populations has come much frustration. The nation is struggling with the inability to deal with difference in race, gender, culture, disability, and class. Difference has become the basis for restriction of access to shelter, medical care, food, security, and, of course, education. Andrew Hacker (1992, p. 4.) spoke of the United States becoming "two nations," while Derrick Bell, in his landmark book, *Faces at the Bottom of the Well: The Permanence of Racism* (1992), spoke with deep conviction of the inability of the country to come to grips with its racially, culturally, and class oriented bias, maintaining instead a view of difference as "the other." He said of his African

American culture, "the fact is that, despite what we designate as progress wrought through struggle over many generations, we remain what we were in the beginning: a dark and foreign presence, always the designated 'other'" (p. 10).

Community college educators in the United States are struggling with this sense of alienation among people of color and other aspects of difference. The current educator understands that the student he or she encounters is unlike those who accompanied him or her to school in the fifties, sixties, and seventies. These "new" students often find the environment of the school and classroom totally alien to their cultural orientation, their method of approaching new information, and, quite simply, their world view. "Many of these students experience culture shock by being in an environment where dominant values, expectations or experiences may be very different than their own and which may be implicitly or explicitly devalued" (Smith, 1989, p. 35). Other students, perhaps not totally new to the environment, including women and students with disabilities, are beginning to acknowledge the different ways in which they engage the learning experience, and are pressing for an educational process that not only acknowledges their uniqueness as groups, but also includes methodologies that are as facilitating to their needs and orientations as those traditionally used for the more linear, usually white male dominated student population. Additionally, roughly 50 percent of all college students, regardless of their ethnic background, do not reach their college goals (Levine, 1983, p.314). That statistic alone creates a special population that is allowed to enter the unskilled workforce. Now these people must be prepared for the new realities of a competent workforce in the United States. If these diverse groupings of students who have unique needs in education are ignored, then the community colleges are complicit in the development of a culturally bifurcated society that is permanently separated between those who have the competency to find work and those who do not. It is incumbent upon these institutions to comprehensively adjust their strategies to ensure an environment for the greatest levels of student success possible.

The community colleges have acknowledged being challenged by these issues, facing a call for strategies that productively engage a wide array of students in learning experiences that give them a greater chance for success. The American Association of Community and Junior Colleges released a report entitled, *Building Communities: A Vision for a New Century* (1988). In the study, the association called for the development of learning environments that are more active, collaborative, and truly engaging. They went on to say,

> We all agree with Mortimer Adler's conclusion that "all genuine learning is active, not passive. It involves the use of the mind, not just the memory. It is a process of discovery in which the student is the main agent, not the teacher."

All students, not just the most aggressive or most verbal, should be actively engaged. It is unacceptable for a few students to participate in the give and take with faculty while others are allowed to be mere spectators. Since active involvement of all students is critical, more "time on task" is needed, with frequent feedback and creative interaction between students and faculty. In such a climate students also learn from one another. (p.25)

The community college report argued for an educational institution that builds a competent student population, confident in its ability to deal with a rapidly changing technical, economic, and cultural milieu that characterizes the United States at this time. If we accept Maxine Greene's definition of personal autonomy as being "self-directed and responsible, . . . capable of acting in accord with internalized norms and principles, . . . [and] insightful enough to know and understand one's impulses, one's motives, and the influences of one's past" (1988, p.118), it would seem necessary to develop methodologies that address the integration of experientially based knowledge with more abstract cognitive processes. Thomas Clark, writing in the journal *Equity and Excellence* (1989), says that the major reason for adult student failure and dropout is the lack of what he calls "intentional connections" between the student's life and the college classroom experience. "The reason many people drop out of college is not that they are not bright, can't do college work, or are not motivated to learn. They drop out because they do not perceive any connection between what they are studying and their own lives. We must not only work to make content more relevant but to point out this relevance so that students can make their own connections" (p. 48).

This lack of relevance and inability to engage students has been discussed from a number of different perspectives. First, the critical pedagogists suggest that the politics of U.S. education lend support to the dominant culture's ethical and political standards, all the while discounting those of nondominant ones. Aronowitz and Giroux put it clearly when they discussed this aspect of institutional alienation:

The dominant school culture functions not only to legitimate the interests and values of dominant groups; it also functions to marginalize and disconfirm knowledge forms and experiences that are extremely important to subordinate and oppressed groups. This can be seen in the way in which school curricula often ignore the histories of women, racial minorities, and the working class. . . . Schools legitimate dominant forms of culture through the hierarchically arranged bodies of knowledge that make up the curriculum as well as the way in which certain forms of linguistic capital and the individual (rather than collective) appropriation of knowledge is rewarded in schools. (Aronowitz & Giroux, 1985, pp. 147–48)

Along with a sense of political alienation, students today who look to the community colleges as a direct route into jobs and career tracks based upon non-baccalaureate educational levels are often frustrated because of the traditional lack of cohesion between programs that are aimed toward transfer and those that are vocationally directed. Historically, the common institutional paradigm held that the goals and objectives of the two academic tracks were widely separated from each other. However, the current educational reality is that there is very little difference between the intellectual requirements of the vocational and the liberal arts student in the two year postsecondary institution. At a recent meeting for community college and high school faculty dealing with a federal "tech prep" program, it was stated that the average reading level of technical manuals today has risen from an eighth grade level of ten years ago to an average of grade fourteen, with concomitant adjustments in numeracy rates as well. Dale Parnell, past president of the American Association of Community and Junior Colleges, laid out the current baseline skills and competencies that the new technologies have placed on vocational education. He listed them as being:

a stronger math and science foundation (better knowledge skills, the ability to solve problems, and the ability to learn new technology in a rapidly changing field),

use of computers (for design, information management, and control of machines such as robots),

combinations of skills (interdisciplinary approaches such as electrical, mechanical, fluid, thermal, or optical systems), and interpersonal and communication skills (team building, customer relations, presentations, and getting along with other workers at all levels). (Hull & Parnell, 1991, p. 37)

Hull and Parnell went on to say that changes in technology should not be emphasized in isolation. Nontransfer community college students also need an array of new liberal arts-integrated competencies. They must be able to:

use basic principles, concepts, and the laws of physics and technology in practical applications;

use algebra, trigonometry, and analytic geometry as problem-solving tools (an understanding of higher mathematics — including computer language and some calculus — may be required);

analyze, troubleshoot, and repair systems composed of subsystems in three or more of the following areas: electronic, electrical, mechanical, thermal, hydraulic/ pneumatic, or optical;

use materials, processes, apparatus, procedures, equipment, methods, and techniques common to technology;

apply detailed knowledge in one field of specialization with an understanding of applications and industrial processes in that field;

use computers for information management, equipment and process control, and design;

record, analyze, interpret, synthesize, and transmit facts and ideas with objectivity — and communicate information effectively by oral, written, and graphical means.

The pathway for community colleges to meet these pressing educational needs; prepare for President Clinton's projections of the number of professions facing the average high school graduate; and facilitate the broadening diversity of student profiles in culture, gender, disability, and learning styles seems to lie in a twofold approach. First, it is clear that the environment of our postsecondary institutions must radically change to meaningfully address the needs of students of difference. There is an array of literature that speaks of the need for the establishment of academic environments that are responsive and nurturing to diverse cultural and ethnic populations. Students who come into a collegiate environment that has an ongoing tradition of methodology, inquiry, staff, and physical environment that relate more readily to the white majority culture's norms than to a student population of diverse origins have to feel at a tremendous disadvantage. Second, it is time to recognize that the question of student learning styles and their relationship to success with traditional postsecondary pedagogical paradigms must be addressed. Other scholars have broadly discussed the issue of campus environment, so the direction of this chapter lies with the consideration of learning styles and their potential for contribution to the increase of student success in the community colleges.

LEARNING STYLES AND THE ADULT LEARNER

Any discussion of learning styles must first recognize that inherent in the establishment of pedagogical strategies for pupil engagement in learning is the ability to systematically acknowledge areas of real student difference and establish clear indications that some students, although equal in intellectual capacity, might have demonstrably different potentials for success in a range of disciplines. Much work has been done in exploring difference in people. David Kolb (1984), a leading proponent of learning style theory, explored John Dewey's idea that the knowledge developed through experience is vital for adult learners returning to the educational process, and for learners from both minority populations and the dominant culture who demonstrate different learning styles than those reflected in the norm. By invoking the personal world view of the students, the interaction in the classroom can develop a true intercultural relationship between diverse groups and provide a methodology of engagement that is nurturing and inclusive to all students. To ignore that personal perspective is to create a stifling environment that isolates and discounts whole groups of students. As O'Connor put it,

It is within the political dynamics of school interactions that the borders of intercultural association are forged. Within these politics, individuals struggle to establish and maintain structured relationships that enhance their success. Favored ways of speaking and acting, as well as valued forms of classroom knowledge, become the cultural capital of educational discourses; they contribute to the control that members of certain groups exercise over the patterns of educational enterprises. The minority group's inability to shape the terms of classroom interaction reduces their likelihood of school success and increases their prospects of alienation and lowered aspirations. Accordingly, the roots of biased education must be seen in the cultural politics of the educational discourse, rather than in cultural or personal attributes of minorities. (1989, pp. 57–58)

Kolb (1984) spoke of learning through experience as being empowering to adult learners, in that it allows them to ignite the learning process from a base that is familiar, unthreatening, and opens the students to a sense of ownership of new material through its connection with the safe and known in their lives. The issue with the reentry adult learner lies in the often dichotomous qualities of the workplace and the classroom. By connecting that daily non-academic experiential knowledge base with the new concepts to be acknowledged, the student is able to engage the material from a position of ownership, rather than one of alienation. Kolb said:

There has been a . . . need for educational methods that can translate the abstract ideas of academia into the concrete practical realities of these people's lives. Many of these new students have not been rigorously socialized into the classroom/textbook way of learning but have developed their own distinctive approach to learning, sometimes characterized as "survival skills" or "street wisdom." . . . Adult learners . . . demand that the relevance and application of ideas be demonstrated and tested against their own accumulated experience and wisdom. . . . For these adults, learning methods that combine work and study, theory and practice provide a more familiar and therefore more productive arena for learning. (p. 6)

There have been numerous studies of learning style as a predictive instrument for various aspects of professional studies, job satisfaction, and specific interest areas dealing with adult learners. However, extensive studies have not been developed particularly exploring the teaching and learning strategies found in community colleges. Examination of the literature dealing with the broad topic of adult learners, however, provides the reader with interesting information that can be, in many instances, overlaid with the more specific mission and objectives of the community colleges. For example, in a study relating to the nature of the adult student, Vondrell (1987) looked to see if identification of student learning styles would assist in predicting "the success in both academic and satisfaction level outcomes of adult students participating in an independent study program" (p. 1962). Such programs of independent learning are proliferating in community colleges. Using the Kolb Learning Styles Inventory (LSI) (McBer, 1986) as the tool for investigation, Vondrell's study found that, based upon identified learning style, adult students could predict relative levels of success and satisfaction, showing that students who were more experientially and experimentally oriented in their learning styles out performed and were more satisfied with the non-classroom format than were those students with the more theory and research based abstract conceptual learning styles.

Kirk's study (1986) was entitled "Assessment of Learning Styles and Cognitive Development of Adult Students in a Higher Education Setting: Implications for Teaching, Administration, and Advisement" (p. 238). Relating learning styles with Perry's model of intellectual hierarchy, the study found that the consideration of the development of thinking along the scale from dualism to relativism, in concert with ascertaining student learning styles, produced better indicators of learning strengths and closer relationships to each other than they did with grade point average (GPA), age, gender, or parental educational level. On the other hand, Rush (1983) completed a study that compared the learning styles of a group of adult students over 50 years of age with a group under the age of 25. Although strong correlative significance was not established between the groups and the different responses to the questionnaire that they answered concerning differential attitudes between the groups and their educational motivations, some areas of clear difference were established. The results of the study showed that "attitudes and the environment may be even more important to classroom success then the identification of learning styles" (p. 351).

In the realm of the adult learner and the development of clearer and more successful career goals, the research tends toward inquiry as to the capability of learning styles to predict the most potentially successful options for adult vocational students and to see if learning style theory could be directly utilized in an intervention process for improving vocational student achievement. Pigg, Busch, and Lacy (1980) developed a study of a designated group of civil servants in Kentucky, to see if the LSI could be used regularly as a predictor of success in the design and implementation of teaching strategies to maximize these employees' success in staff developmental training. Using Kolb's suggestions for the expected style delineations of the sample population, the group found that, although there was marginal relationship to how Kolb anticipated the group to be stylistically distributed, they could not be classified as truly falling into the expected stylistic demographic patterns. The study found that, although "it may be tempting to use the Learning Style Inventory in a mechanistic fashion in the design of educational programs. . . . this would be inappropriate" (p. 242), because the research failed to establish clear relationships between learning style and educational techniques. Additionally, the study stated that there may well be preferences of adult learners for pedagogical models that go against their personal styles, simply because the other methodology (most often lecture) is a known and expected process, while experiential techniques may present an element of the frighteningly different and strange. The authors asserted, however, that:

> Despite these cautions against utilizing inventories such as Kolb's for developing educational programs, the Learning Style Inventory does appear to be a useful instrument. A number of individuals, including these researchers, have reported that the inventory really captured tendencies in their personal learning behavior. Being able to recognize these tendencies, and relate them to behavior patterns is important. Thus, it is concluded that the LSI may be effectively employed as a useful device in the actual conduct of educational programs or in a participatory approach to the development of adult education programs due to its high degree of face validity. (p. 242–43)

Considering the learning styles of practicing nurses and nursing students, another area that directly coincides with community college curricula, studies have been created to see if the medical students could be directed, based upon their personal learning style, toward study in the health related field that would provide them with the greatest satisfaction and success, or if there was a significant relationship between the students' learning styles and academic success in their programs. Johanson (1987) explored the styles of a sample of nursing students at Northern Illinois University and compared them with a sample group from the general student population taken from two different universities. Utilizing the Kolb LSI (Kolb, 1985) as the tool for identifying learning styles, the clear majority of highly successful nursing students (2.9+ GPA) displayed the concrete experience/ reflective observation (diverger) style, while the group with that success level in the general population was identified as abstract conceptual/ active experimentation (converger) style dominant. The preferred teaching style among the students was a more traditional (that is, lecture mode) format, while the general population demonstrated preference for more non-traditional strategies (p. 407). In the other two studies, Nelson (1991) and Dougan (1982), the focus of investigation was centered on job satisfaction and individualizing job career opportunities for nurses through the assessment of learning styles. Nelson found that no relationship could be established between learning styles and job satisfaction, while Dougan found that, although learning styles might be useful in assisting nurses in gaining clearer understanding of themselves as unique learners, "it did not prove useful in correlating preferred learning activities with the abstract conceptualization, concrete experience, active experimentation or reflective observation scales" (p. 2248).

Gypen (1981) investigated the possibility of learning style adaptation as one moves onward in a career activity; Matuszak (1991) researched training intervention in the workplace based upon learning styles; and Smedley (1984) did an analysis of the relationship between professional chemists and their learning styles, specific employment category, and preferred developmental learning format. Working with professional engineers and social workers, Gypen found that: "the results indicate that, as engineers move up from the bench to a management position, they complement their initial strengths in abstract conceptualization and active experimentation with the previously nondominant orientations of concrete experience and reflective observation. As social workers move from direct service into administrative positions, they move in the opposite direction of the engineers. These results are consistent with the Carl Jung's developmental idea of individuation" (p. 136).

Matuszak (1991) found that clear relationships were established between learning styles and the successful creation of a "learning to learn" program, preparing workers for more experiential forms of classroom techniques that were distinctly different from the traditional modalities to which the sample population was most accustomed. By engaging the students from the perspective of their learning styles, the researchers helped the students to understand how they engage the learning process. The results clearly demonstrated higher levels of success in learning techniques for "planning, implementing, and evaluating both personal and workplace learning projects" (p. 2790).

Smedley (1984) explored the preferences of professional chemists in the area of continuing education and found that, as predicted by the study, the profession appears to prefer the active experimentation/reflective observation (converger) style and a laboratory methodology for professional development, with computer assisted and correspondence methodologies in least favor. Clear statistical relationships were established between style and learning formats. No inquiries were made, however, as to concomitant success levels in the preferred over the least preferred methodologies.

In an area not widely explored relating adult students of color to learning style, the Kolb LSI was used in relation to African American student samples. Johnson (1989) developed a comparative analysis of white and African American college freshmen, while Baldwin (1987) explored comparative success rates on the National Council Licensure Examination for Registered Nurses for African American nursing students against self-concept, GPA, and Scholastic Aptitude Test math and verbal scores. Interestingly, in the Johnson study, African American freshmen scored significantly higher in the abstract conceptual mode, with most falling into the abstract conceptual/reflective observation (assimilator) learning style category. The white students were predominantly higher in the concrete experience/reflective observation (diverger) learning style. However, no significant indicators were given to suggest major differences in the relative styles of the two different racial groups (p. 3863). Baldwin found that, although the learning styles information alone did not reflect statistically strong relationships to achievement in the sample, when combined with the other demographic materials they became clear indicators of success. Baldwin stated that, "the speculation that selective noncognitive variables when added to cognitive variables will result in prediction of success on the NCLEX-RN exam for Black students was supported in this study" (p. 2922).

On the negative side of the question of predictability, studies by Hawkins (1987), Grun (1986), Sanley (1987), and Zack (1991) all failed to establish significant relationships between learning styles and achievement. For Hawkins, some relationship was established when the styles were combined with a factor for course difficulty. Her findings reflected that "the levels of academic achievement increase for the following individuals: abstract thinkers, more sober students, more tense students, more conservative students, and older students. The levels of academic achievement decrease for the following individuals: concrete thinkers, more enthusiastic students, more relaxed students, [and] more experimenting students" (p. 766).

Grun's study (1986) resulted in mixed conclusions, finding that learning styles were significantly related to academic performance among education majors, and that learning styles appeared to account for "about ten percent of the total variance in students' performance" (p. 3367). The study did reflect a strong relationship between learning style and student attitude toward classroom methodologies, with the more abstract students demonstrating strong preference for a lecture and research mode, while the more concrete students preferred the more experiential modalities (Grun, 1986).

Finally, Sanley (1987) and Zack (1981) each produced studies, with the first on the relationship between learning style and problem solving abilities as demonstrated in the Whimbey Analytical Skills Inventory, and the latter exploring relationships between freshmen students' style and their choices of academic courses in their initial semester of college work. Both studies strongly reflected no relationships in their results.

LEARNING STYLES AND COMMUNITY COLLEGES

The literature specifically dealing with learning style application in community colleges is, as stated earlier, much less prevalent than that found in categories concerning elementary, secondary, and adult learners. However, some studies have been done. There are three areas of inquiry dealing specifically with community colleges that have emerged, including the identification of range in learning style between differently identified classifications of students, validation exercises that explored the relative competencies of different learning style instruments, and consideration of the interaction between learning styles and pedagogy.

In the area of instrument validation, Gruber and Carriuolo (1991) examined both learner and instructor typologies based upon the Canfield Learning Styles Inventory. In their successful study, 1,400 community college students and 240 community college instructors were tested. In "A Factor Analytic Comparison of Four Learning-styles Instruments," Ferrell (1983) examined almost 500 community college students with four different learning style inventories, finding limited success with all four, but unable to measure all of the areas outlined in the study.

Concerning the area of pedagogical relationships to learning styles, three studies specifically relate to community colleges. In the earliest study, Raines (1976) explored the relationship between student learning styles and teaching styles of 6 math instructors and 575 students at Manatee Community College in Florida. Using the Canfield instrument, student and teacher styles were tested against 17 different teaching and learning style preferences, showing that students who had learning styles that more closely matched their teacher attained higher grades in the discipline than did those whose styles did not. DeCoux (1987), in a study attempting to relate community college associate degree nursing student learning styles and academic achievement against control variables of age, sex, race, GPA, and abstract conceptual T scores, found no significant relationship on any levels "between academic achievement and learning style" (p. 124). The final study in this area was directed toward student success in relation to community college telecourses. Dille and Mezack (1991), using the Kolb instrument, conducted a study to identify predictors of high-risk students enrolled in a community college.

Only two studies have been done primarily relating to learning style identification of specific community college student groupings. Both studies are nearly 20 years old, and each deals with a limited demographic examination of the community college population. In the first, Hunter and McCants (1977) studied 968 community college students, testing for learning style difference and learning environment modality preferences by comparing students 24 years and under with students above that age. The study found that the younger students demonstrated a different learning style matrix than the older ones, preferring a more concrete experiential mode of learning with a strong affiliation with both peers and their instructors, while the older students reflected a stronger relationship to the reflective observation and abstract conceptual learning style elements, with a classroom modality that reflected organization, clear instructions, and competition. The recommendation of the work suggested the institutional addition of a new set of pedagogical strategies to address the emerging needs of the younger group.

The second study exploring specific student groups and their relationship to learning styles dealt with gender differences. Brainard and Ommen (1977), using a learning style inventory, examined a sample of over 3,000 community college students who were divided by gender, and compared the difference in style and learning modalities. Significant differences based upon gender were found in preferences for structure, content, mode of instruction, and for academic expectations.

LEARNING STYLE AND STUDENT ACADEMIC ACHIEVEMENT ACROSS THE CURRICULUM IN COMMUNITY COLLEGES

Recently, a new study was developed in which a sample of nearly 1,000 community college students was examined for the relationship between student learning style and academic success across the entire college curriculum. Concerning itself with the question of whether or not style plays a significant role in the community college environment today, the work by Purkiss (1994) provided some very disturbing statistics to ponder. Rather than look at style matching between teacher and students, or at style as a predictor of choice, the study looked to see if there was a significant relationship between a student's style and academic success in the different range of curricula offered in today's comprehensive community college programs. The results showed that style did play a highly significant role, but it was the abstract conceptual student who benefitted across the span of the curriculum, at the expense of the concrete learners.

The study examined a medium-sized California community college located in Southern California. The student population is approximately 11,000 students in any given quarter. With a current but steadily dwindling white student contingent of about 51 percent, over 60 percent of the student population being female, 15 percent physically handicapped, about 8 percent foreign students, and 8 percent receiving some form of institutionalized financial aid, the college approximates the demographic picture of an average community college in the state. The mean age of the student served was 30, and 38 percent of the student population was in re-entry to the educational environment. Almost 25 percent of the population was comprised of single parents. English as a second language and other basic skills offerings have been expanding at a furious rate for a number of years, with the Department of Immigration estimating that there were at least 80,000 Latino persons in the college service region who needed basic English skills (Purkiss, 1989, p. 5). The average reading and numeracy rate of incoming freshmen rests at about the eighth grade level. The socioeconomic level of the communities surrounding the college has been going through a dramatic transition from a basically lower middle class, blue collar community to a more bifurcated one, consisting of the upwardly mobile employable group on one hand, and an expanding, poorer, currently marginally employable developing underclass that appears to be progressively slipping closer to poverty on the other.

Like most colleges in California, the specific environment of the campus was not initially designed for, nor has it moved to embrace, a rapidly developing diversity with its myriad aesthetic tastes. Built during the great college construction boom of the 1950s, the college reflects the nondescript design concepts of U.S. suburbia that predominated in planning academic facilities during that era. Devoid of any coordinated artistic expression including sculpture, mosaics, or murals, the campus speaks of the uninviting and culturally exclusive attitudes of the United States in the middle of the twentieth century. Additionally, the campus is constructed on a hillside with all of the disciplines widely separated by both distance and altitude, making interdisciplinary activity quite difficult.

From a curricular standpoint, the college has specific classes that reflect an interest in cultural diversity, including "African American History," "Chicano History," and some classes in the area of women's studies. The institution is just now exploring the integration of diversity in the curriculum at large, and a historical predilection toward lecture-oriented pedagogies is being questioned by a number of faculty who feel themselves less able to relate to emerging student populations. Although the effort is sincere, well ensconced traditions die slowly and with great difficulty. This type of short sightedness has led to problems for minorities, women, and other students who do not possess either the language skills necessary to deal with some of the curriculum presented or who have learning styles that may significantly differ from those which predominate among the more culturally integrated students. Claxton described a similar situation when he said of African American students,

> Very little research has been done on the learning style of minority students in higher education, but an examination of the influence of Afro-American culture on child rearing is instructive because we must understand the culture of black children if we are to gain insight into their learning styles. . . schools focus almost entirely on the analytic approach to learning. Thus, children who have not developed these skills and those who function with a different cognitive style will not only be poor achievers early in school, but will . . . also become worse as they move to higher grade levels. . . . Schools in the United States orient their curricula to the analytical style, but black people and lower-income people tend to utilize a predominantly relational style. (Claxton & Murrel, 1987, p. 69)

Within this environment, the study examined 987 incoming freshmen, identifying their learning styles by the Kolb LSI (as adjusted by Sims, Veres, & Locklear, 1991); high school GPAs; and specific demographic data including age, race, and gender. Each student's schedule of classes was ascertained, and the academic success or failure recorded. The demographics of the study provided a sample that resembled those of the college, and the learning styles registered an almost dead even 50.5 percent concrete experiential versus 49.5 percent abstract conceptual learning style orientation.

The courses in the college were separated into six meta disciplines based upon the catalog described area of inquiry. Those disciplines included numbers oriented inquiry (meta #1), language oriented (meta #2), descriptive scientific oriented (meta #3), arts oriented (meta #4), behavioral and humanistic oriented (meta #5), and vocationally oriented (meta #6). The GPAs of the students were then tested by style in meta discipline to see if learning style had a significant relationship to success. The results of the Analysis of Variance examination of all student GPA and its relationship to learning style showed extremely high levels, with $F = 5.823$, and a significance level of $F = .0006$.

The multiple regression exercise performed individually on the meta disciplines did not show the presumed relationship in all cases to the projected learning style. When the study was begun, it was assumed that there would be great difference in student relationship by learning style with various curricular offerings at the college. For example, it was hypothesized that, while the more theoretically oriented students would excel in the numerically based math and scientific areas, the concrete experientially oriented students would do so in the arts, language, behavioral, and descriptive sciences. In actuality, only one style element, the abstract conceptual one, showed dominance in academic achievement across the entire curriculum. Across the disciplines, the abstract conceptual based learning style oriented students exceeded the concrete experiential ones by an average of one full gradepoint.

The shocking aspect of the abstract conceptual dominance of achievement across the college curriculum becomes focused when one considers a few salient points of information:

At entry into the college, the concrete experiential students were equal to, or slightly above, the high school academic record of the abstract conceptual students.

At the end of only one quarter's worth of college work, the abstract conceptual students were a full gradepoint above the concrete oriented ones.

Most significantly, the abstract conceptual dominance held across all control variables, including age, race, and gender.

The implications of this study are significant. It appears that concrete experience style oriented freshman students who came to the postsecondary environment with records of previous success that matched or slightly surpassed those of their abstract conceptual style element colleagues found themselves falling behind when it came to academic success at the community college. Given the realities of success and failure of the dichotomous style element dominated students, the real question is not whether style affects learning achievement, but what is it that happens between what is an equally successful secondary experience for both groups, and a clearly unequal situation in the postsecondary environment?

Research inquiries need to be made concerning why students who came from an apparent equal relationship at the high school level went, in only one college quarter, to one full mean gradepoint below their counterparts. In reviewing the study results, no matter how the data were examined, by comparison with whatever variable grouping, the abstract conceptual students exceeded the achievement of the concrete experience oriented ones. The domination was complete.

Where an assumption was made that curricula that emphasized different forms of academic inquiry would provide venues for varying levels of success depending upon student learning style, the truth was that, no matter what the academic inquiry, the abstract conceptual students outperformed the concrete experience style oriented ones. The most significant accomplishment the concrete experience students recorded was in the arts oriented meta discipline, the discipline that most probably, because of its active and experiential performance goals, had to have some pedagogical processes that provided the opportunity for the concrete oriented students. Indeed, some of the strongest correlations established in the study were negative results involving the concrete students and the disciplines in which they were predicted to succeed. Considering the equality of success at high school graduation demonstrated by the concrete experience oriented students with the abstract conceptual dominated ones, the significant drop in accomplishment by those students in the realm of the postsecondary institution was shocking.

A second area of importance that has been made very clear by this study is the consistency of style achievement across racial and gender boundaries. This study has shown a clear line of consistency between style and learning, regardless of other factors. Consequently, success, as reflected in this study, is not simply an issue of those elements of diversity. Although the hypotheses predicted by this study were not always supported by the data collected, across those different areas of analysis the ongoing theme was established that it is the abstract conceptual student who will more predictably succeed in the academic disciplines, regardless of race, culture, age, or gender. This is not to say that other factors, including socioeconomic status, bias against gender, race, culture, and other forms of difference are not clear factors in academic success or failure. However, it is imperative to reflect upon the undeniable consistencies that are demonstrated here in relationship to learning style. This study suggests it is possible that some of the compelling issues faced by higher education might be in some ways mitigated if learning style became an accepted factor in the development of institutional strategies for greater student success.

This sample, as a representative of current community college student freshmen populations, tells us that these learners are equally divided between abstract conceptual element domination and concrete experience element domination, but that there is generally more difficulty for the concrete experience oriented students, no matter what other aspects of diversity they might have, than there is for comparable students who have abstract conceptual learning styles. Remembering that the concrete oriented students came into the institution reflecting previous academic success that was equal to the abstract ones, the question that has to be asked is, why did these students suddenly fall behind, and concomitantly, why did the abstract conceptual students just as dramatically jump ahead? Something is occurring in the methodology of the college that does not work for the concrete experience element dominated students, because the difference in the curricular intensity of inquiry is not, on paper, that much greater for a college freshman than it is for a college-bound high school senior.

There has been much discussion about the greater levels of success and apparent level of advantage that white students have in postsecondary education, as compared to students of color. However, at the community college level, not only was the highest scorer the Latino group, but more significantly, in all groups the abstract conceptual students scored significantly higher than either their own concrete members of their sub-group, or those of any other group in the study. No concrete style group, no matter what age, race, or gender group, had a higher GPA than any of the abstract student groups. Additionally, it is important to acknowledge that while women and men averaged equal 2.5 GPAs, they also were evenly split between abstract conceptual element dominant and concrete experience element dominant learners, with similar results for each style element in each sub-group. This was not necessarily the case in other sub-groups. While the white students were split almost evenly at 52 percent abstract conceptual element dominated to 48 percent concrete experience element dominated, the Asian-Pacific Islanders reflected almost three quarters (72.8 percent) of its population as concrete experience element dominant, with 66 percent of the African Americans being concrete experience dominant as well. The Latinos and the limited number of Native Americans in the sample were the only sub-groups to reflect much stronger abstract conceptual students, and the GPAs of both groups reflected those delineations.

The underlying meaning of these statistics is clear and more than a little disconcerting. The study strongly suggests that learning style plays a role in student achievement, with the abstract conceptual element dominated styles as the ones who have the unquestionable advantage over the concrete experience learning style element dominated students. This factor covers all sub-groups of diversity. The problem lies in the fact that some groups are more abstract conceptual element dominated than others, giving them a greater advantage in the institution. The emerging demographic profile of the nation's community college suggests that the most significant growth in student populations lies with those groups that have higher percentages of concrete experience style element domination. Additionally, those groups that demonstrated success still had significant numbers of their group who reported themselves as having a concrete experiential oriented learning style. If the college then wishes to continue in a relevant position as to the needs of its student population, the issue of abstract conceptual domination and an emerging concrete experience oriented majority must be successfully addressed.

Finally, it is clear that there is some validity to the claim that style is a predictor of success in different academic disciplines. It is clear that, at least in the examination of the experience encountered by this freshman class, the institution has been more supportive of abstract conceptual learning style dominated students. Real efforts must be made to develop methodologies of engagement that will stylistically democratize the community college and allow all students to step into the learning dynamic as equal partners in the process. If President Clinton's goal of "a place at the table" for each student of every race, culture, gender, age, lifestyle, socioeconomic status, or disability is to become a reality, the uniqueness of learning style, with its opportunities and challenges, should be a significant part of the community college overriding strategy for success.

REFERENCES

Abudu, M. 1990. *United States aggregate demographic data.* Norman: University of Oklahoma, Southwest Center for Human Relations Studies.

American Association of Community and Junior Colleges. 1988. *Building communities; a vision for a new century.* Washington, DC: abstract conceptual JC.

Aronowitz, S. & Giroux, H. 1985. *Education under siege.* New York: Bergin & Garvey.

Bell, D. 1992. *Faces at the bottom of the well: The permanence of racism.* New York: Basic Books.

Baldwin, D. M. 1987. A correlational study of self-concept, learning style, college GPA, and SAT math and verbal scores with academic performance and success rate for Black graduates from traditional Black institutions on the National Council Licensure Examination for Registered Nurses (Doctoral dissertation, Georgia State University), *Dissertation Abstracts International, 48,* 2922.

Brainard, S. R., & Ommen, J. L. 1977. Men, women, and learning styles. *Community College Frontiers, 5*(3), 32–36.

Clark, F. Thomas. 1989. Adult diversity and general education. *Equity and Excellence*, *24*(3), 46–48.

Claxton, C. S., & Murrel, P. H. 1987. *Learning styles*. Washington, DC: ASHE-ERIC.

Cuch, F. S. 1987. Cultural perspectives on Indian education; a comparative analysis of the Ute and Anglo cultures. *Equity and Excellence*, *23*(1&2), 65–76.

DeCoux, V. M. 1987. The relationship of academic achievement to the variables of learning styles, intellectual development, age, and abstract conceptual T scores among associate degree nursing students (Doctoral dissertation, University of Southern Mississippi). *Dissertation Abstracts International*, *49*, 124.

Dille, B., & Mezack, M. 1991. Identifying predictors of high risk among community college telecourse students. *American Journal of Distance Education*, *5*(*1*), 24–35.

Dougan, M. A. 1982. Utilizing Kolb's inventory as a partial base for individualizing learning/career opportunities for registered nurses (Doctoral dissertation, Pennsylvania State University). *Dissertation Abstracts International*, *43*, 134.

Ferrell, B. G. 1983. A factor analytic comparison of four learning-styles instruments. *Journal of Educational Psychology*, *75*(1), 33–39.

Greene, M. 1988. *The dialectic of freedom*. New York: Teachers College, Columbia University.

Gruber, C. P., & Carriuolo, N. 1991. Construction and preliminary validation of a learner typology for the Canfield Learning Styles Inventory. *Educational and Psychological Measurement*, *51*(4), 839–855.

Grun, A. F. 1986. An analysis of learning styles and academic achievement based on experiential learning theory, conceptual level theory, and right-left brain hemisphere theory (cognitive development) (Doctoral dissertation, University of Minnesota). *Dissertation Abstracts International*, *47*, 3367.

Gypen, J. 1981. Learning style adaptation in professional careers: The case of engineers and social workers (Doctoral dissertation, Case Western Reserve University). *Dissertation Abstracts International*, *41*, 4853.

Hacker, A. 1992. *Two nations — black and white, separate, hostile, unequal*. New York: Charles Scribner's Sons.

Hawkins, M. G. 1987. The combined predictive value of learning style characteristics and personality factors on academic achievement (Doctoral dissertation, East Texas State University). *Dissertation Abstracts International*, *49*, 766.

Hull, D., & Parnell, D. 1991. *Tech prep associate degree: a win/win experience*. Waco, TX: Center for Occupational Research and Development.

Hunter, W. E., & McCants, L. S. 1977. The new generation gap: involvement vs. instant information. Topical paper No. 64. (ERIC Document Reproduction Service No. ED 148412). Washington, DC: ASHE-ERIC.

Johanson, L. S. 1987. An investigation of learning styles of baccalaureate student nurses (Doctoral dissertation, Northern Illinois University). *Dissertation Abstracts International*, *49*, 407.

Johnson, W. M. 1989. A comparative analysis of learning styles of Black and White college freshman (Doctoral dissertation, Oklahoma State University). *Dissertation Abstracts International*, *50*, 3863.

Kirk, S. L. 1986. The assessment of learning styles and cognitive development of adult students in a higher education setting: Implications for teaching, administration, and advisement (Doctoral dissertation, University of Northern Colorado). *Dissertation Abstracts International*, *47*, 1981.

Kolb, D. A. 1985. *LSI (Learning Style Inventory): User's guide*. Boston: McBer & Company.

Kolb, D. A. 1984. *Experiential learning: Experience as the source of learning and development*. Englewood Cliffs N.J.: Prentice-Hall.

Levine, A. Ed. 1983. *Higher learning in America: 1980–2000*. Baltimore: Johns Hopkins University Press.

Matuszak, D. J. 1991. Learning to learn in the workplace: A case study of a training intervention in preparation for learning through experience (workplace learning, experiential learning) (Doctoral dissertation, Northern Illinois University). *Dissertation Abstracts International*, *52*, 2790.

Nelson, J. E. 1991. Differences in learning style preferences, environmental press perceptions, and job satisfaction between surgical intensive care and general surgical unit nurses (Doctoral dissertation, University of Arizona). *Dissertation Abstracts International*, *30*, 97.

O'Connor, T. 1989. Cultural voice and strategies for multicultural education. *Journal of Education*, *171*(2), 57–74.

Pigg, K. E., Busch, L., & Lacy, W. B. 1980. Learning styles in adult education: A study of county extension agents. *Adult Education*, *30*(4), 233–244.

Purkiss, W. 1994. Learning styles and their relationship to academic success: a community college perspective. (Doctoral dissertation, The Claremont Graduate School).

Purkiss, W. 1989. Organizational implications of cultural diversity. Unpublished paper. Claremont: The Claremont Graduate School.

Raines, R. H. 1976. A comparative analysis of learning styles and teaching styles of mathematics students and instructors. (Doctoral dissertation, Nova University).

Rush, I. E. 1983. Comparative study of learning styles and related factors between traditional and nontraditional students at the University of Akron (Doctoral dissertation, University of Akron). *Dissertation Abstracts International*, *44*, 179.

Sanley, J. D. 1987. An examination of student learning styles and learning modalities on problem-solving success (Doctoral dissertation, University of Nebraska). *Dissertation Abstracts International*, *48*, 2028.

Sims, R. R., Veres, J. G., & Locklear, T. S. 1991. Improving the reliability of Kolb's revised learning style inventory. *Educational and Psychological Measurement*, *51*(1), 143–150.

Smedley, L. C. Jr. 1984. An analysis of the relationship of Kolb's learning styles to employment category, preference for continuing education format, and selected demographic variables of professional chemists (Doctoral dissertation, West Virginia University). *Dissertation Abstracts International*, *46*, 585.

Smith, D. 1989. The challenge of diversity: a question of involvement or alienation. Unpublished monograph. Claremont: The Claremont Graduate School.

Vondrell, J. H. 1987. Learning style as a predictor of success for adult students participating in an independent study course (Doctoral dissertation, University of Cincinnati). *Dissertation Abstracts International*, *48*, 1962.

Zack, C. W. 1991. The relationship between self-knowledge of personal learning style and academic choices made by freshmen college students (Doctoral dissertation, Pennsylvania State University). *Dissertation Abstracts International*, *52*, 4241.

6

The Importance of Learning Styles in Total Quality Management-Oriented College and University Courses

J. E. Romero-Simpson

Learning style is a construct contained in Kolb's (Kolb, Rubin, & Osland, 1991) 1984 Experiential Learning Theory (ELT). Both total quality management (TQM) and ELT are conceived in this chapter as meta models and have proved useful in the design and delivery of an Organizational Behavior (OB) course. A meta model may be defined as "a model describing many other models. As such, the purpose of meta-modeling is not to present new information, but to organize and synthesize existing information systematic patterns. Out of these patterns one can sense an underlying, inherent organization that was 'there' all the time" (Ivey & Matthews, 1984). It is relevant to conceptually explore the nature of the relationship between ELT and TQM. The comparison will mainly focus on TQM's plan-do-study-act cycle and ELT's learning styles.

The purpose of this chapter is to illustrate the role of learning styles in an OB course delivered under a TQM approach. This chapter will also offer a set of suggestions to those interested in implementing a course under a similar approach.

WHY TOTAL QUALITY MANAGEMENT IN A HIGHER EDUCATION COURSE?

TQM holds great potential for improving the economic situation of the United States and of other countries in the global marketplace (Dobins, 1991). This is why its teaching in business schools has become imperative. In 1989, Christopher Hart, a Harvard Business School professor, stated: "For quality . . . there is as yet no predetermined body of knowledge to be taught and there is a crying need for organized course material."

An analysis of the field of OB led the author to confirm Hart's assertion. The emphasis on listening to customer needs for quality products and service, key to the TQM philosophy, was missing entirely in OB. Productivity and worker satisfaction appear as single overt concerns of the field.[1]

OB's conventional topics had been traditionally taught by the author in a modular way, rather independently from each other. A broader conceptual framework such as TQM appeared ideal to integrate the covered topics. As such, TQM may also be considered a meta model as defined by Ivey and Matthews (1984), meaning that TQM also organizes and synthesizes existing information into systematic patterns. TQM has also been described as a philosophy by both scholars and practitioners (Gitlow & Gitlow, 1987).

REVIEW OF LEARNING STYLES AND TOTAL QUALITY MANAGEMENT

Human beings have been traditionally conceived as "finished structures" (Lersch, 1962). Kolb's ELT offers a refreshing alternate view, where people are perceived dynamically, as learners or problem-solvers, constantly adapting to their environment. According to Kolb (1984), learning follows four specific and consecutive stages: (1) concrete experience or "feeling," (2) reflective observation or "observing," (3) abstract conceptualization or "thinking," and (4) active experimentation or "acting." Accordingly, in Sims' (1983) words: "the learner must be able: (1) to get involved fully, openly, and without bias in new experiences; (2) to reflect on these experiences and interpret them under different perspectives; (3) to create concepts that integrate these observations in logically sound theories; and (4) to use these theories to make decisions and solve problems leading to new experiences. These general abilities encompass specific skills."

Learning Styles

The concept of learning or problem-solving style is a natural extension of Kolb's normative four-stage model (ELT). It stems from the dominance of feeling over thinking or vice versa and the dominance of observing over acting or vice versa within a specific person. Smith and Kolb (1985) have described each style.

The converger "combines the learning stages of Abstract Conceptualization and Active Experimentation. People with this learning style are best at finding practical uses for ideas and theories." They tend to be effective problem solvers and decision makers. However, they may be solving the wrong problem in a very effective way and may get involved in hasty decision making.

The diverger "combines the learning stages of Concrete Experience and Reflective Observation. People with this learning style are best at viewing concrete situations from many different points of views." They are also good at understanding people. Divergers, however, tend to be paralyzed by alternatives and, thus, cannot make decisions.

The assimilator "combines the learning stages of Abstract Conceptualization and Reflective Observation. People with this learning style are best at understanding a wide range of information and putting it into concise, logical form." They are good at planning, creating models, and developing theories. However, they may build "castles in the air, and not find practical applications to their ideas."

The accommodator "combines the learning stages of Concrete Experience and Active Experimentation. People with this learning style have the ability to learn primarily from 'hands-on' experience." They are good at getting things done, taking risks, and assuming leadership. The problem is that they may be involved in trivial improvements or meaningless activity.

Smith and Kolb's (1985) first suggested strategy for improving learning and problem-solving skills is to develop learning and working relationships with people whose learning strengths and weaknesses are opposite to one's own.

Develop supportive relationships: This is the easiest way to improve your learning skills. Recognize your own learning-style strengths and build on them. At the same time, value other people's different learning styles. Also, don't assume that you have to solve problems alone. Learning power is increased by working with others. Although you may be drawn to people who have similar learning skills, you'll learn better and experience the learning cycle more fully with friends and co-workers of opposite learning skills.

How? If you have an abstract learning style, like a Converger, you can learn to communicate ideas better by associating with people who are more concrete and people-oriented — like Divergers. A person with a more reflective style can benefit from observing the risk taking and active experimentation of someone more active — like an Accommodator.

The two remaining strategies for learning and problem-solving skills development offered by Smith and Kolb (1985) are improving the match or fit between learning style and life situation, and making flexible learners by developing learning weaknesses.

Total Quality Management

TQM is an alternative paradigm[2] to that of traditional management, a new way of perceiving and doing business. The author defines TQM as "the unyielding and continuous efforts of an organization to constantly understand, meet and exceed its customers' needs. This is accomplished by controlling and improving different processes through the involvement of the entire workforce" (Romero, 1993).

TQM is a holistic philosophy that views human, technical, and engineering subsystems as intertwined through a closely knit set of values clearly oriented to satisfying the customer. It represents a drastic paradigm shift from the traditional way that management has been conceived thus far: structurally and separate from the customer.

Traditional management theory has conceived the organization and the customer as separate entities, almost as if there were a wall between them. On one hand, the organization was conceived structurally, as a pyramid or organization chart, while the customer was not given much attention or was considered a "necessary pest" (Dobins, 1991). Thus, any managerial improvement was aimed at changing the structure of the organization, with little concern for the customer's true needs. The new management paradigm has removed that wall and views the business and the customers as dynamically related in a continuous flow. The previous management paradigm reflects a product out mentality, whereas the newest one may be labelled a market-in one.

Deming's School of Thought

TQM is presented here as conceived by W. Edwards Deming, the American physicist and statistician to whom the "Japanese miracle" is attributed. Deming's (1986) doctrine was originally contained in his 14 points and later in his "Profound System of Knowledge" (1993). At the core of Deming's school of thought is a working model originally developed by Walter Shewart on May 16, 1924 (Killian, 1988), which eventually became known as the "Deming Cycle" or "P-D-S-A Cycle" (Plan-Do-Study-Act).

Deming's System for Profound Knowledge stems from four interconnected subsystems: appreciation for a system, theory of knowledge, knowledge about variation, and psychology.

Appreciation for a System

"A system is an interconnected complex of functionally related components that work together to try to accomplish the aim of the system" (Deming, 1993, p. 61). Deming states that management of a system requires knowledge of the interrelationships between all the components of the system, including the people that work in it. He adds that "the aim of an organization [system] is for everybody to gain — stockholders, employees, suppliers, customers, community, and environment — over the long term" (Deming, 1993, p. 62).

Knowledge about Variation

Deming (1993) views variation as something inherent in every system: "Variation, there will always be, between people in output in service, in product. The key issue, however, is 'What is the variation trying to tell us about a process, and about the people that work in it?'" (p. 65). An initial step, according to Deming, is to bring a process into a state of stability, as measured by statistical control. This stability will make the system performance predictable.

Theory of Knowledge

The third part of Profound Knowledge is the Theory of Knowledge — a branch of philosophy concerned with the nature and scope of knowledge, its presuppositions and bases, and the general reliability of claims to knowledge. Deming emphasizes that there is no knowledge without theory and that experience alone does not establish a theory. To copy an example of success without understanding it with the aid of theory may lead to disaster. Without theory, one has no questions to ask. Hence, without theory, there is no learning. Theory is a window into another world. Theory leads to prediction. Without prediction, experience and examples teach nothing.

Psychology

Psychology helps to understand people, interaction between people and circumstances, interactions between leaders and employees, and any system of management. People differ from one another. A leader must be aware of these differences and use them to optimize everybody's abilities and inclinations. Many managers operate under the supposition that all people are alike and treat them as interchangeable components of a process. However, people learn in different ways and at different speeds and perform at different levels. Some learn a skill by reading, some by listening, some by watching still or moving pictures, some by watching someone do it.

Many of the issues contained in Deming's system of Profound Knowledge are not original. They are, however, intertwined in a unique way. The concept of common and special causes of variation was developed by Shewart in the 1920s; behavioral theories to which Deming subscribes were developed in the 1960s; systems theory was refined by management scientists from the 1950s through the 1970s; and scientists in all fields have long understood the relationships among prediction, observation, and theory. Deming's contribution was in tying together some basic concepts. He recognized the synergy among these diverse subjects and developed them into a theory of management.

Deming's (1986, 1993) 14 points have their basis in Profound Knowledge. The 14 points are:

1. Create a constancy of purpose toward improvement of product and service with a plan to improve competitive position; stay in business, and provide jobs.
2. Learn the new philosophy, top management and everybody.

3. Understand the purpose of inspection, for improvement of processes and reduction of cost.
4. End the practice of awarding business on the basis of price tag alone.
5. Improve constantly and forever the system of production and service.
6. Institute modern methods of training on the job.
7. Teach and institute leadership.
8. Drive out fear. Create trust. Create a climate of innovation.
9. Optimize toward aims and purposes of the company the efforts of teams, groups, and staff areas.
10. Eliminate arbitrary numerical goals, posters, and slogans for the work force which seek new levels of productivity without providing methods.
11. Eliminate work standards that prescribe numerical quotas.
12. Remove barriers that rob people of pride of workmanship.
13. Institute a program of vigorous education and retraining.
14. Create a structure which will push on the prior points every day.

COMPATIBILITY BETWEEN EXPERIENTIAL LEARNING THEORY AND TOTAL QUALITY MANAGEMENT

Kolb's 1984 ELT model and Deming's school of thought — as operationalized in his working methodology via the P-D-S-A cycle — may be conceived as two sides of the learning coin. Furthermore, many concepts derived from ELT could significantly contribute to strengthening and complementing Deming's System of Profound Knowledge, particularly its psychological pillar.

TQM emphasizes a *modus operandi*, meaning "a way of working" in Latin: This *modus operandi* is reflected in the P-D-S-A cycle. ELT, on the other hand, focuses on the operator, the way someone works, learns, or solves problems.[3] According to the ELT normative model, people learn differently, depending on their orientation to the different learning stages of the ELT model.

Common Features of the P-D-S-A Cycle and the Experiential Learning Theory Model

A careful examination of P-D-S-A and ELT shows some commonalities between both meta models (see Figure 6.1): both are process-oriented; both are normative, advocating a prescribed learning sequence; both models show a counterpart of the combination of Kolb's reflective observation and abstract conceptualization stages.[4]

The reflection-action flux in Kolb's model is contained in his reflective observation and active experimentation stages, which are complemented by his concrete experience and abstract conceptualization

FIGURE 6.1
Reflection and Action Cycles in Kolb's and Deming's Learning

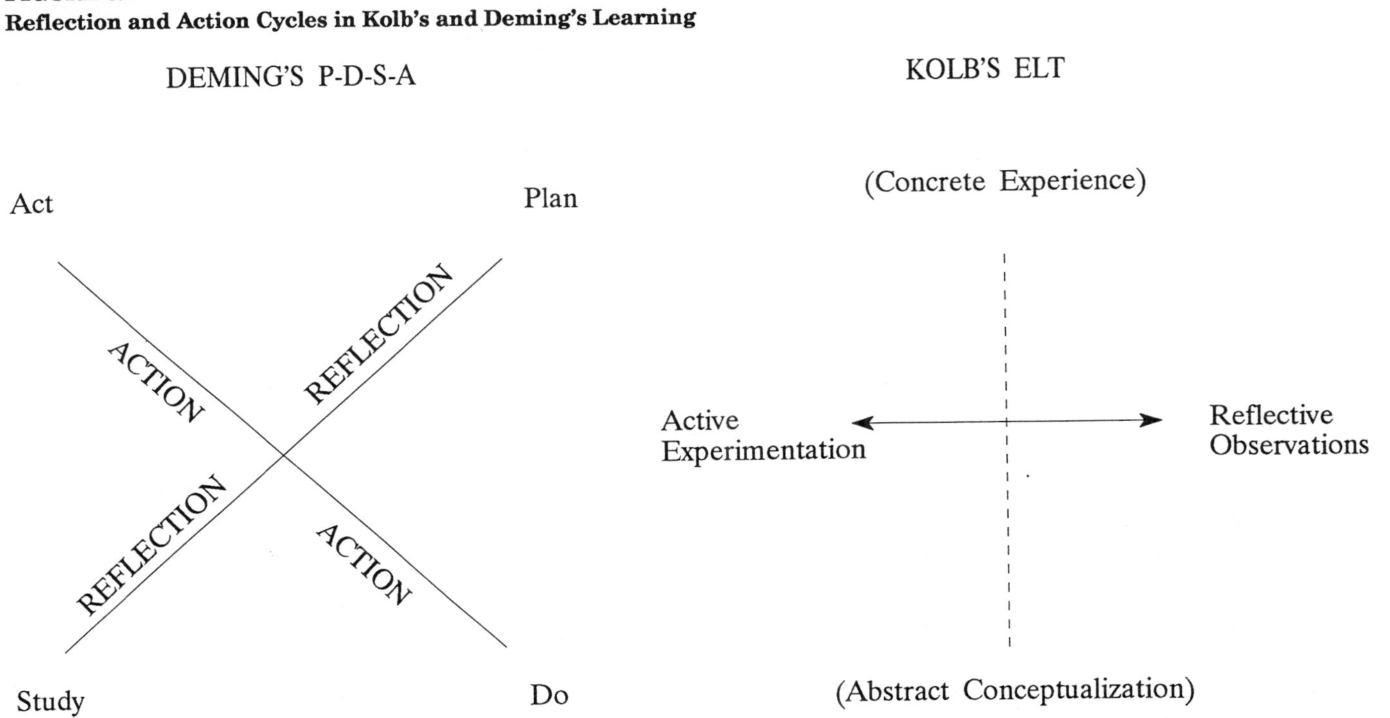

stages. These are a part of a cycle because "learning is really relearning" (Kolb, 1991).

Deming's P-D-S-A cycle's reflective stages (plan and study) are followed by action stages (do and act). By including reflection and action components twice, Deming, like Kolb, is stressing the complementary and cyclical nature of these two components.

Differences Between the P-D-S-A Cycle and the Experiential Learning Theory Model

There are two key differences between the P-D-S-A cycle and the ELT model. TQM emphasizes a way of tackling problems or learning in a rather objective or detached way, as seen from outside, whereas ELT describes the problem-solving or learning stages from the learner's standpoint. Yet both models are dealing with the meta process of learning. Deming does not openly include the words "concrete experience" or "feeling" in his cycle, as Kolb does.[5] It may be argued, however, that planning is a natural consequence of experiencing a problem followed by a desirable end state (this is known as the "sweat-leadership theory") or the motive to reach a desired state as represented by a vision (known as the "vision-leadership theory"). It is not surprising, however, that Deming, as a statistician, would have omitted the word "feeling" in his charts or graphic models.

Learning Styles and the System of Profound Knowledge

Learning styles can be pulled together in a team to develop synergy. The four subsystems contained in Deming's (1993) System of Profound Knowledge — the theory of knowledge (or learning), the notion of a system, variation, and psychology — may be easily conceptualized as characteristics of an effective team. A multiple-style learning team is a system containing interrelated and yet different subsystems; people of diverse and yet complementary problem-solving styles join in a common effort of accomplishing a task.

TOTAL QUALITY MANAGEMENT IN THE CLASSROOM — MANAGEMENT 307

TQM calls for a different set of values and norms, such as, cooperativeness instead of competitiveness and team effort instead of competition and individual effort only. It also calls for different roles for the instructor and the students. The former acts as a learning facilitator, and the latter are expected to increasingly assume responsibility for their own learning and the improvement of the entire learning system. It should be stressed, however, that the ultimate responsibility for the course lies with the instructor. Only the instructor can have a historic or evolutionary perspective of the course.

TQM guidelines applicable to instruction include:

listening to the customer's (student's) needs;

top management's (instructor's) commitment to quality and willingness to accept responsibility for the system's well-being, control, and improvement;

an increasing conviction of TQM's value by learners;

the critical role of education and self-improvement for accomplishing change;

the sense of "KAIZEN," or constant improvement through efforts of the entire work force (or class);

process orientation rather than results-only orientation;

enhancement of a stimulating environment, free of fear;

synergy of individual differences through teamwork;

overcoming obstacles through communication, not through inspection; and

the use of statistical thinking and tools to measure variation.

Course Description and Purpose

Advanced Organizational Behavior was offered to management majors who had already taken an introductory OB course and, thus, were familiar with its different topics. The procedures for the course are: finding key TQM assumptions and principles; developing instructional guidelines based on assumptions and principles; selecting pertinent instructional materials; implementing the course; and having users evaluate course and course components. The course, the attending members, the instructor, the classroom, and the available resources are viewed comprehensively as a learning organization comprised of several interconnected teams modeling a quality organization. Topics considered particularly critical for management majors were covered by student teams through exercises and simulations.

Course Mission

The basic mission of the course is twofold. First, it should help students improve as learners and helpers of fellow team and class members. It should also control and improve the quality of the learning system (course) by listening to its customers' suggestions and recommendations (pertaining to its content, modules, and procedures, among others). Constant improvement is done to make sure that the new generation of students (external customers) is exposed to an improved system.

A former student of Advanced Organizational Behavior described the course as follows:

MGT 307 is the firm in which the product is information which becomes knowledge through our interaction in a multiple-style team; the clients are the students, and the manager is Dr. Romero, the professor in charge of delivering information. Knowledge will enable us as students to better our managerial skills and to apply them in the future. The course experience and the output of histograms, "pinches," and other ways of expressing our opinion . . . are the means through which our professor will improve the product (MGT 307) by polishing the information it grants for future clients.

Course Content

The course covered its different units from a TQM perspective. The course's initial unit, worker-organization bonding (organizational socialization), offers an ideal opportunity to expose the students to a different philosophy from the very beginning of the course.

The Role of Individual Differences

TQM authors recognize the importance of individual differences when referring to working skills. Kolb's concept of problem-solving style adequately fits with TQM's assumptions and methods. Kolb's model stresses the differences among human learners in their way of adapting to the environment and acting upon it (Kolb, Rubin, & Osland, 1991).

The concept of problem-solving styles is particularly useful when analyzed within a multiple-style problem-solving team perspective. Each student's style was originally determined by the Learning Style Inventory (Kolb, Rubin, & Osland, 1991).[6] The four styles — accommodator, diverger, converger, and assimilator are labelled by the author as bee, dolphin, beaver, and owl, respectively, for didactic purposes. Students found the above nomenclature easy to memorize and quite useful in terms of their contribution to the team.

Personal Application Assignments

Personal Application Assignments (PAAs) were used as learning tools. Students are required to answer in writing four questions that reflect the four normative stages contained in Kolb's ELT model: (1) concrete experience, (2) reflective observation, (3) abstract conceptualization, and (4) active experimentation. The PAAs are used to assess student learning and their value is unquestionable.

Standard Student Learning Routine

The learning routine of students began with their studying the material related to the topic in question and joining a team for an exercise. It ended with their presentation of the PAA described above.

The sequence of the learning routine is as follows:

1. study and do exercise before class,
2. join a multiple-style team,
3. experience a topic-related situation,
4. participate in a team exercise,
5. share team conclusions with the class,
6. participate in class-wide discussion,
7. write a PAA based on class or work, and
8. present the PAA the following week.

Initial Course Evaluation

The course was initially only evaluated at its conclusion by multiple-style teams to get more balanced reactions. This was done through a questionnaire containing certain items related to Deming's fourteen points and applicable to a learning setting.

As can be observed in Table 6.1 and Figure 6.2, six of the eight items related to the course received an evaluation higher than 4 (out of 5) by the participants. Two items were evaluated low. These items were number three, assuming responsibility for one's own learning, and number five, quizzes.

TABLE 6.1
Team Evaluations of Eight Crucial Items Related to the Course

	Team Number					
Item	*1*	*2*	*3*	*4*	*5*	*X*
1. Absence of fear	5	4	5	5	5	4.8
2. Learning useful things	5	5	4	5	4.6	4.7
3. Responsibility for own learning	3	4	4	4	2.5	3.5*
4. Improving problem-solving skills	5	4.8	4	5	4	4.6
5. Quizzes	5	5	1	4.6	3	3.7*
6. Working in teams	5	4	5	5	5	4.8
7. Leadership exercise	5	5	5	3	3	4.2
8. Films	4	5	5	4.5	2	4.1
					X =	4.3

*under 40

Several specific course components were highly valued by students.

Teams proved to be useful "ice breakers" and useful feedback systems. The balance of learning styles in teams significantly reduced fear and enhanced effective problem solving.

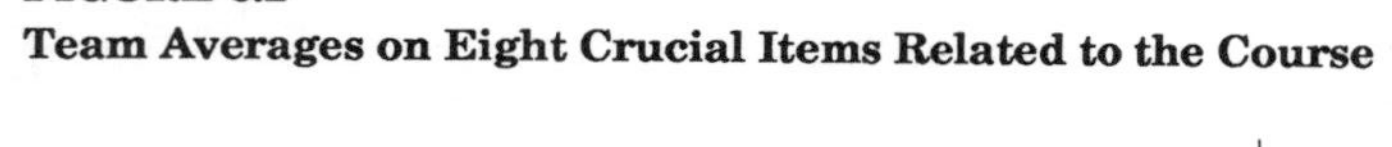

FIGURE 6.2
Team Averages on Eight Crucial Items Related to the Course

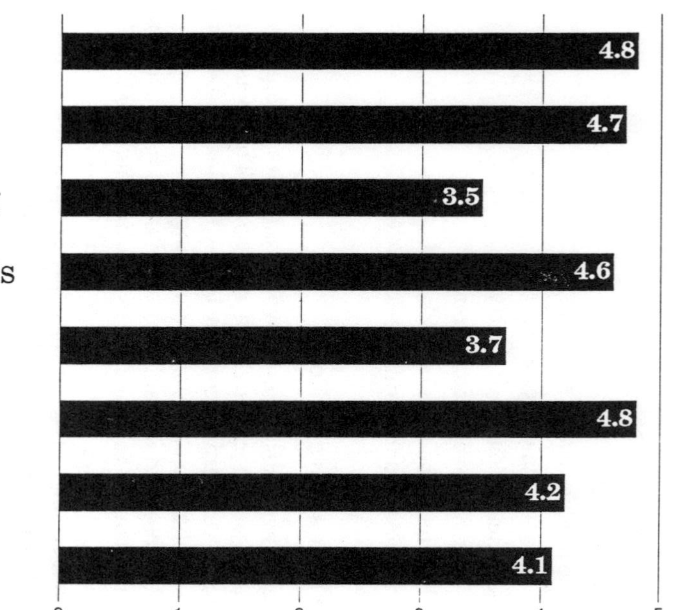

The non-threatening atmosphere or free-to-learn climate allowed each student to bring out in the open their "pinches" (that is, feelings of discomfort, concerns, doubts, and frustrations about the readings, exercises, and other factors).

Student concerns were taken care of as soon as possible by the facilitator. There was an official channel for pinches in topic evaluation forms and an informal channel in their oral presentation in class. The availability of an escape valve for the students may partially explain the lack of serious discipline problems in the classroom.

PAAs proved to be highly useful and compatible with the TQM philosophy due to its process and problem-solving orientation.

The initial evaluation was a one-shot type of evaluation. It basically measured the overall impression that students had of the course after it was delivered. In other words, it measured the outcome of a process but did not really describe or measure the process that lead to those outcomes. It was, therefore, hard to determine how the process could be controlled and further improved. Students also evaluate each topic at its conclusion and, during the following week, the facilitator shows the results of these evaluations through histograms and pulls together the comments by content.

More sophisticated and subjective causes were furnished by students through their final assignments. The present system addresses two key areas:

1. Helping students become better learners. Part of the course's mission is to help students become better learners through the mastery of a learning model: Kolb's (Kolb, Rubin, & Osland, 1991) experiential learning model. This model is applicable to diverse OB situations. The course's emphasis shifts from rote learning to learning how to learn. This is accomplished through teamwork, individual effort, and learning assessed through PAAs, which reflect the ELT model.

2. Improvement of the learning system (course). The other part of the course mission deals with the control and improvement of the learning system as a whole through the integrated efforts of the entire work force (students and instructor). Any course of action is followed by a careful reflection of its consequences with the help of the P-D-S-A cycle and statistical tools (histograms).

By the end of the course, a composite of the histograms is presented to the students. The mapping of the course with its strengths and weaknesses helps the student customers get a better grasp of the learning process.

Advantages of the New Learning System

The new system enhances continuous improvement of the course from one semester to another. The visual displays of the course's process through statistical figures followed by student comments are extremely helpful for maintaining those course aspects that facilitate learning and for eliminating those that do not. The system is constantly refined by new generations of learners. Also, time spent in preparing each topic is considerably reduced.

The sense of ownership of the course that students gain leads them to give their best efforts to improve it for the sake of future students who will be taking it.

The balance of learning styles in teams is highly appreciated by the learners. According to them, it enhances effective problem solving and promotes a healthy climate. This climate allows the discussion of concerns before presenting them to the facilitator. The PAAs consistently reflect the benefits of teamwork.

A multiple-style team is a true reflection of Deming's entire Profound System of Knowledge. It is a system containing interrelated subsystems: people of different, yet complementary, problem-solving styles join in a common effort of accomplishing a task.

Teams also respond to Deming's assumption that people are different from one another and that a manager should be aware of such differences and use them to optimize everybody's abilities and inclinations.

Effective teams empower their members and, in doing so, generate intrinsic motivation in them.

The new evaluation system — after each unit, as opposed to after the course — considerably involves learners in the design and development of their learning processes. At the end of the course, when students receive their composite containing all the unit evaluations, they are able to trace back the processes involved in each one easily.

The team learns to generate knowledge from experience by following a prescribed action-reflection flow.

There is a shift from the use of power by the instructor (external control) to the empowerment of the team member (internal control). The instructor gradually releases control of the learning process and allows his or her students to become responsible for it. Students are responsible for evaluating their learning-oriented process and for offering suggestions toward their improvement. An interesting side effect of this is that the assumption of responsibility by the students considerably enhances the mastery of concepts and pertinent points related to each unit.

The number of students showing up in the author's office asking questions about the assignments, PAAs, and other course-related aspects is estimated to have decreased at least by 80 percent. The present system clearly spells out what is expected of each learner and offers a standard *modus operandi*. It also provides a mechanism for voicing concerns or pinches on a weekly basis in an orderly way through either the topic evaluation forms or orally in class.

Disadvantages of the New Learning System

The initial stages of the course development take time and patience because the instructor has to keep track of every single detail related to the processes leading to learning. Furthermore, students are not used to taking responsibility for monitoring those processes conducive to their learning. They are puzzled as to what is happening in the classroom and why. Some seem to bring along a sense of mistrust from previous courses that could be reflected in the following thoughts: "I wonder what the instructor is really up to!" "Where's the catch?" or "How will this affect my grade?" The process of shifting from power and external control by the instructor to empowerment of the learning process by its true constituents takes time.

The instructor or facilitator has to feel strongly motivated because the complex efforts displayed in controlling and improving the course processes are of little interest to most of the academic community, whose primary concern has traditionally been research and publication. This is why efforts such as this one should be in context and, thus, promoted and acknowledged by the broader educational system.

The complexity of the process, particularly at its initial stages, and the fact that it is time-consuming, almost forces the instructor to rely on someone else, like a graduate assistant or one of the students, to help him or her to convert the quantitative and qualitative information to statistical charts and graphs.

The advantages of the new learning system, mainly the positive learning outcomes of the course in terms of content mastery and process awareness and the healthy climate in which the students participate, clearly outweighed the disadvantages mentioned by the author.

RECOMMENDATIONS GEARED TO FUTURE LEARNING STYLES AND TOTAL QUALITY MANAGEMENT-ORIENTED COURSES

It is important to realize that the responsibility for the well-being of a TQM-oriented course lies with the instructor, the only person who has a time perspective of the course across the different semesters. The facilitator is also responsible for the course's evolution.

The presence of fear in the classroom should be acknowledged, openly discussed, and properly managed throughout the entire semester. Students bring different kinds of fears from the educational system they have been involved in since the early stages of their lives.

They also have an orientation to grades as opposed to learning itself. Students seem to have a love-hate relationship with quizzes because they have been conditioned to study and memorize, which they usually dread, to get good grades.

The facilitator has to induce the students, as early as possible, to understand the relationship between grades and learning. Because the present educational system is deeply rooted in grading, the instructor's role in reconciling both is key. High grades should ideally reflect true learning. In this sense, the value of PAAs is unquestionable. A love for learning should be instilled from the very first session of the course.

It is convenient to set the boundaries of the course with respect to the broader system. The TQM-oriented course (subsystem) is unique with respect to its surrounding subsystems. On one hand, students discover through the course a new approach to learning and an unsuspected freedom. On the other hand, students are taking and will be taking other courses offered in a more traditional way. It is important that students realize that they cannot expect the same climate or the same results experienced in an ELT-TQM course. In most university courses, memorization, rather than learning, is emphasized, unless the entire system consistently behaves in a similar way.

It is highly desirable that the facilitators and innovators contribute to changing the overall educational system toward an ELT-TQM approach, particularly if they are convinced of the merits of the joint venture of these two meta models.

CONCLUSION

Kolb's ELT model and Deming's TQM school of thought as represented in his P-D-S-A cycle, are two sides of the learning coin. Deming focuses on a *modus operandi*, or way of working that prescribes the right way to approach a task, whereas Kolb focuses more on the stages that the operator or learner goes through in the problem-solving process. Both models share an action-reflection flow and, thus, may be perceived and analyzed jointly from an even broader perspective — that of learning. From a learning perspective, TQM focuses on the tangible, objective steps of problem-solving, whereas ELT focuses on the more subjective stages that each learner goes through in his or her problem-solving process. The benefits of these two intertwined meta models have been clear to the author.

NOTES

1. To test Hart's assertion, the author examined 12 representative Organizational Behavior textbooks. None of the textbooks covered its topics from a quality improvement perspective. The references to quality were fragmented and consistently related to "quality circles" and "quality of work life."

2. The word "paradigm" is understood here as a pattern or filter through which we perceive reality having a specific boundary and a specific set of rules, as described in Thomas Kuhn's *The Structure of Scientific Revolutions*, University of Chicago Press, 1962.

3. Way of working and problem solving are considered complementary concepts here.

4. Deming insists on the use of statistical thinking and statistical tools when analyzing different phenomena (processes).

5. Deming does, however, include the word "feeling" and other related words such as "pride of workmanship" in his 14 points and in his Theory of Profound Knowledge.

6. A different version of this instrument has been used recently in Romero, J. E., Tepper, B. J., and Tetrault, L. 1992, Spring. *Educational and Psychological Measurement*, *52*(1), 171–180.

REFERENCES

Deming, W. E. 1993. *The new economics for education, government, and industry*. Cambridge, MA: Massachusetts Institute of Technology Press.

Deming, W. E. 1986. *Out of the crisis*. Cambridge, MA: Massachusetts Institute of Technology, Center for Advanced Engineering Studies.

Dobins, L. 1991. Quality . . . or else! Public Broadcasting Service Tape (video).

Gitlow, H., & Gitlow, S. 1987. *The Deming guide to quality and competitive position*. Englewood Cliffs, NJ: Prentice-Hall.

Ivey, A. E., & Matthews, W. J. 1984. A meta-model for structuring the clinical interview. *Journal of Counseling and Development*, *63*, 237–243.

Killian, C. 1988. *The world of W. Edwards Deming*. U.S.A.: CEE Press Books.

Kolb, D. A., Rubin, I. M., & Osland, J. M. 1991. *Organizational behavior*. Englewood Cliffs, NJ: Prentice-Hall.

Lersch, P. 1962. *Der Aufbau der Person*. Leipzig: Joann Ambrousius.

Romero, J. E. 1993, March. Applying TQM in the classroom. Presentation, University of Mississippi, School of Education, Jackson.

Sims, R. R. 1983. Kolb's experiential learning theory: A framework for assessing person-job interaction. *Academy of Management Review*, *8*(3), 501–508.

Smith, D., & Kolb, D. A. 1985. *User guide for the learning-style inventory: A manual for teachers and trainers*. Boston, MA: McBer and Company.

7

Adapting Faculty and Student Learning Styles: Implications for Accounting Education

William T. Geary and Ronald R. Sims

Few disciplines can match the commitment to change in educational practices that is evidenced in accounting. The process of change in accounting education is distinguished by both the breadth and depth of the effort. Organizations such as the American Accounting Association, the American Institute of Certified Public Accountants, and the Institute of Management Accountants have joined with accounting firms, publishers, and educators to provide leadership, funding, and widespread dissemination of information about initiatives and outcomes in accounting education. During this period of great change and experimentation, it has become clear that change will continue to characterize accounting education. If the emphasis during this evolution is placed on understanding the learning process and learning objectives, then accounting education can avoid the fate of once again becoming stagnant.

As faculty promote growth and development in students, they struggle to improve themselves and to become more effective classroom leaders, planners, presenters, and facilitators. This challenge for faculty development is very intense in accounting. Faculty must not only respond to the demands created by very complex professional and technological environments but also reexamine their choice of pedagogy and their assumptions about the learning process. Rather than using only the teaching style with which they may be most comfortable and familiar, faculty must learn to use new techniques and approaches to respond to a variety of educational goals and a variety of student approaches to the learning process.

This chapter will focus on the challenge of creating a learning environment that employs diverse faculty resources to relate what needs to be learned to a student population that is characterized by individual differences in their approaches to the learning process.

APPLYING LEARNING STYLES TO ACCOUNTING EDUCATION

The Future Committee of the American Accounting Association made the following assessment of accounting education in 1986:

> Fifty years ago, the method of lecture together with routine-problem-solving was generally used. Today, that same method tends to dominate accounting teaching methods, although class discussion in the form of teacher-question and student-answer is given more emphasis. The current pedagogy also emphasizes problems with specific solutions. As the number of authoritative pronouncements has expanded, textbooks and faculty have required students to learn more factual rules and procedures to be applied in a rather rigid fashion. A primary focus in many cases has been on the acquisition of knowledge needed to pass professional examinations. (AAA, 1986, p. 177)

More recent changes in the development and execution of the accounting curriculum demonstrate a widespread and positive response to the problems of accounting education articulated by the Future Committee. Learning objectives (for example, master a computer skill, think analytically, communicate effectively) must be clarified and made explicit. These objectives must be coordinated with the ways students learn (for example, lecture, group discussion, independent project).

In the process of restructuring accounting education, it is important to avoid the "one size fits all" philosophy observed by the Future Committee in 1986. Students learn in different ways, and different learning objectives are more or less compatible with various approaches to the learning process. Failure to provide for differences in student learning styles may mean that a gain to some students from a change in method will be offset by losses to other students. Also, failure to provide experience with a variety of learning approaches may severely limit a student's professional effectiveness because of an inability to address a wide range of problems that require different approaches.

Learning is an interactive process that involves both teachers and students. It is important to acknowledge that the reality of the classroom is more complex than the simple pursuit of knowledge. Students may want to be entertained in the class, engage in dialogue with other students, simply achieve a particular grade, send a message to a parent, or attain some other goal not directly related to the learning process. Faculty may also be interested in diverse goals, such as obtaining good student evaluations, being well-liked, getting students to enroll in more advanced courses, obtaining more majors in accounting (especially in a time of stable or declining overall enrollments), and so forth. While motives such as these are commonplace, the planning process should continue to focus on the learning objectives as the central focus of concern.

The exchange between faculty and student will be more effective if there is a "fit" between teaching styles of instructors and cognitive or learning styles of students (Kolb, 1985; Goldstein & Blackman, 1978). A greater understanding of successful teaching may emerge from answers to the following questions:

Are there certain teacher style profiles that work best with specific learning styles? If so, what are they?

Are there certain teacher style profiles that work best with specific learning objectives? If so, what are they?

Do effective instructors adapt their teaching style to match both the learning style of specific students and the learning objectives?

How can faculty learn to adapt teaching styles to student learning styles?

Can learning environment profiles be identified? If so, can the learning process be managed in accounting programs?

Answering these questions will provide a beginning for the planning process needed to support curriculum development.

Teaching styles are personal and develop over time. If an instructor's preferred teaching style (for example, highly structured lectures, group discussion, experiential learning, case studies) is highly incompatible with either the students' learning styles or the learning objectives, the instructor will need to make a more successful accommodation. For this to occur, instructors must be aware of both alternative pedagogies and useful insights that will allow them to differentiate the ways in which accounting students learn.

INDIVIDUAL DIFFERENCES

An understanding of individual differences is indispensable to the effective design and delivery of accounting education. With a better understanding of individual differences, learning opportunities can be designed that match the student's learning strengths and weaknesses with the learning objectives. The challenge is to identify those factors that are most valuable and readily employed, to permit educators to make distinctions that lead to meaningful differences. The Experiential Learning Theory developed by Kolb, the Learning Styles model developed by Grasha-Reichmann, and the theory of psychological type collectively comprise a very powerful and readily available approach to understanding and responding to individual differences in learning styles. While these theories are not mutually exclusive (see Kolb [1985, pp. 78–85] for a discussion of the Learning Styles model and Jung's theory of psychological type), each perspective makes an important contribution to understanding and responding to individual differences. In addition, ongoing research should continue to enhance both our understanding of individual differences and the methods to apply this understanding in the classroom.

Kolb's (1984) Experiential Learning Theory is based on his understanding of how people extrapolate from their experiences to generate the concepts, rules, and principles that guide their behavior in new situations, and how they modify these concepts, rules, and principles to improve their effectiveness. Kolb approaches learning as a circular process in which concrete experience is followed by reflection and observation; this in turn leads to the formulation of abstract concepts and generalizations, the implications of which are tested in new situations through active experiments. By combining parts of the four stages, Kolb identified four main styles of learning (accommodator, diverger, assimilator and converger) and used his Learning Style Inventory (LSI) to establish an individual's relative emphasis on each of the four styles. The revised LSI (Kolb, 1985) describes the way a person learns and how he or she deals with ideas and day-to-day situations in his or her life.

Any accounting education program, course design, or classroom session can be described using Kolb's four styles. The strength of the convergent learning style is the practical application of ideas to problem solving and decision making. Kolb notes, "We have called this learning style the converger because a person with this style seems to do best in situations like conventional intelligence tests where there is a single correct answer or a solution to a question or problem" (1985, p. 77). The divergent learning style, on the other hand, emphasizes imaginative and unconventional responses and is naturally inclined toward the "generation of alternative ideas and implications" (1985, p. 78). The assimilation style emphasizes the primacy of inductive reasoning and concepts over the deductive and more pragmatic approach of the divergent style. The adaptive emphasis of the accommodative style is focused on "opportunity seeking, risk taking, and action" (1985, p. 78). When faced with a conflict between theory and reality, the accommodative style will adapt to the reality resorting to trial and error approaches rather than a priori reasoning.

The Grasha-Reichmann Learning Styles Questionnaire (GRLSQ) (Reichmann, 1974) can be used to further differentiate approaches to learning. It provides the basis for classifying three distinct approaches to learning: dependent, collaborative, and independent. A person who scores high as a dependent learner generally prefers a teacher-directed, highly structured course with explicit reading assignments, explicit class assignments, and a predetermined number of tests. A person who scores high as a collaborative learner prefers a discussion class with as much interaction as possible. A student who scores high as an independent learner likes to have significant influence over the content and structure of the course.

The implications of these three approaches are straightforward. A person who is a dependent learner would most likely prefer a lecture without term papers, but if a term paper is to be assigned, the dependent learner would want the topic to be assigned by the teacher, with fairly detailed instructions. A person who is predominately a collaborative learner would prefer group projects and collective assignments, such as case studies, that require interaction and collaboration. The independent learner prefers to have a voice in the determination of the material covered, the number of tests given, and so forth. Also, independent learners prefer that the teacher serve as a resource person rather than as a formal lecturer. If a paper is to be assigned, independent learners will prefer to choose their own topics instead of having the teacher assign specific topics.

A third and complementary perspective on the learning process is drawn from the theory of psychological type originally developed by Carl Jung and popularized by Myers and Briggs through the Myers-Briggs Type Indicator (MBTI). The MBTI assesses four bipolar dimensions: extraversion-introversion (orientation towards the outer and inner worlds), sensing-intuition (ways of perceiving), thinking-feeling (ways of making choices), and judging-perceiving (ways of responding to the outer world).

Students and faculty with a preference for extraversion will generally prefer learning approaches that emphasize participation and interaction (for example, an opportunity to ask and answer questions). Students and faculty with a preference for introversion will generally prefer individual work that emphasizes the importance of reflection.

Sensation and intuition refer to cognitive approaches for acquiring knowledge. Sensate learning emphasizes facts, patterns, rules, procedures, and a mastery style of learning; intuitive learning is focused on new possibilities, unstructured problems, and an understanding style of learning. Accounting education has been characterized by highly structured problem solving (sensate) activities. Geary and Rooney (1993, p. 66) report that accounting students, based on data obtained using the MBTI, when compared to norms for college students, are much more likely to prefer sensate thinking.

Thinking and feeling refer to the process of making choices. A decision based on feeling will emphasize subjective factors such as personal values and inclinations, group values, and concern for particular issues and people. A decision based on thinking will stress the importance of justice and objectivity. Effective use of the feeling mode can greatly enhance communications and contribute to success in teamwork and developing new business. Correspondingly, effective use of the thinking mode will promote logical reasoning and the pursuit of just and correct solutions to problems.

Judging and perceiving describe how individuals process information. A person with a preference for judging will seek closure, structure, and resolution. A person with a preference for perception is inclined to gather more information and postpone making decisions.

Historically, the accounting profession has been closely identified with sensate and thinking based teaching methods, with the result that accounting education has overemphasized both sensate and thinking based approaches. The complex forces reshaping the profession demand the application of intuitive and feeling based approaches to meet the goals articulated in *Perspectives on Education: Capabilities for Success in the Accounting Profession*. Students, for example, are expected "to use creative problem-solving skills in a consultive process," "to solve diverse and unstructured problems in unfamiliar settings," and "to comprehend an unfocused set of facts; identify and, if possible, anticipate problems; and find acceptable solutions." In addition, the ability to work "effectively in groups with diverse members to accomplish a task is essential. The practitioner must be able to influence others; organize and delegate tasks; motivate and develop other people; and withstand and resolve conflict" (Arthur Andersen & Co. et al., 1989, pp. 6–7).

Like their students, accounting professors have different styles that will be reflected in how they approach education. For example, faculty will vary in terms of how explicitly they give instructions, how much they expect students to learn on their own, and how actively they encourage group work. The GRLSQ can be used to assist faculty in examining how they use dependent, collaborative, and independent teaching styles. Similarly, the LSI and the MBTI can be used to help instructors assess how they plan their classes and how they utilize their own strengths and preferences in the classroom.

SELECTING APPROPRIATE PEDAGOGIES

Perhaps the most sophisticated innovations introduced into the classroom during the past decade are the computer-assisted approaches to accounting education. These approaches run the gamut from drill-based programmed learning to complex simulations. Drill-based programmed learning is ideal for teaching rules and algorithms (for example, analyzing transactions or preparing financial statements). In addition to providing continuous reinforcement, programmed learning accommodates individual differences in the rate and manner in which students master the subject material. Simulations, on the other hand, stretch the ability of students to understand how to respond to complex and unstructured problems. The best simulations will allow students to experience decision making under uncertainty in a complex setting. The goal of these simulations is to understand how concepts are applied rather than to master predetermined algorithms.

Innovations in the accounting classroom are certainly not limited to computer-based strategies. Many universities support programs and projects that provide students with opportunities to gain direct experience with an accounting application. The experienced-based learning can take place within the framework of a formal internship or cooperative learning program, or it can incur less formally through participation in course projects or field-based learning, where students are required to analyze problems in the context of actual organizations. Other techniques for bridging the gap between the classroom and the business environment include the use of cases, role plays, business games, collaborative learning, and organized adventure games. Often the intent of these approaches is to simultaneously address the goals of learning the accounting content and developing communication and interpersonal skills. For example, a project focused on international accounting may require students to pool resources and work together as a team and then demonstrate the knowledge they have acquired by making an oral presentation to a group that plays the role of the board of directors.

The opportunities for accounting faculty to employ a wide range of pedagogical styles are impressive. Because of the leadership provided by academic organizations, accounting firms, and publishers, support materials are widely available at affordable prices. This is a dramatic change that can be expected to accelerate as contemporary publishing methods continue to increase the range of choice at ever more affordable prices. To take full advantage of these opportunities, faculty must achieve congruence between their learning objectives, their choices in pedagogies, and the individual learning styles and preferences of their students.

ANALYZING LEARNING ENVIRONMENTS

Fry (1978) argues that the learning environment can be assessed by observing the following variables in the context of a course: the purpose of the major activities, the primary source or use of information, the rules guiding learner behavior, the instructor's role, and the provision for feedback. These are useful dimensions to guide faculty in planning classroom interactions, provided that provision is made for individual differences encompassing both faculty and students.

Each of the three theories considered in this chapter is supported by assessment instruments (the revised LSI, the GRLSQ, and MBTI). When faculty decide to make individual differences an explicit consideration in designing and presenting a class, assessment instruments are a great advantage. Faculty, for example, can set aside time to complete assessment indicators in preparation for a discussion of how their personal preferences affect their choice of pedagogy and how they complement or fail to complement the efforts of their colleagues across the accounting curriculum.

These authors have also had considerable success in employing assessment instruments as an integral part of their courses. Almost always, the use of assessment indicators with students has allowed the students to appreciate their strengths and to value the opportunity to develop in less preferred areas where they have the greatest potential for growth. If students see the learning objective as legitimate and consistent with their well-being, tackling an assignment that requires them to develop new strategies for learning can be approached with a positive rather than resentful attitude. This places the faculty in the role of the supportive ally as opposed to the more patronizing role of the expert who knows what is best for the uninitiated.

While the availability of assessment indicators is an advantage, using indicators is not essential to the design and implementation of the accounting curriculum. However, given the wide range of objectives and the many different pedagogies currently supported, it is essential to develop a comprehensive plan that is supported and implemented by the faculty. Using the three models considered in this chapter, there is almost no limit to the possibilities to create a tailored plan that incorporates ever-evolving learning objectives, a dynamic and changing faculty team, and the characteristics of the many students and populations served by the college or university.

To illustrate this planning process, consider how Kolb's four approaches to the learning process can help frame an approach to the design of the accounting curriculum. The convergent learning style is most likely to prevail in the introductory accounting course, where traditionally students seek a single correct answer to a highly structured problem. It is exactly this type of student who is most likely to feel betrayed and unprepared when there is a dramatic shift in the intermediate accounting sequence to a learning style that emphasizes deductive reasoning and concepts. There are other ways to develop the introductory courses and to smooth the transition.

Traditional courses in financial accounting, auditing, managerial accounting, tax accounting, and information systems have not emphasized the strengths of the divergent learning style. Yet, there is a steady chorus from the profession asking for inventive and imaginative thinkers who are not constrained by the molds of the past. Has accounting education driven away the divergent learners with these preferences? How has the curriculum made a place for the opportunity seeking, risk taking, and action oriented student with the accommodative style? Without contributions from students with divergent and accommodated styles, it would not be surprising if the learning environment becomes biased in favor of structured and risk adverse responses to problems.

The GRLSQ can be equally important in designing a development plan that will encourage students to learn to adapt to situations that require dependent, independent, and collaborative strategies. Students who score high as dependent learners will find favor with their counterparts on the faculty, and together they may exert considerable influence in shaping student expectations of faculty. The dependent learner seeking uncertainty reduction and a subordinate relationship will not respond well to the freedom to follow his or her interests in unstructured advanced-level courses, and, perhaps, this student will see an instructor who advocates an independent approach as deficient. The advanced-level instructor, on the other hand, may see her or his role as that of a resource person dedicated to promoting independent habits of thought and work.

The importance of collaborative learning also must not be overlooked. Perhaps it is the collaborative learner who is most at home in the professional world and least comfortable in the classroom environment. A collaborative learner is a natural team player who prefers discussion, group projects, and collaborative assignments such as group case studies. There is very little opportunity to develop a collaborative adaptation in a curriculum that is focused on individual achievement on a certification examination.

In developing a plan for an accounting curriculum, it should be expected that both faculty and students will differ in their preferences and experiences with regard to the dependent, independent, and collaborative approaches. It is also clear that each approach has its place in the curriculum. While entry-level positions will continue to emphasize a subordinate relationship, the preparation of accountants must not overvalue dependent approaches and fail to prepare students to develop independent habits of thought and work relationships. Similarly, students must be prepared for work environments whose scale and complexity make it essential for them to work collaboratively as a member of team.

In developing a plan for the growth and development of accounting students, Jung's theory of psychological type is especially well-suited because it is inherently a theory of personal development. For example, Jung described the development task of introverts as acquiring extroverted strategies to be used in coping with the external world while retaining an underlying preference for introversion. Thus, requirements for class participation and oral presentations can become opportunities for introverts if the introverts value the experience they gain in working outside their normal preference. Similarly, the preference commonly encountered in the accounting classroom for highly sensate learning that allows a student to master the material by learning all the facts can be balanced by assignments that require students to address unstructured problems that require an understanding of principles that can be applied in an environment that is far too complex to anticipate and master. Students who prefer thinking over feeling also predominate in accounting classes, and these students are likely to believe that knowing the right answer is enough. Those students who fail to appreciate the importance of group process and communications fall short of the goals set for accounting education by the profession. Finally, differences in the approaches to tasks that characterize judging and perceiving types can provide very valuable insights into why people clash in their approaches to completing a project.

IMPLICATIONS FOR ACCOUNTING EDUCATION

A better understanding of the role of learning and teaching styles in relation to the learning objectives can make an important contribution to accounting education. A planned curriculum that factors in the effects of individual differences and multiple learning objectives across the boundaries of individual courses is much more likely to achieve the ambitious outcomes now associated with accounting education.

Faculty confront an array of objectives that encompass many dimensions of student growth and development. This objective set is far broader than in past periods. To address these objectives, many new and innovative approaches and accompanying textual materials have been developed. In addition, many individual faculty members are continuing to experiment and develop strategies and materials for use in their classrooms.

The inconclusive results reported in surveys of the literature on student evaluations of teachers may occur, not because a new teaching method is bad, but because students with different learning styles will react differently to different methods. Thus, some students may gain, but others may lose, from using a new teaching method. Taking different learning styles into account may provide more conclusive results of the evaluations of different teaching methods. Researchers may be able to discover which types of students gain (or lose) from different types of teaching methods.

Perhaps the most important outcome to be gained from employing strategies that explicitly recognize critical differences in student and faculty approaches to the learning process are the benefits gained by recognizing diverse objectives and diverse approaches associated with accounting education. Explicit recognition of the fact that diverse approaches are both inescapable in the learning process and essential in the achievement of diverse goals can dramatically alter the ways faculty and students make the most of their opportunities in the classroom.

REFERENCES

American Accounting Association, Committee of the Future Structure, Content, and Scope of Accounting Education (The Bedford Committee). 1986, Spring. Future accounting education: Preparing for the expanding profession. *Issues in Accounting Education*, pp. 168–195.

Arthur Andersen & Co., Arthur Young, Coopers & Lybrand, Deloitte Haskins & Sells, Ernst & Whinney, Peat Marwick Main & Co., Price Waterhouse, and Touche Ross (The Big Eight). 1989, April. *Perspectives on education: Capabilities for success in the accounting profession*. White Paper. New York.

Fry, R. E. 1978. *Diagnosing professional learning environments: An observational framework for assessing situational complexity*. Unpublished doctoral dissertation, Massachusetts Institute of Technology.

Geary, W. T., & Rooney, C. J. 1993. Designing accounting education to achieve balanced intellectual development. *Issues in Accounting Education*, *8*(1), 60–70.

Goldstein, K., & Blackman, S. 1978. *Cognitive style: Five approaches and relevant research*. New York: Wiley.

Kolb, D. A. 1985. *Learning style inventory: Technical manual*. Boston: McBer and Company.

Kolb, D. A. 1985. *Learning style inventory* (rev. ed.). Boston: McBer and Company.

Kolb, D. A. 1984. *Experiential learning: Experience as the source of learning and development*. Englewood Cliffs, NJ: Prentice-Hall.

Reichmann, S. 1974. *The refinement and construct validation of the Grasha-Reichmann student learning styles scales*. Unpublished master's thesis, University of Cincinnati.

8

Using Experiential Learning Theory and Learning Styles in Diversity Education

Mary Ann Rainey and David A. Kolb

Diversity education is an increasingly important priority for schools, the work place, and the community. Its purpose is to raise awareness and understanding of differences in race, ethnicity, gender, physical ability, and social class, as well as in less visible differences of sexual lifestyle, education, personal style, and way of knowing. Diversity education promotes two fundamental democratic values — equal rights for all regardless of difference and the right to recognition of individual difference. The idea is that learning flourishes when learners have equal opportunity to develop and utilize their talents and perspectives to the fullest. Learning to value differences and to be receptive to diversity pose difficult educational challenges.

1. Diversity education requires not only acquisition of knowledge but also attitude change, appreciation of multiple perspectives, and willingness to bring about change. It must address emotional, perceptual, cognitive, and behavioral issues. The definition of prejudice, for example, includes not only ignorance of those who are different but also an emotional investment in maintaining that ignorance. Freire's (1974) pedagogy of "critical conscientization" sought to enable the oppressed masses of Brazil to understand their plight as well as to change it.
2. Resources of diversity education must be organized to be maximally responsive to what each learner wants to learn and the manner in which that learning is to be achieved. An African American female may enter a diversity class seeking to understand the institutions of racism and sexism, a goal that may require her to read related concepts and theories. A white male, on the other hand, who wants to learn what it

means to himself and others that he is white male, might engage in self reflection and dialogue with his classroom peers. Such individualized learning sometimes comes into conflict with the democratic value of equality in education when individualized learning is interpreted as proposing a politics of difference, and equality is perceived as espousing a politics of sameness.

3. Perhaps, because diversity education addresses core feelings and values, it requires a climate of psychological safety and trust. Learners must feel empowered and in control of their own learning. When learners feel threatened, they adopt defensive and conformist postures. Teaching, then, is experienced as coercive and manipulative, and learning becomes secondary.

Diversity education summons to the classroom social issues and the act of learning in unique combination. Teaching about human differences compels a framework that is considerably broader than traditional classroom methodology — one that recognizes the relevancy of education to the learner's life situations. Theories of experiential learning provide educational strategies for responding to the challenges of diversity education.

1. Experiential learning theory (ELT) describes learning as the holistic engagement of affective, perceptual, cognitive, and behavioral processes (Kolb, 1984). Learning results from the interplay of these processes, which are positioned along two primary dimensions of knowledge. Prehension, knowing by taking in data, involves the affect of concrete experience and cognition of abstract conceptualization. Transformation, knowing through modification of data, requires perception in reflective observation and behavior in active experimentation. ELT is an inclusive paradigm that allows for a range of responses to the learning requirements of diversity education.

2. ELT in the concept of learning style offers a perspective for addressing the dilemma between equality in education and individualized learning. Learners are each unique in the way they learn and equal in their contribution to a larger holistic learning cycle that values, acknowledges, and includes all ways of knowing. There is no one best way to learn. The assumption is equal worth in all ways of knowing. ELT also provides guidelines for creating learning environments that address the special learning needs of each learning style.

3. ELT proposes that the foundation of learning resides not in schools, books, or even teachers; rather, it rests in the experience of the learner. This democratic approach to education emphasizes self-directed learning and the role dialogue plays in the creation of a psychologically safe climate of learning.

In this chapter, we apply the experiential learning theories of Kolb and Freire to formulate ideas about delivering effective diversity education. These ideas are in part shaped by findings from interviews with diversity educators about their successful and unsuccessful diversity education experiences. They were asked to describe their experiences concretely, to reflect on them, to conclude why the experiences were successful or unsuccessful, and to recommend actions that can improve diversity education as it is now practiced.

HOLISTIC LEARNING

ELT is distinct from traditional approaches to learning. Unlike the epistemology of behavioral theory or cognitive and other rationalist theories, experiential learning theory is based on the epistemology of radical empiricism — a knowledge theory that affords equal status to multiple ways of knowing. Its intellectual roots are traceable to the pragmatism of John Dewey, the Gestalt and action research perspectives of Kurt Lewin, and Jean Piaget's structural dimensions of cognitive development. According to ELT, learning proceeds as a cycle and results from the integration of four learning modes — concrete experience, reflective observation, abstract conceptualization, and active experimentation (Kolb, 1984). Learners must be able to fully and openly engage in new experiences; reflect on, observe, and consider these experiences from various perspectives; create concepts that assimilate these experiences into sound theories; and appropriately apply these theories to their life situations.

Of significance in this knowledge theory is that the four learning modes constitute two primary dimensions of knowing. The first dimension, prehension, represents concrete experience and abstract conceptualization. Knowledge acquired through concrete experience — affective, immediate, and intuitive — is called apprehension. Knowledge gained through abstract conceptualization — cognitive, rational, and symbolic — is referred to as comprehension. The second dimension of knowing, transformation, represents reflective observation and active experimentation. Knowing through reflective observation — perceptual, appreciative, and diffuse — is intentional. Knowing through active experimentation — behavioral, focused, and goal directed — is extensional. The synthesis of these four forms of knowing results in higher levels of learning.

Research and theory illustrate distinctions of apprehensive and comprehensive knowledge and suggest that these distinctions could be gender related. Females are associated with a "diffused awareness" that emphasizes acceptance and wholeness, and males are depicted as having a "focused consciousness" that is characterized by separation and change (de Castillejo, 1973). Related research contends that females rely on intuition, personal meaning, and self understanding, which is at odds with the more socially accepted way of knowing that establishes truth in a rational and dispassionate manner (Belenky, Clinchy, Goldberger, & Tarule, 1986). The voice of females is subjective, holistic, and contextualized in contrast to the objective, rational, structured voice of males (Gilligan, 1982). More than half (59 percent) of 801 females emphasized concrete experience over abstract conceptualization, while 638 males (59 percent) preferred the reverse, abstract conceptualization over concrete experience (Smith & Kolb, 1986).

The transformation dimension of knowing is well illustrated in the two primary psychological dimensions of introversion (intention) and extraversion (extension) in dialectic relationship (Jung, 1971). The radical pedagogical concept of praxis — "reflection and action upon the world in order to transform it" — depicts the interplay between intentional knowing and extensional knowing (Freire, 1974, p.36).

INDIVIDUALIZED LEARNING

"The scientific study of human individuality poses some fundamental dilemmas. The human sciences, unlike the physical sciences, place an equal emphasis on the discovery of general laws that apply to all human beings and on the understanding of the functioning of the individual case" (Kolb, 1984, p. 62).

Educational institutions continue to search for ways to deliver effectiveness in diversity education. The challenge of teaching to a diverse group of students is the ability to respond to the unique qualities and peculiar needs that each brings to the classroom. Compounding the situation is the delicate nature of the topic of individualized education.

The democratic principle of equality has propelled to the forefront the current demand for recognition by females, persons of color, and other subaltern groups (Taylor, 1992). Equality for these individuals is far from being realized in the political, social, and economic realms, as well as in the educational domain. At issue is a politics of sameness that espouses equality in education versus a politics of difference that proposes individualized instruction. Opponents of recognition of difference in education question its value. They proceed from a vantage point of difference blind that is the appropriation of neutrality in response to diversity education — treat and consider all students the same. Separatism invites prejudice and ill will, the consequence of which is increased racial and ethnic conflict over inequality in education that serves little purpose (Schlesinger, 1992). Alternatively, difference blind suppresses identity and is discriminatory (Taylor, 1992). Diversity education faces the classic dilemma of total system versus subsystem optimization. Will it be sameness or difference, universalism or peculiarism, individuality at the sacrifice of equality?

Learning Style

Educators have yet to fully discern what equality looks like in diversity education. They do know it is unequal when Native Americans, for instance, are excluded or portrayed in an unbalanced way in textbooks, even though they and others are taught from the same textbooks (Minnich, 1990). Educators are also beginning to realize the extent to which cultural, ethnic, and gender differences influence learning and achievement.

Students from various areas of American subculture — African American, Chinese American, Greek American, and Mexican American — have different patterns of preferred learning strategies (Dunn, Gemake, Jalali, & Zenhausern, 1990). Statistical differences were found in the learning styles of Asian students at a Singapore college and Caucasian students at a U.S. university (Lam-Phoon, 1986). Studies suggest that Native Americans possess strong spatial ability and visual memory (Kleinfeld & Nelson, 1991). As stated earlier, females have a slightly higher preference than males for concrete experience over abstract conceptualization and vice versa (Smith & Kolb, 1986).

Diversity educators must be mindful of learning differences among students and the methods used to assess these differences (Sims & Sims, 1993). It is through the concept of learning style that ELT provides a mediating perspective on the dilemma of equality and personalized education. Experiential learning theory allows for recognition without judgment of both common and unique characteristics of learning and in so doing destructures whatever hierarchical arrangement that exists between the politics of sameness and the politics of difference in education.

The Learning Style Inventory (LSI) evaluates the relative preference an individual holds for the four learning modes (Kolb, 1984). The LSI reveals four statistically prevalent learning styles — diverger, converger, assimilator, and accommodator. The diverger is imaginative, understands people, perceives relationships between situations, and is good at brainstorming. The converger, who is the opposite of the diverger, likes deductive reasoning and is good at decision making and problem solving. The assimilator develops models and theories, plans well, and is systematic. The accommodator, opposite of the assimilator, takes risks, gets things done, and is comfortable with assuming leadership.

Learning Environments

Individualized learning in diversity education must also be considered from the perspective of course design. Content, context, conduct, and character are key dimensions of designing a course on understanding and appreciating diversity (Schor, 1993), each dimension having its own pedagogical consideration. What will be included in terms of course content? What is the appropriate context or learning environment to foster? What is the process or conduct to use? What is the character or role of the instructor?

Particular learning styles seem better suited for particular learning environments (Fry & Kolb, 1979). Students perform better in environments and with approaches that complement their learning styles than in environments or approaches that are inconsistent with their learning styles (Dunn, Beaudry, & Klavas, 1989). Mexican American students, to illustrate, are likely to achieve better in small groups than when working independently (Dunn & Dunn, 1978). In addition to conceptualizing individual learning styles, experiential learning theory provides a structure for the learning environment in a manner consistent with the learning cycle (Fry & Kolb, 1979) and appropriate for diversity education. Figure 8.1 depicts the relationship between learning modes, learning styles, and learning environments.

Four learning environments are identified and oriented toward the four learning modes — an affectively oriented environment corresponds to concrete experience, a perceptually oriented environment corresponds to reflective observation, a symbolically oriented environment (hereafter referred to as a cognitively oriented environment) corresponds to abstract conceptualization, and a behaviorally oriented environment corresponds to active experimentation. Each environment is measured by observing key variables: purpose, primary source, rules guiding learner behavior, nature of feedback, and teacher role. These variables, when considered, create four distinct components of a learning ecosystem. Table 8.1 structures each learning environment against the five variables with examples of activities for each.

Affectively Oriented Learning Environment

This learning setting focuses on attitudes, feelings, values, and opinions generated from "here and now" experiences. Tasks and activities often change from prior design and are more emergent as a result of learners' immediate needs. Procedures and guidelines are geared toward free expression of personal feelings, values, and opinions. Feedback is personalized with regard to the personal needs and goals of the learner rather than comparative and comes from both teachers and peers. Teachers serve as role models and colleagues. Typical activities are exploring feelings with students at a particular time or asking the class what might be useful to do given the dynamics of the moment.

Perceptually Oriented Learning Environment

This learning setting emphasizes appreciation and understanding of relationships between events and concepts. Students are encouraged to view topics from multiple perspectives and in different ways in the service of clarifying their own position. Emphasis is on how things get

FIGURE 8.1
Learning Modes, Learning Styles, and Learning Environments

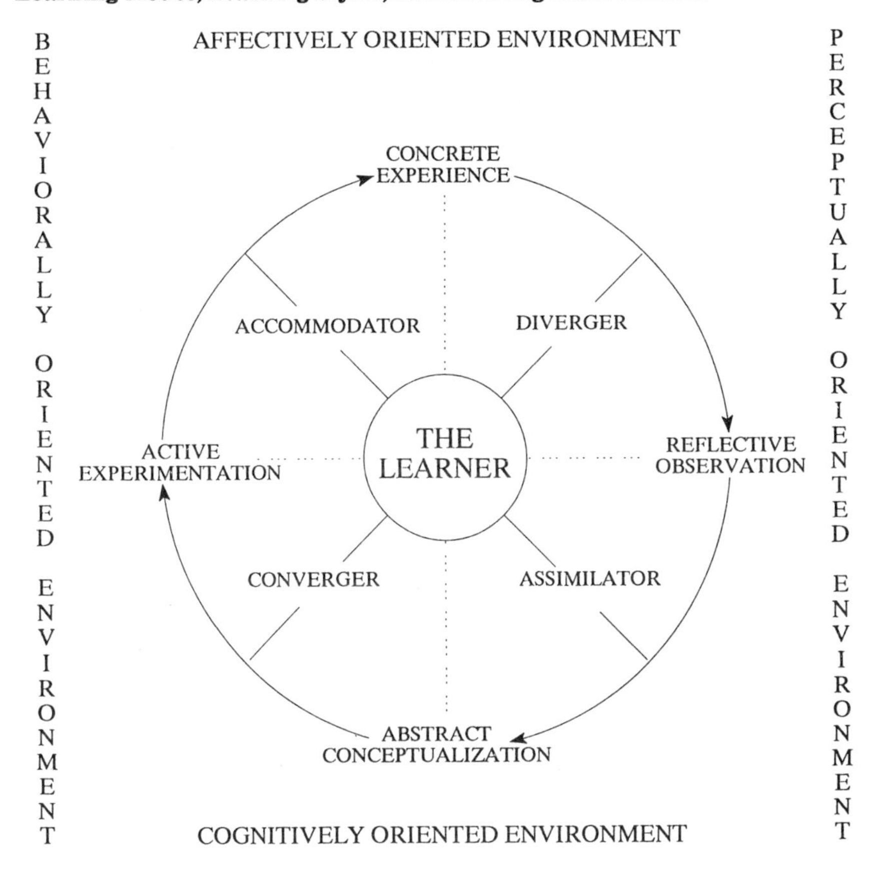

done, the process, rather than on solutions. Learners are evaluated on methodology of inquiry versus getting a particular answer. Teachers serve as process facilitators. Inviting students to step back and attempt to appreciate opposing viewpoints or engaging the class in a causal mapping of the concept of oppression are examples of activities.

Cognitively Oriented Environment

This environment is one characterized by skill mastery. Activities are directed toward problem solving based on "there and then" objective data. Learner output is evaluated as correct or incorrect using objective criteria. Teachers function as interpreters of a field of knowledge. Lecturing on identity development or asking students to create their personal theories about gender differences are typical activities.

TABLE 8.1
Learning Environments and Their Distinct Variables

	Learning Environment			
	Affectively Oriented	*Perceptionally Oriented*	*Cognitively Oriented*	*Behaviorally Oriented*
Purpose	Develop personal awareness and insight	Appreciate and understand how and why things relate	Acquire and master knowledge and skills	Actively apply learning to real life situations
Information source	"Here and now" concrete experience	Multiple data sources viewed in different ways	"There and then" abstract concepts and facts	Activities directed toward requirements of task completion
Rules of behavior	Free expression of feelings, values, and opinions	Emphasis on process and inquiry	Adherence to prescribed objective criteria	Minimal rules in support of learner autonomy
Nature of feedback	Personalized and immediate from teachers and peers	Non-evaluative suggestions rather than critiques	Evaluation of correct or incorrect learner output	Learner judges own performance based on established standards
Teacher role	Role model and colleague	Process facilitator	Interpreter of a field of knowledge	Coach and advisor
Activities	Check-in, guided imagery to create experience, or debate	Causal mapping, maintaining a diary, or brainstorming	Presenting concepts, developing personal theories, or traditional testing	Developing action plans, a simulation, or leaderless work teams

Behaviorally Oriented Environment

This setting is geared toward application of knowledge and skills to solve real life situations. Activities are directed toward what is necessary to plan to complete a task. Learners are left to judge their own performance based on criteria they establish. Teachers serve as coaches who provide friendly advice and leave responsibility for outcome to the learner. Assigning students to develop strategies for using their learnings about differences in their everyday lives or developing role plays that demonstrate effective interaction in the workplace among the culturally different are illustrations of activities.

PSYCHOLOGICAL SAFETY, DIALOGUE, AND DIVERSITY EDUCATION

"We have cast our own lot with learning, and learning will pull us through. But this learning must be reimbued with the texture and feeling of human experiences shared and interpreted through dialogue with each other" (Kolb, 1984, p. 2). Diversity education requires attitude change — an unprecedented and daring undertaking for the classroom. Teaching and learning about human differences evoke high anxiety in their most seasoned citizens — teachers, learners, and administrators alike. As a subject matter, diversity education has few equals in terms of uncertainty of outcome. Awareness of the strong tone of emotion generated when social issues are discussed leads to expressions of dismay at a trend that focuses on course content in diversity education without attending to issues of process. "It is very difficult to talk about race, class, or gender in a meaningful way without also talking and learning about racism, classism, and sexism. The introduction of these and other issues of oppression often generates in students powerful emotional responses ranging from guilt and shame to anger and despair. These emotional responses, if not addressed, can result in student resistance" (Tatum, 1992, p. 19).

Feeling safe in the classroom takes on added significance in diversity education. Students must feel supported and believe that they can make choices about the process of learning as they venture into what for many is unchartered territory. New experience is the foundation of learning; however, a sense of security must be attained before learners can begin to consider the unfamiliar (Fry & Kolb, 1979). Trust is critical and enhanced by guidelines and group norms that encourage participation, risk taking, self disclosure, mutual support, and dialogue (Schor, 1993).

Diversity education without dialogue is programmed for failure. Providing a forum for dialogue is one of the most proactive gestures educators can do to enhance relationships among the culturally different (Tatum, 1992). Diversity is a source of learning and good conversation is a means of acquiring learning from diversity. Ideal speech, ideal listening, discourse in relationship, and promotion of the different voice are necessary components of good conversation among those who are different (Baker & Kolb, 1993).

The merits of dialogue are its practicality, its ability to weaken totalitarianism, and its cathartic qualities (Simpson, 1994). Dialogue, however, must subscribe to what is termed "the new decorum," which requires us to listen across boundaries of difference and engage in a moderate tone of conversation. Caution must be heeded against "conversation stoppers" from both the political left and right who engage in monologues, either by claiming to be victims of the system or who define identity on one source of human characteristic. Attention is quickly directed toward the fact that it is not the goal of the new decorum to suppress passion or promote a false congeniality, but, rather, it seeks to teach not one culture but human similarities, differences, and cross-connections (Simpson, 1994).

Dialogue plays a role in identity formation. Self awareness is facilitated by self disclosure and interaction with others (Jourard, 1971). When, in the process of dialogue, each party recognizes the identity of the other, both then will become able to understand better their individual identities. Through dialogue we create a broader horizon that serves as the backdrop against which we operate in the world. This broader horizon results from the "fusion of horizons" — situating one possibility, our usual standard, along side other possibilities, new and unfamiliar standards (Taylor, 1992).

ELT insists that genuine learning only occurs when students are engaged in "praxis" — political action informed by reflection (Freire, 1973). A fundamental aspect of praxis is the process of "naming the world." Naming the world is achieved through dialogue among equals, a dual process of inquiry and learning. Progressive education rejects the banking concept of teaching, where students are passive receptacles for deposits of fixed content from teachers. The idea is to instill "critical conscientiousness" in learners where the meaning of abstract concepts is explored through dialogue among peers. Dialogue is key to human emancipation of the oppressed (Freire, 1974).

Dialogue is good conversation. It must adhere to rules of the new decorum. Dialogue serves many purposes. It facilitates self-awareness and awareness of others, is a source of learning, is liberating, and lends to the creation of a climate of safety for teaching about human difference.

ELT supports knowledge in diversity educa-tion through the provision of a holistic model and process of learning, a structure and tool for assessing learning preferences, a framework for creating effective learning environments, and dialogue as a vehicle for creating psychological safety in the classroom. The significance of ELT in diversity education extends beyond these factors. Diversity education typically focuses on visible human characteristics such as race, ethnicity, and gender. ELT offers learning style as an invisible yet significant human difference. It breaks the glass box of diversity education that focuses entirely on that which is observable. Learning style acknowledges diversity on the inside and highlights the relevancy of unobservable human characteristics in diversity education.

THE INTERVIEWS

A study was conducted to gain better understanding of factors contributing to effective diversity education and to validate the challenges it faces as advanced in this paper. Fifteen individuals participated in one on one interviews: four African Americans (two males), four Asian Americans (one male), six Caucasian Americans (three males), and one Latino male. These individuals were between 30 and 55 years of age and had from two to 16 years of experience as diversity educators. Each person described a peak and a nadir experience of diversity education by responding to the following protocol based on the experiential learning cycle (Kolb, 1971).

The question stated, "Think about a time when you were either a participant or trainer in a cultural diversity education session that was particularly (ineffective or effective) in terms of your learning and the learning of others."

A. Concrete Experience
   Tell me about the experience — what happened, your thoughts, feelings, perceptions at the time of the experience?
B. Reflective Observation
   Since the time of the experience, what have been your key reflections — how do you make sense of the experience, now?
C. Abstract Conceptualization
   What are your conclusions as a result of the reflection and sense making?
D. Active Experimentation
   What rules of thumb and guidelines would you include in any future diversity education designs?

Data were analyzed for recurring comments or themes, which are listed in Table 8.2. Findings are presented without interpretation. Factors that contribute to effectiveness in teaching about differences are storytelling, trust and safety, dialogue, gaining personal insight, broadly defining diversity, teaching more than cognition, class lasting more than one day, clear expectations and goals, and a diverse group of students and teachers. Characteristics of ineffectiveness are negative perceptions of faculty, lack of closure of emotional issues, lack of trust, race and gender as a sole focus, feeling helpless to make a difference, feeling personally attacked or blamed, and class lasting one day or less.

TABLE 8.2
Aspects of Effective and Ineffective Diversity Experiences

Effective Experiences	*Ineffective Experiences*
1. Storytelling	1. Negative perceptions of faculty
2. Trust established	2. Lack of closure of emotional issues
3. Feeling safe	3. Lack of trust
4. Dialogue among students	4. Race and gender as a sole focus
5. Gaining some personal insight	5. Feeling helpless to make a difference
6. Diversity broadly defined	6. Feeling personally attacked or blamed
7. Teaching more than cognition	7. Insufficient time (class one day or less)
8. Class more than one day	
9. Clear expectation and goals	
10. Diverse group of faculty and students	

Females and males were evenly split in identifying storytelling and dialogue as useful learning tools. The two activities are related. Storytelling, it seems, affects students in ways that arouse curiosity and a desire to engage in dialogue and often leads to personal insight. Females spoke about trust as a component of effective diversity education, while males associated feeling safe (from attack and blame) with a satisfying experience. Broadly defining diversity positively affects the experience of males more than females. Expanding the context of diversity creates the opportunity for students to personally relate to experience of difference and positions them for more receptivity to the more controversial aspects of diversity such as racism and sexism. This opinion is expressed across ethnic and gender boundaries of persons interviewed. A couple of individuals suggest gradual movement toward the discussion of race. Diversity education is less satisfying for many of the individuals in this study when limited to race and gender.

Diversity educators in this study emphasized the importance of teaching more than cognition in a class on difference. Efficacy in diversity education is "unlike competency or skill building where you can be very objective and still do a good job. It touches everyone's feelings." Effectiveness also necessitates more time. Persons interviewed felt that a day and a half is the minimum time for teaching diversity. Less time often leaves students with unresolved issues. Lack of closure of emotional issues is an aspect of ineffective diversity experiences. One teacher provides individual counseling for students taking classes on differences.

Experiences of diversity education are more positive for persons interviewed when ground rules and goals are clarified, particularly when this occurs at the beginning of the semester. One educator is committed to what he refers to as community building, where objectives, ground rules, and roles are explicit and total group as well as subgroup is seen as important. Identifying personal goals for some individuals is just as critical as goal setting for the class in general.

Having a diverse team of faculty models the concept of diversity. A multicultural class of students provides richness of discussion and diminishes feelings of isolation and loneliness. Teacher skill was more a concern for males than females. Negative perception of faculty was a key aspect of ineffective diversity experience. Elements of this theme are perceptions of faculty as coercive, lacking in process skills, unclear about their own cultural identity, and when as a team working at cross purposes.

Themes from the interviews confirm the challenges confronting diversity education as presented in this paper. Persons interviewed underscore the need for dialogue, psychological safety, and learner-directed education. In singling out a requirement for more than cognition, the usefulness of a more comprehensive method of teaching is also highlighted.

EXPERIENTIAL LEARNING THEORY AND LEARNING STYLES IN DIVERSITY EDUCATION

If ELT offers diversity education a framework that integrates personal experience and practical application with perceptive appreciation and understanding of concepts, what then is required to deliver diversity education? We offer some suggestions based on interviews and ELT.

Position Diversity Education as a Holistic Process

It is useful to inform students that a diversity course based on experiential learning might belie some of their assumptions about the teaching process and their role in it. Unlike traditional approaches to learning, where teachers are experts and students are passive recipients of the information that is disseminated, here responsibility for learning will be shared by teacher and learner. In that a course on human differences is not merely a new content area, it summons all of who learners are — their intelligence, their perception, their practicality, and, most importantly, their emotions. The approach to learning must be guided by a holistic framework and include a range of activities including experiential exercises, discussions, readings, and role plays.

Clarify the Role of the Instructor

Generally, and particularly in diversity education, ELT requires a different role of the instructor from the one typically seen. That role needs to be clarified. As mentioned, the teacher's role is less one of purveyor of knowledge and more one of managing a classroom as a learning organization. We have stressed that, at any given time, the instructor could be a role model and colleague who supports awareness of human experience in the moment, process consultant who keeps on track an engaging discussion of sexual lifestyle, interpreter of knowledge who does a brief lecture on types of group identity, or coach who supports the planning of transfer of learnings.

Clarify the Role of the Student

Experiential learning is individualized and self-directed learning. Students who are unaccustomed to this approach may have difficulty with assuming responsibility for achieving their learning objectives. Instructors will need to work with students so that they see value in their own experiences and applying new knowledge, skills, and attitudes to their life situations.

Assess the Learning Styles of Students and Faculty

Learning style immediately creates an alternative view of difference. The LSI gives individuals data about which aspects of the learning process they prefer. It also has implications for classroom activities, faculty role, feedback, student engagement of material, and faculty to student dynamics. The LSI, when administered in class using the LSI grid, provides data about the learning community that is immediately available to everyone. It is intriguing to watch students act out their learning style during the discussions. Some struggle with feelings they have, others question the pragmatics of the model or challenge the theory behind it, and others just watch and take it all in (see Kolb, Rubin, & Osland, 1991, Chapter 3, for administration of the LSI as a classroom activity).

Establish a Psychological Contract

The importance of psychological safety and feelings of trust in diversity education is emphasized in the literature and interviews conducted for this chapter. The concepts of learning environments and dialogue have been presented as constructive mechanisms toward creating the ideal climate of learning. The act of negotiating a psychological contract is good for establishing trust and should take place during the first class session. The Sherwood and Glidewell (1972) model captures the dynamic nature of psychological contracts and suggests strategies for renegotiation when pinches or disruption of shared expectations occur. It is designed to be a real agreement among members of the learning community — students and teachers alike — that guides their behavior for the entire term (see Kolb, Rubin, & Osland, 1991, Chapter 1, for a guide to establishing a psychological contract). Planning the progression of discussion of sensitive topics, particularly the "isms" — racism, ethnicism, sexism, ageism, nationalism, ableism — is another way of building trust (Schor, 1993). Gender issues are presented before issues of ethnicity; ethnic issues are discussed before racial issues, which are the most emotionally charged.

Identify Guidelines of Behavior

Guidelines complement the contracting process and, like the psychological contract, should be identified on the first day of class. Identifying guidelines, of course, is a joint activity between students and teachers. Ones to consider include honoring confidentiality, affording mutual respect, speaking from personal experience, and engaging in interpersonal conversation. Confidentiality creates a dilemma for students whose learning is supported by discussion outside the classroom, which we encourage and sometimes request. We ask students to refrain from attaching names to opinions or experiences shared by their classmates. Simply put, mutual respect is behavior consistent with the Golden Rule. It is the act of acknowledging that we all hold perspectives of the world that, even when they differ, are valid for each of us.

Encourage Dialogue

Design activities that allow for discussion and processing of experience. Dialogue itself begins with speaking from personal experience and owning experience through the use of first person language — "I," "my," "me," "mine." First person language is more engaging in dialogue than the more distant and abstract third person. It lends to "straight talk" — use of clean, clear, direct communication that fosters connections between two parties of equal status (Jamison, 1987). Good conversation requires both speaking and listening and in this regard is not monological. Gestalt principles emphasize calling the other by name as a first step toward good interpersonal contact. Calling someone by name serves to plant a seed for relationship building. Another Gestalt approach to good conversation is to find ways to engage, not two or a few, but all students in total classroom discussion.

Utilize a Variety of Group Structures

Mix groups based on the difference represented in the class, for example, race, gender, learning style, and organization type, and also in a variety of structures of pairs, trios, small groups, and total community. We find especially useful the small group structure we call "learning teams" that meet during the formal structure of the class as well as outside of class. Time constraints, class size, and other related factors do not allow for the appropriate and thorough processing of student experience within the classroom setting. Learning teams allow for continued processing of experience and serve as support groups for identification of goals and monitoring of progress toward goal achievement. They enrich the learning process, provide a stable reference group, and facilitate trust that spills over into the classroom.

The Personal Application Assignment

Readings, essays, term papers, thought pieces (a written stream of consciousness in reaction to readings or experiences), and group projects are mechanisms for teaching and learning about differences and evaluation in diversity education. We like the Personal Application Assignment (PAA) that is used for evaluation of student progress by the student and teacher. The PAA is a paper that corresponds to the experiential learning model (Kolb, 1971) as it is designed to indicate:

a real situation (concrete experience),

understanding of the situation (reflective observation),

use of models and concepts to frame understanding of the situation (abstract conceptualization),

behavioral plans for similar situations in the future (active experimentation), and

integration of the four preceding perspectives (synthesis).

The PAA is typically used several times during the course of a semester and is similar to the interview guide of open-ended questions that students respond to as a way of monitoring their development over the course of the class (Tatum, 1992). Used in this manner, the PAA contributes to equalization of power between learner and teacher.

SUMMARY

In this chapter, we submit ELT as a guiding framework for effectively responding to three key challenges facing diversity education — providing a holistic education, addressing the dilemma of individualism and equality in the classroom, and providing a safe climate for learning. The dual knowledge theory of ELT depicts learning as a holistic and integrated process that attends to what learners think as well as what they feel, perceive, and do. Through the concepts of learning style, ELT responds to the dilemma of particularism and universalism in teaching. ELT provides some of the whats and hows of the psychologically safe environment through the concept of the learning environment and dialogue among peers of equal status. Based on popular and academic literature and the experiences of professionals in the field of diversity, we outlined several strategies for using ELT in teaching about human differences.

The efficacy of diversity education rests on the degree to which all participants are able to own who they are as individuals, as group members, as citizens of a global community, and as learners, seeking knowledge and appreciation of self and other. Experiential learning is a theory of life and learning that celebrates human potential. As a paradigm of diversity education, it appropriately prepares learners for life in an ever changing society.

REFERENCES

Baker, A., & Kolb, D. A. 1993. Diversity, learning, and good conversation. In R. R. Sims and R. F. Dennehy (Eds.), *Diversity and differences in organizations: An agenda for answers and questions* (pp. 17–32). Westport, CT: Quorum Books.

Belenky, M., Clinchy, B. McV., Goldberger, N. R., & Tarule, J. M. 1986. *Women's ways of knowing*. New York: Basic Books.

de Castillejo, I. C. 1973. *Knowing woman: A feminine psychology*. New York: Harper & Row.

Dunn, R., Beaudry, J., & Klavas, A. 1989. Survey of research on learning styles. *Educational Leadership*, *46*, 7.

Dunn, R., & Dunn, K. 1978. *Teaching students through their individual learning styles: A practical approach*. Reston, VA: Prentice-Hall.

Dunn, R., Gemake, J., Jalali, F., & Zenhausern, R. 1990. Cross-cultural differences in learning styles of elementary-age students from four ethnic backgrounds. *Journal of Multicultural Counseling and Development*, *18*, 68–93.

Freire, P. 1974. *Pedagogy of the oppressed*. New York: Continuum.

Freire, P. 1973. *Education for critical consciousness*. New York: Continuum.

Fry, R., & Kolb, D. 1979. Experiential learning theory and learning experiences in liberal arts education. *New Directions for Experiential Learning*, *6*, 79–92.

Gilligan, C. 1982. *In a different voice*. Cambridge, MA: Harvard University Press.

Jamison, K. 1987. Straight talk: A norm-changing intervention. In W. B. Reddy and C. C. Henderson, Jr. (Eds.), *Training theory and practice* (pp. 209–223). Arlington, VA: National Institute for Behavioral Science.

Jourard, S. M. 1971. *The transparent self*. New York: Van Nostrand Reinhold.

Jung, C. 1971. Psychological types. In J. Campbell (Ed.), *The portable Jung* (pp. 178–269). New York: Viking. (Original work published 1921. Original translation 1923).

Kleinfeld, J., & Nelson, P. 1991. Adapting instruction to Native Americans' learning styles: An iconoclastic view. *Journal of Cross-cultural Psychology*, *22*(2), 273–82.

Kolb, D. A. 1984. *Experiential learning: Experience as the source of learning and development*. Englewood Cliffs, NJ: Prentice-Hall.
Kolb, D. A. 1971. Individual learning styles and the learning process. Working paper. Massachusetts Institute of Technology, Alfred P. Sloan School of Management.
Kolb, D. A., Rubin, I. M., & Osland, J. 1991. *Organizational behavior: An experiential approach*. Englewood Cliffs, NJ: Prentice-Hall.
Lam-Phoon, S. 1986. *A comparative study of southeast Asian and American Caucasian college students of two Seventh-Day Adventist campuses*. Unpublished doctoral dissertation, Andrews University.
Minnich, E. K. 1990. *Transforming knowledge*. Philadelphia: Temple University Press.
Schlesinger, Arthur M. 1992. *The disunity of America: Reflections on multiculturalism*. New York: W. W. Norton.
Schor, S. M. 1993. Understanding and appreciating diversity: The experiences of a diversity educator. In R. R. Sims and R. F. Dennehy (Eds.), *Diversity and differences in organizations: An agenda for answers and questions* (pp. 73–92). Westport, CT: Quorum Books.
Sherwood, J. J., & Glidewell, J. C. 1972. Planned negotiation: A norm setting OD intervention. In W. W. Burke (Ed.), *Contemporary organization development: Orientations and interventions* (pp. 35–46). Washington, DC: NTL Institute.
Simpson, C. R. 1994, March 16. A conversation, not a monologue. *The Chronicle of Higher Education* (Pull-Out Section), p. 2.
Sims, S. J., & Sims, R. R. (1993). Diversity and difference training in the United States. In R. R. Sims and R. F. Dennehy (Eds.), *Diversity and differences in organizations: An agenda for answers and questions* (pp. 73–92). Westport, CT: Quorum Books.
Smith, D., & Kolb, D. A. 1986. *A user's guide for the Learning Style Inventory: A manual for teachers and trainers*. Boston: McBer & Co.
Tatum, B. D. 1992, Winter. Teaching the psychology of racism. *Mount Holyoke Alumnae Quarterly*, pp. 19–21.
Taylor, C. 1992. *Multiculturalism and "the politics of recognition": An essay by Charles Taylor*. Princeton, NJ: Princeton University Press.

9

Experiential Learning: Preparing Students to Move from the Classroom to the Work Environment

Serbrenia J. Sims

When most of us think about the concept of experiential learning and its applications to higher education, ideas of co-operative education, internships, community service-learning, field studies, cross-cultural programs, and practicum immediately come to mind. Yet experiential learning goes far beyond these hands-on experiences that are designed to prepare students for their future work environment. Experiential learning involves a directed process of student initiated questioning, investigating, reflecting, and conceptualizing based on experiences both in and outside the formal classroom setting. Key to its success as a learning tool is the active involvement of students in the learning process. Students are free to choose and directly experience the consequences of their learning choices.

Hutchings and Wutzdorff (1988) substantiate findings that students are unable to apply what they have learned in the classroom to the actual work environment. This gap in application of knowledge has often been blamed on an inadequate education offered by colleges and universities, when in fact it might be more appropriate to attribute the shortcomings of our educational system to the students and their passive as opposed to active involvement in their educational experience. In the past, emphasis has been placed solely on changing the educational offerings and increasing the number of resources (such as library holdings, computers, and faculty) available to students in an effort to address the question of inadequate education. The purpose of this chapter is to offer some suggestions on how to correct the problem of the link between classroom learning and the work environment by emphasizing the need for the student to be an active participant in her or his education.

How can colleges and universities move from a pedagogy approach to an andragogy approach that promotes flexibility and independent learning? Keffe (1988) suggests that emphasis be placed on three areas: the individual student; the classroom and instructor; and the institution. These three areas are considered paramount to a successful plan for implementing experiential learning into an educational environment.

This chapter will review the concept of experiential learning as it can be applied across disciplines and courses in the curriculum at colleges and universities by first examining the history of experiential education in institutions of higher education; second, by reviewing ways to integrate experiential learning into the existing mission and values of colleges and universities; third, by increasing faculty involvement in an attempt to increase quality and effectiveness of experientially based education; and fourth, by increasing student awareness of their role in their education in an effort to strengthen the link between classroom learning and work force requirements.

HISTORY OF EXPERIENTIAL LEARNING

The history of experiential learning and its successes is firmly based in the study of individual differences — differential psychology. The emphasis is placed on providing a range of instructional styles to maximize learning for all individuals. An outdated assumption that still guides teaching and curriculum development at colleges and universities is that all learners will perform equally given a single form of instruction based on the pedagogical model of instruction. The method of instruction at ancient universities was lecture, with rote memorization and recitation of facts. The chosen form of instruction today is primarily lecture and discussion, which might be supplemented by outside readings or projects. Efforts should be made to move away from this model to a model such as the andragogy model that requires more student involvement in his or her own education. Hiemstra and Sisco (1990) review both models. The pedagogical model of instruction was originally developed in the monastic schools of Europe in the Middle Ages. Young boys were received into the monasteries and taught by monks according to a system of instruction that required these children to be obedient, faithful, and efficient servants of the church (Knowles, 1984). This tradition of pedagogy, which later spread to the secular schools of Europe and America, became and remains the dominant form of instruction.

Pedagogy is derived from the Greek words *paid* (child), and *agagos* (learning). Thus, pedagogy has been defined as the art and science of teaching children. In the pedagogical model, the teacher has full responsibility for making decisions about what will be learned, how it will be learned, when it will be learned, and whether or not the material has been learned. Pedagogy, or teacher-directed instruction, as it is commonly known, places students in a submissive role and requires them to obey the teacher's instructions. It is based on the assumption that learners need to know only what the teacher teaches them. The result is a teaching and learning situation that actively promotes dependency on the instructor.

Until very recently, the pedagogical model had been applied to the teaching of both children and adults. This involved an obvious inconsistency. As adults mature, they become increasingly independent and responsible for their own actions. They are often motivated to learn by the need to solve immediate problems in their lives. Additionally, they have an increasing need to be self-directing. In many ways the pedagogical model does not account for such developmental changes in adults, and thus produces tension, resentment, and resistance in them (Knowles, 1984, p. 231).

Numerous researchers tend to refute this one method of instruction. Studies on learning styles designed to determine how students learn, think, and solve problems have been conducted for several decades. These studies reveal that a variety of factors affect an individual's preferred learning style to include heredity, personality development, motivation, and environmental adaptations. In addition, style is relatively persistent in the behavior of individual learners. It can change, but it does so gradually and developmentally (Keffee, 1988).

In early works of Argyris and Schon (1974, 1978), a link was explored between classroom learning and application of that learning to a particular job to be accomplished or decision to be made. Studying graduate interns, Argyris and Schon suggested that actions are guided by two theories: espoused theory and theory in use. Espoused theory is values and strategies that we proclaim in public. Theory in use is values and strategies that inform our actions and of which we are largely unaware and over which we have little control.

More recently, Kolb (1984) offered a learning style inventory designed to create an awareness that learners differ and to be a starting point for integrating knowledge and experience. Kolb's Learning Style Inventories suggests that students learn in a variety of ways, from concrete experience to abstract conceptualization, and from reflection to active learning. None is deemed superior to the other.

Knowledge of different learning styles allows us to organize learning environments and activities in a manner that involves telling, showing, and doing in an attempt to maximize the learning potential of all students at one time or another in the learning process. The result is more effective learning for all involved (Hiemstra & Sisco, 1990).

COLLEGE MISSIONS AND VALUES

Institutions of higher education, just as all organizations, tend to resist change. Generally speaking, the vast majority of the over 3,000 institutions of higher education in the United States are satisfied with the results that are being obtained from the traditional pedagogy approach to education. Yet, there are some who are restless and espouse what they feel is a better way to educate, that colleges could move far beyond their current levels of educational achievements if only they would dare to break away from tradition.

The primary assumption of this chapter is that it is possible to alter a college's curriculum and faculty teaching styles to accommodate differences in ability, style, or interest among individual students to improve learning outcomes and their abilities to adapt college learning to actual work applications. Jonassen and Graboeski (1993) offer the following theories that underlay this assumption:

Different learning outcomes require different skills and abilities.

Individuals differ in their abilities to process information, construct meaning from it, or apply it to new situations. (p. 19)

Colleges and universities must become more responsive to the needs of the diversity of students who wish to matriculate at their institutions and the needs of the workplaces that employ these students. Institutions are finding that, as financial problems become more evident, students are no longer looking to fill the role of the traditional full time residential learner. Instead, the student body on most college campuses is changing. Students are often working part time or full time. Many students have families and other obligations and, thus, need an educational system to suit their needs. This need for a flexible educational system was recognized over 20 years ago in England and is just now taking root in the United States.

Hiemstra and Sisco (1990) identified four societal forces that have contributed to the need for flexibility in teaching and college curriculum. The first force identified is the "ever increasing rapidity of social change, the constancy of technological advance, and the expanding awareness of global conditions." These factors have all contributed to the need for adults to maintain high levels of education preparation and skills. A second force identified by Hiemstra and Sisco (1990) is job obsolescence. This results in the need for retraining and career changes. The third force, an aging population and workforce, provides a large supply of adults interested in the learning opportunities offered by colleges and universities. Finally, a change in life styles for most Americans has contributed to the need for further education. These changes include single parent families, families where both parents work, and emphasis on individual development, just to name a few.

Thus, there is a need for flexibility in education and a new approach to adult learners.

Flexible education is based on a college curriculum that provides a wide variety of learning opportunities through a more flexible arrangement of course times and contents. Students are expected to be mature enough to guide their own educational experience. One institution that dared to pioneer in the area of flexible education and student-directed learning is Hampshire College. Hampshire College, a member of Five Colleges Incorporated (a consortium between Hampshire College, Smith College, Amherst College, Mount Holyoke College, and the University of Massachusetts) dared to expand their mission by developing an innovative approach to education in the late 1960s. More specifically, Hampshire College has implemented a student-directed education model that allows the student to facilitate actual class sessions, determine the syllabus, regulate commitment by all students, decide topics to be covered, coordinate both individual and group projects, and give course evaluations (Warren, 1988).

At Hampshire College, students are the directors of the course, as opposed to the instructor. This allows the students to feel a sense of involvement and control over their education while at the same time serves as a mechanism for the college to reach its goal of promoting independent learning.

The road to a student-directed education was not easy. It began with a 350-page document entitled *The Making of a College* as a guide to the direction to be taken by the institution within the consortium. Realizing that the existing system of courses and credits was not sufficient for liberal arts colleges and their evolving mission was a stimulus for the generation of a new college plan. The following is an excerpt taken from the initial letter of transmittal dated November 14, 1958, that outlines the college's plan:

At New College subjects will be covered, not by providing complete programs of courses, but by training students en masse to recognize fields of knowledge. The systematic and sustained effort will be made to train students to educate themselves. As freshmen they will start with seminars especially designed as the first step, not the last, in independence.

Other devices, such as student led seminars associated with all lecture courses will follow to reinforce this initial experience. Throughout, the program will provide for a type of social interaction which will create a climate favorable to intellectual activities.

Students will study only three courses at a time, an arrangement making possible concentration of effort and high levels of achievement. The faculty, on their side, will give only one lecture course at any given time; the rest of their energies will be devoted to the several kinds of seminars which characterize the curriculum. The student's program will be built on a large freedom of choice among areas of learning, and will be tested impersonally, by field examinations set according to recognized professional standards, frequently with the participation of outside examiners.

The college's total offering of lecture courses will be small. But it will be supplemented by other kinds of study and testing. It will also be supplemented to some degree by the collateral use of the course offerings of the sponsoring institutions and there will be each year a month-long mid-winter term after the Christmas vacation, during which the whole college will join in studying two courses which will provide a common intellectual experience. (Birney, 1993, pp. 10–11)

Although the initial values and mission expressed by leaders of Hampshire College are noteworthy, some modifications were necessary as a result of high student attrition and problems associated with maintaining central records. In addition, on a yearly basis instructors are faced with a freshman class that is a product of the traditional pedagogy or teacher-directed system. Thus, there is a continuing need for assistance in adjusting to student-directed learning. Yet the institutions's accomplishments have been numerous.

Hampshire College has engaged nonscience students, especially women students who have avoided science, in the sciences and mathematics.

Hampshire has encouraged and fostered growth in the capacity to work and think independently. This is frequently noted by graduates. Some who have experienced graduate school remark that they were not as well prepared factually as their contemporaries from other schools, but were better prepared in how to search and evaluate evidence, ask questions, and trust their own judgements.

Hamphsire graduates are more likely to pursue careers in public service, become entrepreneurs, participate in social and community organizations, and be involved in policies or civil rights, give money to causes in which they believe, etc. They are active, involved citizens.

Hampshire has developed a collaborative learning faculty that is highly productive and has created a culture that is very supportive of the institution's mission to develop active learners with a strong social consciousness. (Birney, 1993, p. 21)

FACULTY INVOLVEMENT IN EXPERIENTIAL SETTINGS

Often, teachers tend to conduct class based on the pedagogy model simply because this is the way they have been taught. Knowledge of experiential learning and learning styles can lead to improvements in teaching styles. Their role in experiential settings is to serve as a facilitator of learning, as opposed to the director of learning. As the facilitator of learning, the instructor is responsible for designing experiences for students on which to base learning, rather than the role of teacher, responsible for lecturing on theory and concepts. This role of facilitator should be developed and established early in each course, especially when there are students present who are not familiar with an andragogous teaching setting.

Early Class Sessions

The primary role should be to guide students in their understanding of the student-directed classroom and what responsibilities are entailed in their roles. This can be accomplished by providing a concise course description and a detailed introduction to both the need for the course and the objectives to be accomplished. The first few class sessions should also be geared to helping students adjust to student-directed learning by providing some initial structure, ground rules, and tools for working in groups.

The initial structure for an experiential student-directed classroom is the foundation for internalizing student-directed learning experiences. The teacher sets the direction of the course by offering course goals and objectives. The actual task of creating the curriculum then becomes the focus of student involvement in an effort to reach established course goals. The students are expected to look to the instructor for guidance in how to present information in a creative and challenging manner.

The first few class sessions should also be used to establish some basic ground rules for conducting the course. These ground rules might include involvement of all students regardless of their interest in a particular subject, sensitivity to diverse opinions, no interruptions during presentations, or offering suggestions for bettering the process. These rules serve as a device for including all students and as an assurance that their views will be respected.

The experiential learning approach to teaching and learning can be even more successful if the first class sets the tone or climate for future classes. The first class should introduce students to a way of learning that requires them to learn from their own experiences and those of others. In addition, the first class should establish a learning climate that encourages risk taking as students begin to think about different ways that people go about learning. Finally, the first class should set the standard for active participation by getting students started in sharing experiences and learning how to apply concepts and theories (Sims and Lindholm, 1993).

By taking the time to set the climate or tone for learning in the first few classes, the instructor has established a foundation for the appreciation of diverse ways of learning. In addition, the instructor has started developing student skills in four activities that are paramount to successful learning through experiential learning. According to Kolb's (1984) experiential learning model (ELM), students as learners need to be able to enter into an experience directly and openly (concrete experience), be able to stand back and reflect on the experience from many perspectives (reflective observation), be able to create concepts that integrate the reflections and observations with sound theory (abstract conceptualization), and, finally, be able to use that knowledge in new situations (active experimentation). In Kolb's (1984) view, learning involves a dual concern for action and conceptualization and an ability to move from specific involvement to general analytic detachment.

Because experiential learning activities are often conducted through group exercises and discussions, the instructor should also provide students with some tools or skills for working in groups. Warren (1988) suggests that instructors offer the following skills to better enable students to work in group situations:

Skills in Thinking in a Group

In order to come up with what they want to learn, students are introduced to brainstorming and prioritizing strategies and quickly find these to be of use in synthesizing their syllabus.

Decision-making Skills

Consensus decision making is explained and tested out. Practicing with smaller decisions at first, the group builds proficiency in the empowerment stage and is able to orchestrate very complex decisions in the self-determination stage.

Leadership Skills

Because a group needs leadership rather than set leaders to function effectively, the teacher points out available leadership roles such as timekeeper, feelings articulator, minority opinion advocate, summarizer, and gate keeper.

Problem-solving Skills

Through a series of simple initiative problems, the group is equipped with the tools as well as the belief that they can creatively solve problems together.

Feedback and Debriefing Skills

Because debriefing is critical to experiential education, the teacher's job is to ensure it happens. Insisting on quality feedback time early in the course sets an expectation for continuation during the latter sessions.

Mid-class sessions

After the initial class sessions have served their purposes in establishing the foundation for the course, the students should turn their attention to actually achieving course objectives. Students should be encouraged to finalize an ordered topic for each class. At this stage the teacher becomes a resource person for suggested readings, speakers, films, and programs to be reviewed for each topic to be covered. Students, however, are not required to limit themselves to the instructor-suggested resources.

Later Class Sessions

Later class sessions should serve as a review to course accomplishment and to student-directed learning. Students should be assisted in determining the worth of self-directed learning for themselves and their future endeavors. The end of the course is also a time to assess what has been learned in the course. This can be done by both oral and written testing based on course objectives and major events that happened during the class.

STUDENTS AND EXPERIENTIAL LEARNING

Focusing on the student begins by identifying the preferred learning style of each individual. Results should then be shared with the students in order to acquaint them with their range of skills, learning preferences, and interests. It should be stressed that the results of their learning styles do not relate to superior or inferior intelligence but should be viewed as a method to enhance their learning potential. For example, some students prefer to work in groups while others prefer individual attention. Both are acceptable preferences.

It is important to obtain this information so that students can prepare for their educational programs. Students need to understand that their learning styles might not always match the teaching styles of their professors. When this occurs, both students and professors are better prepared to alter their styles to suit the immediate situation in order to succeed.

Ideally, administrators and instructors should gather information on student learning styles during orientation or the first few classes, with an eye toward introducing students to experiential learning, to begin to build a learning climate, and in particular courses to introduce the students to the topics to be covered during the course and to emphasize the importance of active student involvement in the learning process.

With the above objectives in mind, one approach to introducing the concept of learning styles and experiential learning in a first class may be of use to administrators, instructors, and staff in their efforts to introduce experiential learning and learning styles.

Students first complete and score one of the many available learning style instruments, such as Kolb's Learning Style Inventory II (LSI II) (see Chapters 2, 3, and 12 for a detailed description of some of the more popular learning style instrumentation). The LSI II measures four individual learning style preferences and is based on the theory that habits of learning emphasize some aspects of the learning process over others. After completion and scoring of the LSI II, giving a short lecture on Kolb's ELM is useful in advancing the notion of learning styles and the experiential learning approach.

After the lecture, the students and instructors share the results of their Learning Style Inventories with each other. In our experience, students respond in different ways to this sharing experience. Some students vehemently reject the results of the Learning Style Inventories; most, however, are in total agreement with the results. Further discussion on similarities and differences between the students and how different people go about learning and problem solving should be encouraged by the instructor. This sharing experience is intended to encourage participation from all students and open discussion on potential opportunities and problems that differences in learning styles might lead to in classroom and work situations. An interesting aspect of using this approach in the first class is the fact that students will be acting out a particular part of the learning process according to Kolb's ELM. In other words, some will form an abstract conceptualization issue — for example, the validity of the LSI II, Kolb's ELM, or questioning what is the right or best way to learn. Others (active experimentation) will focus on issues of pragmatic usefulness — for example, how Kolb's ELM can be used to help a student or employee. The concrete experiencers are often struggling to deal with the feelings they are having, and the reflective observers will be doing just that — being silent and observing.

Students should then be placed in groups with other students who have the same learning style. At this point, students are given a copy of the syllabus, which lists the topics to be covered during the course. Each group of students is asked to define what each topic on the syllabus means. For about 15 or 20 minutes, each group should not only work toward a clearer understanding of the course topics but also point out differences in how each group went about accomplishing the topic definitions. Energy levels of the students seem to peak as they begin to realize some differences in how each group behaved during that experience. For example, those categorized as concrete experiencers tend to demonstrate a more playful attitude during the exercise, whereas those categorized as abstract conceptualizers tend to be more serious. Each group should then be given about 10 or 15 minutes to complete a personal application assignment and to answer in writing the following four questions based on Viega's (1975) journal-writing exercise.

1. Behaviorally, what happened in class today? (concrete experience)
2. Reflecting on your experiences today, what are you led to believe or feel about this course? (reflective observation)
3. How do your reflections and conclusions relate to a particular topic we will be studying in this class? (abstract conceptualization)

4. Based on your experiences today, plus your conclusions and analysis, what thoughts about the future classes do you have that will make you a more effective learner and this a better class? (active experimentation)

This assignment is followed by a total class discussion based on the four questions. To ensure maximum participation, a minimum of four people from each group must participate during the discussion. Because an implied goal of this first class and experiential learning exercises is learning how to learn, it is particularly relevant and valuable to help students understand the importance of each phase of Kolb's ELM. Therefore, this closing discussion not only serves as a means of integrating the total first class learning experience, it also introduces a mechanism for students to examine and improve their ability to learn, their understanding of learning styles, and how to learn from experience.

The above framework has been successfully used in a variety of settings (different courses, during orientation, and in training sessions). The whole process takes about 90 minutes; however, it can be completed during a 60-minute class.

In using this framework, students can begin to develop a set of skills that they can use throughout their educational life: skills in observing; skills of self-insight; skills of understanding the behaviors, learning styles, and motives of others; and skills of adapting behavior to the requirements of a task and the needs of individuals.

Hiemstra and Sisco (1990) offer the concept of learning contracts to help students take control of their learning. A learning contract is essentially an agreement between instructors and individual students as to what they will learn from a particular course. The contract consists of five parts:

1. the knowledge, skills, attitudes, and values to be acquired by the learner (learning objectives);
2. how these objectives are to be accomplished by the learner (learning resources and strategies);
3. the target date for completion;
4. the evidence that will be presented to demonstrate that the objectives have been completed (evidence of accomplishment); and
5. how this evidence will be judged or validated (criteria and means for validating evidence).

The learning contract serves as a foundation for student-directed learning in that it establishes a minimum standard for success in a course. However, it should not be written in stone. Students should be allowed to alter their contract in accordance to a change in views of plans for a course. When this is done, instructors should ensure that learning objectives are still being met in light of new situations or approaches to learning (Hiemstra & Sisco, 1990). It serves a variety of uses for both the student and the instructor of a course.

ADVANTAGES AND DISADVANTAGES TO INSTITUTIONALIZING EXPERIENTIAL LEARNING

Several advantages exist in institutionalizing experiential learning at colleges and universities. The main advantage will be the benefits derived from students who are able to take charge of their own learning and who can easily adapt to new learning environments. It is impossible for any college curriculum to teach everything that students will need to know as they enter the workforce; however, colleges can teach students to take charge of their own learning by giving them the needed tools and experience with self-directing experientially based education.

The second advantage to an experientially based education system will be the challenge to faculty to remain fresh and up to date on course topics, teaching, and learning styles. Challenges posed by students who are actively involved in their own education will serve to provide a stimulus for increased interaction with different points of view and approaches to presenting information to a class.

One final advantage to accrue from experiential education systems will be those that serve to increase the reputation for excellence for the college or university. This could mean an increase in the number of applicants who are looking for a solid education, not to mention the advantages of providing parents with assurances that their son or daughter will be properly stimulated in exchange for tuition.

The disadvantages or problems with institutionalizing experiential learning in college environments parallel the areas of emphasis that are reviewed in this chapter. First, colleges and universities that are not committed to the process and do not feel that students are mature enough to take charge of their own learning will have difficulty in institutionalizing the process. At these institutions, it is best to take an incremental approach to implementing experiential based education that can be phased in over several years, until the institution is comfortable with the concept of student-directed learning.

Second, many instructors tend to be rigid in their teaching style. This is evident by their continuous lecture and discussion approach to every subject and class session. They tend to use the same lecture notes and examination questions from year to year, yet feel that students should be penalized for not giving 100 percent to their assignments. We encourage teachers who have reservations about implementing experiential exercises in their courses to take a slower approach by allowing students to direct select topics within the curriculum until they feel comfortable relinquishing control of the courses to the students. However, teachers should still be aware that students will depend on them heavily as a resource person and as a guide on difficult topics.

Students must be willing to be more flexible in their learning style preferences in order to adapt to changing classroom and work environments. Having firsthand knowledge of their own learning styles allows students to recognize situations, work choices, and possible career moves that are more suitable to their preferred styles. For example, a student who clearly enjoys a hands on approach to learning or working with others might not enjoy a job that takes him or her away from this core, such as a research position that involves extensive solitude and reading.

REFERENCES

Argyris, C., & Schon, D. 1978. *Organizational learning: A theory of action perspective.* Reading, MA: Addison-Wesley.

Argyris, C., & Schon, D. 1974. *Theory in practice: Increasing professional effectiveness.* San Francisco: Jossey-Bass.

Birney, R. C. 1993. Hampshire College. *Important lessons from innovative colleges and universities.* V. Ray Cardozier (Ed.). New Directions for Higher Education, no. 82. San Francisco: Jossey-Bass.

Hiemstra, R., & Sisco, B. 1990. *Individualizing instruction: Making learning personal, empowering, and successful.* San Francisco: Jossey-Bass.

Hutchings, P., & Wutzdorff, A. 1988. Knowing and doing: Learning through experience. *New Directions for Teaching and Learning*, no. 35. San Francisco: Jossey-Bass.

Jonassen, D. H., & Graboeski, B. L. 1993. *Handbook of individual differences, learning and instruction.* Hillsdale, NJ: Lawrence Erlbaum Associates.

Keffe, J. W. 1988. *Profiling & utilizing learning style.* Reston, VA: National Association of Secondary School Principals.

Knowles, M. S. 1984. *The adult learner: A neglected species* (3rd ed.). Houston: Gulf Publishing.

Kolb, D. 1984. *Experiential learning: Experience as the source of learning and development.* Englewood Cliffs, NJ: Prentice-Hall.

Sims, R. R., & Lindholm, J. 1993. Kolb's experiential learning model: A first step in learning how to learn from experience. *Journal of Management Education, 17*(1), 95–98.

Viega, J. 1975. Experiential learning: A universal approach to management education. In Proceedings of the Academy of Management Eastern Division (Sec. 3). Academy of Management, Ada.

Warren, K. 1988, Spring. The student directed classroom: A model for teaching experiential education theory. *Journal of Experiential Education, 11*(1), 4–9.

10

The Nature of Adult Learning and Effective Training Guidelines

Robert L. Hewitt

A primary mission of the human service educator or trainer is to develop or enhance the development of human service workers (that is, social workers, counselors, psychologists, child and family welfare workers, teachers, probation officers, etc.), students, and workshop participants for professional practice. This educational process requires that students develop self-awareness, helping skills, assessment skills, and knowledge for social problem solving. Consequently, courses, workshops, and curricula in human services place a major emphasis on the helper-client unit (individual, family, group, organization, or community) interaction and the client unit's active involvement in the problem-solving process. The establishment of a working relationship and engagement of the client unit as an active participant in problem solving are central principles of social work and other human service practices.

Unfortunately, human service educators and trainers often do not practice what they espouse. Students have an opportunity to become active participants in the fieldwork component of their education. However, classroom teaching and learning focus on the transmission of knowledge, with the student as a passive recipient of information. Some discussion is utilized, but the primary form of educational methodology is the lecture. The teacher is the transmitter of knowledge and the student is the receiver (Hokenstad & Rigby, 1977).

Methodology (the process by which material is presented) in social work education is as important to the learning and teaching process as methodology in social work practice is to the problem solving process. In order to be an effective educator or trainer when working with adults, one must embrace the idea that if classroom adult students or workshop participants are not able to learn the way the teacher teachs, then the teacher must teach them the way they learn best.

The mystery of what factors make the teaching and learning process effective has left many educators and trainers of adult learners with many questions and situations at various times. For example:

Have you had an adult learner in your classroom who told you that he or she failed a previous version of this course, and then ended up with a strong A or B in your class?

Have you conducted training sessions in which significant theories and skills were presented, yet evaluations of the training reported that the information was "good" but not particularly "useful"?

Have you wondered why some adult learners appear to understand the material you have presented in class or in a training workshop, yet do poorly when an examination is given?

Has an adult student come to you in frustration that he or she is not comprehending the concepts that you are teaching, despite his or her dedicated study time to the material?

Have you had employees who attended a training workshop to learn and build particular skills, yet returned to work somewhat unsure of how to apply what they were taught to their work?

While explanations to these questions can certainly not be reduced to any one significant study, in the last 20 years studies have explored in depth the role that learning styles play in such situations. It has been found that people have varying ways of understanding and learning, and, subsequently, different ways of processing information. Knowles (1973), among others, has written that understanding how a person learns and helping people understand how to learn is a major requisite for a successful educational program.

This awareness is especially important for adult education or community educational programs that teach adults to use a skill. Smith and Haverkamp (1977) state that educators should seek to match learners with learning situations that are commensurate with their learning styles. Indeed, there is a real need for human service educators to more diligently work toward developing multi-assignments or structured exercises that will present or package the curriculum material in ways that take into consideration the different learning styles and the nature of adult learning.

ASSUMPTIONS ABOUT ADULT LEARNING

Sometimes teaching and training have a negative connotation. The *American Heritage Dictionary* (1992) notes that to train or teach is "to bring a person or animal to a desired state or standard of efficiency, etc.

by instruction;" "to teach a person or animal to do an action;" and "to cause a plant to grow in required shape." These definitions can be amusing, but most people do not want to be considered a plant or animal and do not want someone else to bring them to a state of efficiency that they neither believe in nor want. Therefore, assumptions about adult learning and ways of teaching adults need to be very different from the ways most children are taught (Pasztor, Nickens, & Blome, 1984). Table 10.1 highlights some assumptions about adult learning adapted from Knowles (1973, pp. 32–39).

TABLE 10.1
A Comparison of Pedagogy and Andragogy

Learning Criteria	*Pedagogy*	*Andragogy*
The individual's self concept	Dependent	Self-directed
The importance of life experiences	Not important	Very important
The time frame for relevant application of learning	Postponed for later use	Must be immediately
The focus of learning	Centered on the person	Centered on solving a problem
The readiness for learning	Related to physical growth and emotional development	Related to tasks and skills required
The importance of peers in learning process	Little emphasis on peers as resources	Peers are considered important resources
The responsibility for responsible learning	Teacher is responsible	The learner is responsible while the teacher makes resources available and helps the learning process

The above comparison of children and adult learning styles makes it quite clear that understanding the differences in learning styles of individuals, especially the fact that adults learn differently than children, can assist in efforts to develop effective teaching strategies and models that will provide the necessary connections in the teaching and learning process that will individualize, personalize, and give ownership of the learning and motivation for learning to the adult learner.

The adult learning style approach helps the teacher and adult learner to know themselves better. When we use the adult learning style approach to teaching and the creativity that it brings to the training site setting, the end result is that educators have more freedom to teach and adult learners have more freedom to learn.

In keeping with Knowles model of adult learning, presented below are some suggested guidelines for facilitating instruction to adult learners.

FACILITATION GUIDELINES FOR EFFECTIVE ADULT EDUCATION

Motivation Techniques

The learning climate that is established at the beginning of the training can be one of the most effective tools for motivating adult learners. A climate that both motivates participants to learn and fosters active involvement is characterized by a number of the same qualities necessary in the establishment of a direct intervention helper-helpee relationship in social work and other human service professions.

Openness: When an open attitude is displayed toward the adult participant, the trainer demonstrates a receptiveness to ideas from the other participants.

Mutual trust: When adult learners know they are not being judged and the trainer demonstrates that he or she respects confidentiality, the group will feel more free to take risks, ask questions, and state opinions.

Mutual respect: By acknowledging the contributions of all members of the group, the trainer builds an acceptance of differences and a foundation for mutual trust. Encouraging feedback and openly airing and discussing issues demonstrates the trainer's willingness to establish a climate of mutual respect.

Support/challenge/excitement: After establishing an atmosphere of trust, project enthusiasm for the topic and present challenges to the group.

Mutual concern: By respecting feelings as they are shared, the trainer sets a positive example for the group. By promoting a sense of belonging and acceptance, the trainer can foster a strong investment in the group itself.

Goal Setting

Goal setting is very important when instructing adults. Adult learners are better able to state how they learn and are more aware of what their learning needs are. Each participant brings important resources, concerns, and interests to the training site. To ignore this will invite frustration, hostility, tension, and resistance.

Open dialogue in the beginning of the training to negotiate such things as ground rules and limits clarifies expectations of each other and defines desired results for the training. Paramount to this process will be the role of the instructor and his or her flexibility and ability to make changes as needed. One way of doing this is to hand out a pre-training questionnaire such as the following:

Clarification and Expectation Questionnaire

1. Why are you taking this course?
2. Name two learning goals that you have as they relate to this training.
3. How do you plan to use the information/skills gained from this training?
4. What do you need to do as a participant in this training in order to accomplish your stated desired learning goals? Please be specific.
5. How do you learn best? (state your learning style).

In a recent three-day training session, which was sponsored by the Center for Juvenile Training and Research of Pennsylvania and facilitated by this author, entitled "Skill Building: A Model for Interviewing and Assessing Adolescents," the above questionnaire was handed out to the 29 juvenile probation officers and other juvenile justice practitioners participating in the training. The questionnaire was given to the participants, completed, and returned to the trainer in the early part of the first day of the training.

This brief and straightforward questionnaire helped the trainer to gain an awareness of the specific and general expectations of persons attending the training, their motivation for taking the training, how each participant planned to use this new learning experience in his or her job situation, and how each person planned to take responsibility for his or her own learning. The questionnaire put the adult learner in the position of having to think seriously about how he or she could make this a "practice-useful" learning experience.

A complete three-day agenda had been prepared prior to the commencement of the actual training. As the training continued, adjustments in the agenda were made by the trainer in response to the learning styles, learning expectations, and learning needs stated by the adults in this particular training group. Adjustments were made in a way to capture the general needs represented in the questionnaire responses.

Adult learners need to be able to apply the training content to their own life and work experiences. Handouts and other worksheets should be prepared so as to be of use to the adult learner on the job. Materials that offer explicit examples of possible ways to do things, as they relate to the topic being presented, are most helpful to the adult learner.

Adult learners need to feel that the training is relevant to their own personal and professional growth and development. The more the training materials and exercises help the participants to deal with problems experienced on the job or provide the skills needed in order to be more effective, the more successful the training efforts will be.

Organization

In teaching a practice skills training (that is, individual interviewing and assessment of adolescents, conducting home visits, developing group skills, etc.), it is important that the trainer prepare and divide the material into manageable portions in a systematic way. Organization also refers to the need for the trainer to keep the group on task. For example, if a discussion is getting sidetracked, the instructor has the responsibility to stop and remind the group of the original task at hand. When ground rules are being introduced, the role of the trainer is a topic that should be discussed (Pasztor, Nickens, & Blome, 1984).

Presentation of Content

Training is more effective if the material is presented meaningfully. First, the content has to be meaningful in the participant's perception. Second, it has to be presented in a way that makes sense. Sensible methods of presentation involve a number of factors (Collins, Thomlison, & Grinnell, 1992). There is a need to integrate ideas with practice. For example, when providing training on the topic of interviewing skills it is important not only to understand that there are four parts to an interview and that the building of a professional relationship is critical to being able to assist a client but also to know what to do with that information. Training will be enhanced when the trainer and the participants bring their own work experiences into the discussion. Difficult material should be presented more slowly and in phases as well as repeated more often than easier material. Repetition should include different ways of presenting the same thing to make use of different learning styles. As mentioned, material should be presented in stages, building from the simple to the complex, each stage relating to the stage that went before it. Periodically, everything presented up to that date should be summarized and discussed to ensure that all persons are on track.

Positive Training Site: Atmosphere and Environment

The setting and atmosphere must be conducive for positive learning. The trainer needs to create an atmosphere where the participant feels comfortable to exchange ideas and discuss feelings about the issues raised through activities. An atmosphere of give and take, support, challenge, encouragement, risk-taking, and participant involvement is necessary. Positive learning will take place when there is trust and caring among participants, self-examination, experimentation, involvement, permission to disagree, breaks used to rest rather than to avoid work, and responsibility on the part of everyone for the success of the training (Pasztor, Nickens, & Blome, 1984).

Presentation of a Variety of Materials

Diverse materials and assignments should be offered. This includes the creative use of video tape and audio tape assignments, role playing, discussions, value clarification exercises, and skill games. Encourage the participants to come up with their own ideas to enhance the learning.

Examinations, quizzes, or practice exercises (applying the material covered) can be useful to ensure that the participants are gaining a functional understanding and usefulness of the material being offered. If given, the practical exam or quiz should not be overly rigorous or demanding. When constructing an examination or quiz, the trainer should always take into consideration the factors of time and repetition as they relate to learning a new skill or series of skills. Remember, learning a new skill or series of skills takes time, and the steps to learning the skills must be repeated over and over again.

Opportunity For Evaluation and Feedback

Encourage the participants to offer periodic feedback on the quality of the instruction and the meeting of mutual expectations. Use formal and informal evaluation and feedback methods (Wilson, 1986). Besides handing out a formatted evaluation at the end of the training to be completed by the participants, whenever possible and practical, it is wise to check with the participants in order to find out if learning styles, needs, and goals are being met. During or after breaks, or at the end of the day (if the training is to be longer than one day) are good times to seek feedback.

Trainers Do Not Have to Have All the Answers

Assuming the role of a professional trainer carries with it tremendous responsibilities. As they seek to develop more effective methods to educate and enhance the skills of human service practitioners, they should not feel that just because they are the trainers they must have all the answers. Group members can work for themselves and challenge each other. Interviewing and counseling work with persons who are experiencing social problems often evoke strong emotional responses. Learning new skills and information and the possibility of not understanding the material also can bring out those feelings in adult learners. Some adult learners will demonstrate the following feelings:

fear of failure;

fear of looking foolish in front of their peers;

fear of losing credibility;

fear of others finding out their spelling, writing, or oratory skills are not strong; and

fear that the skills possessed are less than acceptable for the number of years of experience.

Whenever possible, deal with feelings before fact. In an effort to help participants to free their minds to learn, this author, in his role as trainer, often will discuss the nature of adult learning or discuss some of the factors that can get in the way of learning new skills, and how everyone learns differently and at different paces.

It is a good strategy to remind the participants of the ground rule that states everyone will show support for each other. This author often verbalizes the idea that an expert is usually a person who lives at least 30 miles away from wherever the training is being held. The point here is that every adult participant in the room has something to offer from his or her own perspective and life experience to the topic being presented. Some are better writers, some are better spellers, some are better orators, some are better practical demonstrators, but all have something to offer. In the case of the training done with the juvenile justice professionals that was mentioned earlier, these are individuals who do interviews and assessments of adolescents daily. They took the training because they wanted to become better at doing their jobs, but they each had much to offer from their own varied experiences in their work with adolescents. Recognizing this fact and, more importantly, stating this fact to the participants has served as an effective way of dealing with "feelings first" and empowering the learners to dare to share and, in essence, to begin to see themselves as having something worthwhile to offer, to become the expert, and to teach. In the same vein, the participants can begin to see that they can gain much new information from the other members in the training group.

One final comment must be made as it relates to the idea of dealing with feelings before facts about the training topic. If the material to be covered is of a potentially sensitive nature to some participants (that is, adult children of alcoholics, incest, other issues of sexual violence, child abuse), the topic and the feelings that it can evoke should be briefly discussed along with appropriate follow-up guidelines.

KNOWLEDGE BASE NEEDED BY TRAINERS WHO PROVIDE INSTRUCTION TO ADULT LEARNERS

Educators who train adults must have a working knowledge and understanding of the nature of the population with whom they are attempting to develop and manage a teaching and learning relationship. At the very least, they should be able to answer the following questions:

What are the different learning styles?

What is adult learning?

How does adult learning differ from the way children learn?

When teaching human service skills (for example, interviewing or counseling), what factors should the trainer consider?

What are the training benefits of being aware of and sensitive to the idea that we all learn differently?

What is the responsibility of the trainer in the teaching and learning relationship?

What are the learning needs of the direct care human service practitioner and the nature of the human service profession?

Characteristics Needed By the Effective Trainer of Adult Learners

Many successful college and university professors who teach in social work or other human service related programs often struggle with making the transition from teaching the eighteen- and nineteen-year-old student, who usually has little or no practical human service experience and is preparing to enter the social work field, to providing training to the adult learner, who is presently in human service practice and who often has as much or more human service experience than the trainer. The following is a list of characteristics, skills, and guidelines that can assist those who either desire to become instructors of adult learners or are teachers of adults but seek to become more effective providers of practice-useful training:

solid knowledge of the topic or skill;

ability to teach a skill;

practice skills;

human relations skills;

desire to impart knowledge;

commitment to the education process;

creativity, imagination, and flexibility;

desire to connect with the learner as a fellow human being;

self-awareness (knowing strengths and challenges or limitations);

group work skills;
energy;
compassion;
understanding of the nature of adult learning;
variety in presentation (to respond to different learning styles);
empathy, warmth, and respect for the learner and the learning process;
respect for the learner's experience and knowledge;
the ability to say "I don't know, but I will find out" or "I don't know, but can someone else in here help?";
good sense of humor; and
giving the learner a useful learning experience.

Learning Styles and Self Awareness and Preferred Style of Practice

Learning styles, especially when used in conjunction with the nature of adult learning, do not begin and end in the training classroom. They become a natural part of education and life.

In the study of a discipline, such as social work practice, knowing one's preferred style of learning is closely related to getting in touch with the self on a number of other levels.

For adult human service practitioners, having a sense of how one learns and how one learns best serves to not only promote self-confidence but also enhance self-awareness, which is one of the most important prerequisites for human service practice. The major instrument used in human service practice is the self. Anderson (1988) uses the following analogy to underscore this fact: "Just as the violinist needs to know his or her particular violin and keep it as finely tuned as possible to produce music, so must the social worker know the self and tune that self to resonate effectively with others in practice situations" (p. 63).

A key area of self awareness, which is closely related to the idea of a preferred way of learning, is recognition of the preferred style of interacting with others. One's knowledge of one's preferred learning style, personal values, and beliefs greatly influences style. We prefer certain positions, functions, and roles to others because we perceive them as more consistent with our strengths.

A great deal of research in social work, education, and other helping professions indicates that one's learning style and personality style lead to particular theoretical approaches and behavior in practice (for reviews see Mullen, 1969; Rice, Fey, & Kopecs, 1972). This research suggests that more introverted persons prefer less direct approaches and techniques, while more extroverted persons prefer more confrontive approaches and techniques. Some are more comfortable in providing support; others are more comfortable in providing challenges in the problem-solving processes.

Thus, adult learners in human service must be aware of how their own styles affect their preferences in the use of self in practice situations. This awareness requires that they identify their style's strengths for, and obstacles to, providing help in both general and particular situations.

DIFFERENT STYLES OF LEARNING IN PROFESSIONAL EDUCATION

The educational strategy that will be effective must start with student assumptions or motivation for learning the material and the different styles of learning that adult learners bring. The trainer must have some sense of what motivates the student to learn.

Psychologist Jerome Bruner (1961) points to several motivating factors that influence the desire to learn. External factors include such tangible items as teacher feedback (performance evaluation) and career opportunities. The desire to receive a diploma and to obtain the necessary qualifications for employment certainly are motivating factors for students in social work programs. For the human service training participant, the external factors are quite similar (advancement in the form of a promotion, certification, etc.). However, Bruner also gives attention to internal factors that motivate learning. The desire to achieve competence can be a stimulus. Intangible needs such as curiosity and reciprocity (the need to respond to others and cooperate with them toward a mutually defined objective) also can stimulate student responsiveness. Again, the same or very similar internal factors hold true for the human service training participant who is working in the field. The desire and need to increase professional skills and ability in a specific area (for example, individual interviewing and assessment skills with adolescents) is a highly motivational factor. Because it is difficult for the trainer to rely solely on external factors, consideration of these internal factors is essential in the design of training strategies (Hokenstad & Rigby, 1977).

Knowledge of how learning takes place in general further serves to facilitate effective teaching. Learning takes place in many different ways. It can take place through the discussion of ideas, the analysis of theory and data, or the organization and restructuring of concepts (Hokenstad & Rigby, 1977). Learning takes place through the process of integrating new information and experiences with past knowledge and experience. Learning also takes place by systematically viewing another person's model or demonstrating the desired behavior to be learned.

It is clear that not everyone learns in the same way or at the same pace. Thus, knowledge of the different types and ways of learning provides added understanding of the needs of the learner and greatly influences the practical usefulness and overall effectiveness of the teaching or training being offered. What is the person's style of learning? Is the person a visual learner (that is, a student who learns best when everything is in print)?

Is the person an auditory learner? These students learn best when they can compare ideas and learn by saying what they think and, especially, hearing what they say, how they sound, and how they come across to the instructor and other classmates (that is, discussion and verbal instruction). Is the person a kinesthetic learner? This is a student who learns best by doing hands-on projects (that is, role-playing, using applied academics). This type of learner does best in classes of less than 21 students. This information can guide the trainer in developing learning experiences and assignments that stimulate learning and enhance the effectiveness of the training.

Mary Louise Sommers (1971) identifies three major types of learners:

1. the theorist, who uses a deductive approach to learning;
2. the empiricist, who uses an inductive approach; and
3. the practitioner, who learns through doing.

It has been the social work educators' experience that the majority of the social work students and other adult human service training participants have been most responsive to the practitioner style of learning. This style is highly compatible with the students' career goals and their commitment to practice-oriented approaches to problem solving. It is also very consistent with the needs of the adult human service training participant who desires to improve his or her ability to do or to practice human service work. Certainly, some human service training participants also may be motivated by theoretical and empirical approaches. But the practitioner style of learning in the training session should not be disregarded (Hokenstad & Rigby, 1977).

According to psychological research, there are scientifically supported and logically consistent principles drawn from various theories that can aid in the development of a training strategy (Bigge, 1964; Hilgard & Bowen, 1966). The selection of a specific theoretical base model or principles, as stated in the preceding line, taken from different models after the trainer has considered the motivational factors and styles of learning, can aid the structuring of a training strategy.

Hilgard and Bowen (1966) discuss three psychological theories familiar to many teachers of social work practice. They provide useful rules that can be applied to the teaching and learning transaction. These include stimulus-response principles drawn from behavioral theory, cognitive principles derived from gestalt psychology, and motivational principles emanating from ego psychology and other personality theories. These learning principles can be helpful in the formulation of a teaching strategy.

Stimulus-Responsive Principles
The learner's responses must be reinforced.

Positive reinforcement is more likely to be successful than negative reinforcement.

Frequency (repetition) is important in the incorporation of knowledge and acquisition of skills.

Cognitive Principles
Goal setting enhances the learner's motivation.

New ideas and experiences will have a lasting impact if they can be incorporated into the learner's cognitive structure (thinking framework).

Inventive solutions should be encouraged as much as logically correct answers.

Motivational Principles
Different learners are motivated by different needs (some are motivated by achievement; others by duty or affiliation).

Group atmosphere as well as the teacher and learner interaction will affect the learning process.

The learner's culture and subculture will affect the pattern and style of learning. (pp. 562–564)

Although the above listed principles are not all inclusive, they are some of the principles that may be used to develop an effective teaching strategy for the adult. Remember that, no matter which of the many principles or models one selects, those principles or models must begin with the learner's needs and style of learning and then move to the role of the trainer in facilitating learning (Hokenstad & Rigby, 1977).

ASSUMPTIONS ABOUT TEACHING AND LEARNING

A myth is a half truth in that some parts of it are true, but the whole truth is not present. There are many myths when it comes to the relationship between teaching and learning. A myth that has greatly hindered and at times rendered ineffective the teaching and learning process is the acceptance of the myth that training essentially involves the transmitting of information and ideas from the trainer to the learner, who somehow grasps it, understands it, adopts it, and uses it later. The myth further states that all that a good educator needs is a solid knowledge of the material and the ability to clearly present the information to the learner by organizing ideas well, articulating them systematically, and then illustrating them. As in most myths, there is some truth in this one.

A study of university level teaching (Shurlman, 1993) found that having knowledge and the ability to transmit it were associated most highly with effective instruction. The next most important variable, however, was the instructor's ability to empathize with students, and the fourth was the ability to present ideas so that they are open to challenge. These findings suggest that there may be more to teaching than just knowing a subject and presenting it to students. In fact, the findings support what many experience as consumers of teaching: teachers who were very knowledgeable and clear presenters from whom we learned very little, and teachers who were less certain of their grasp of the subject and more hesitant in their presentation from whom we learned a great deal.

The above suggests that the teaching and learning process is not simple but, rather, is quite complicated and influenced by a number of factors related to the subject area.

The latter factor is elaborated by John Dewey, who maintains that "the organism is not simply receiving impressions, and then answering them. The organism is doing something, it is actively seeking and selecting certain stimuli" (Dewey, 1916, p. 46).

The teacher's knowledge of the subject matter and his or her ability to communicate it are very important factors in the teaching and learning process. The problem is that these two factors alone will not ensure effective teaching. The learning style of the learner and the nature of adult learning are central factors that must be included in the equation.

Recent educational research shows that adult learners are characterized by significantly different learning styles: they preferentially focus on different types of information, tend to operate on perceived information in different ways, and achieve understanding at different rates (Barbe & Milone, 1981; Claxton & Murrell, 1987; Corno & Snow, 1986). Those in human service must be aware of how their own styles affect their preferences in the use of self in practice situations.

THE ADULT LEARNER CENTERED TRAINING MODEL AND TEACHING STRATEGY

In general, classroom teachers have used an educational approach that focused on the transfer of knowledge from the teacher to the adult participants. Knowledge and information has been transmitted verbally or in written form. In higher education, the lecture has served as the main vehicle for imparting knowledge. This classroom knowledge is utilized in the field practicum, and it is assumed that the outcome will be integrated into the student's overall learning experience (Hokenstad & Rigby, 1977).

This particular approach to teaching and learning has proven to be less than adequate on all levels of education. This especially holds true in training courses designed for professional practitioners. This approach is not only at odds with many of the principles discussed earlier, but it also undermines the principles of how adults learn best.

Adult learners need to be actively involved in the instructor and learner process. The interactive participatory approach is highly suited for effective training with adult learners, especially focusing on the professional human service practitioner.

A model utilized by this author, with much success, is an adult learner centered approach to training social work skills and practice methods. It is a three-stage methodology:

1. Tell the participants. Introduce the clarification and expectation at the beginning (or before the training date if practical) of the training. Provide didactic instruction on the skills through lecture, readings, classroom discussions, and term papers. Present and explain the skills and related theories.
2. Show the participants. Demonstrate the practice skills (that is, case studies, live trainer demonstrations of the skill, outside expert demonstration, video tape simulation, or field trips when practical).
3. Involve the participants. Construct participant role plays using practice skills (that is, simulations of a social work practice situation, video taped interviews done by the participants, worksheets, critical incident solutions, brainstorming, and problem solving).

This participation model requires an active role for the instructor as well as for the adult learner. The instruction of direct social work skills, utilizing the principles discussed earlier, must be based in the theory and foundation principles of the skill being taught.

The three-part methodology, when examined in detail, consists of small steps within each stage:

Tell: clarification and expectation questionnaire; the introduction of skill/topic; motivation; break into smaller parts; and check for questions/comments.

Show: model the skill; explain; and check for questions/comments.

Involve: participants practice the skill; feedback; and transfer of learning.

The clarification and expectation questionnaire (discussed earlier in the chapter) engages the adult learner early in the teaching and learning process. The questions in the questionnaire deliver a powerful statement to adult learners that the instructor is open to hearing each person's story about learning and recognizes that each story is unique and has worth. Such a message serves to build trust, the foundation for effective work in the teaching and learning process.

Learning new skills, relearning old skills, or breaking old habits can be stressful and uncomfortable for adult learners. This approach embraces the fact that, even though adult learners do have a general learning style, within the adult learning style are individual motivations, capacity for change and understanding, and a unique style of learning. This model related the need for the training instructor to demonstrate consistently an appreciation of these facts, patient guidance, clear positive feedback, and tolerance for resistance that comes naturally when people are out of their comfort zone. Training instructors of interactive skills want to encourage humor and set up a climate that offers permission to try.

The third stage, which includes transfer of learning, is critical for adult learners because the skills and information being learned are for immediate use. General studies of learning and integration of learning support the idea that when adult participants are allowed to review the material covered, take time to clarify what has been learned, and integrate that learning in their lives, it serves to enhance the long term memory and use of that learning (Gehris, 1992).

The practical experience of this author has been that, if adult participants identify, write, or verbally state a plan of action incorporating a learning or intent, they are more apt to implement that plan of action.

In this stage of the model, at the end of the workshop or at the end of the day, an activity should be designed to give adult participants time to mentally review the training, call up learnings, state them, and plan some ways to use them with their clients if the participants are practitioners or with their staff if the participants are supervisors or trainers. One example is for the training instructor to ask the participants to mentally review the training. Show them the agenda — going over each day — allowing them time to think about and write some things they learned or relearned about the workshop topic or subtopic. Ask them also to think about and write at least one strategy they gained as a result of this training that they plan to use with the population they are working with. When an appropriate time has elapsed, ask people to share a learning and something they plan to do. Affirm and encourage each offering (Gehris, 1992).

CONCLUSION

Clearly the teaching and learning process is complex at best. The effective human service training instructor must be skillful, knowledgeable, sensitive, and aware on many different levels. Interactive one-on-one and group skills, as well as expertise in the specific topic being taught, are musts. In order for the process to work effectively with adult learners, the training instructor's understanding of learning styles and the nature of adult learning is critical.

The participation model offered in this chapter provides a teaching and learning framework that promotes an active role for the instructor as well as for the adult learner. The instructor is empowered to teach effectively because he or she is free to guide the teaching and learning process creatively in a collegial, structured style. In the same vein, the adult learner has the opportunity to shape the training, ensure its practical usefulness, and pursue the learning in the manner in which he or she learns best.

This approach to adult training allows the training instructor and the adult participants to develop initial trust, credibility, training focus, and respect for the groups as well as all individuals involved in the teaching and learning process.

This is turn promotes a key ingredient to all successful teaching and learning interactions — the ability of the instructor and adult participants to develop an atmosphere that makes it safe for the adult learner to not only dare to risk in the learning process but also to begin to see the learning situation not as a risk but as an opportunity for new knowledge, reaffirmation, practical skill enhancement, and growth.

REFERENCES

American Heritage Dictionary, The. 1992. Boston, MA: Houghton Mifflin Company.

Anderson, J. 1988. *Foundation of social work practice*. New York: Springer.

Barbe, W. B., & Milone, M. N. 1981, February. What we know about modality strengths. *Educational Leadership*, pp. 378–380.

Bigge, M. L. 1964. *Learning theories for teachers*. New York: Harper & Row.

Bruner, J. 1961. *Toward a theory of instruction*. Cambridge, MA: Belknap Press.

Claxton, C. S., & Murrell, P. K. 1987. *Learning styles: Implications for improving educational practice*. ASHE-ERIC Higher Education Report No. 4. College Station, TX: ASHE.

Collins, O., Thomlison, B., & Grinnell, R. M. 1992. *The social work practicum: A student guide*. Itasca, IL: F. E. Peacock.

Corno, L., & Snow, R. E. 1986. Adopting teaching to individual differences among learners. In M. Wittrock (Ed.). *Handbook of research on teaching* (pp. 27–28). New York: Macmillan.

Dewey, J. 1916. *Democracy and education: An introduction to the philosophy of education*: New York: Free Press.

Gehris, D. 1992. *Shippensburg University prevention project: Fundamentals of alcohol and other drug prevention education for educators*. Washington, DC: U.S. Department of Education.

Hilgard, E., & Bowen, G. 1966. *Theories of learning* (3rd ed.). New York: Appleton Century Crofts.

Hokenstad, M., & Rigby, B. 1977. *Participation in teaching and learning: An idea book for social work education*. New York: International Association of Schools of Social Work.

Knowles, M. 1973. *The adult learner: A neglected species*. Houston, TX: Gulf Publishing.

Mullen, E. J. 1969. Differences in worker style in casework. *Social Casework, 50,* 347–349.

Pasztor, M., Nickens, B., & Blome, S. 1984. *The Army family advocacy program: Child abuse and neglect training for child development services and youth. Activities personnel: A training manual.* Washington, DC: Department of the Army, Nova University Institute for Social Services to Families.

Rice, D. G., Fey, W. F., and Kopecs, J. G. 1972. Therapist experience and "style" as factors in co-therapy. *Family Process, 11,* 142–160.

Shurlman, L. 1993. *Teaching the helping skills: A field instructor's guide.* Alexandria, VA: Council on Social Work Education, Inc.

Smith, R., & Haverkamp, K. 1977. Toward a theory of learning how to learn. *Adult Education, 28,* 3–21.

Sommers, M. 1971. Dimensions and dynamics of engaging the learner. *Journal of Education for Social Work,* 7(3), 51–53.

Wilson, R. 1986. Improving faculty teaching: Effective use of student evaluations and consultants. *Journal of Higher Education, 57,* 196–211.

11

The Learning Model for Managers: A Tool to Facilitate Learning

Kenneth L. Murrell and Richard W. Bishop

The world is becoming a global village. Technology, and international trade are changing the distribution of power, leveling the competitive market place, and forcing diverse groups into close proximity. The potential to improve the quality of life on earth has never been greater. However, the uncertainty and fear caused by rapid change, restructuring, and misunderstanding also present the potential to move in ineffective and self-defeating directions.

The increasing diversity of the U.S. workforce has been well documented, but diversity within national boundaries is only a small part of the picture. Today's international marketplace is bringing extremely different groups and cultures into close physical and economic proximity for the first time. This new proximity between diverse groups and cultures often causes stress and conflict that is felt by everyone involved in interaction. Frequently these dynamics lead to a crisis, panic, and action by one or more of the individuals or groups involved in interaction. As we see every day in the news, crisis, panic, and ineffective and self-defeating action cause great difficulty. What is needed are bridges across stress, conflict, and crisis that can prevent or at least reduce panic and ineffective or self-defeating action. Bridges promote understanding, tolerance, and the conscious realization that it is in each of our best interest to create empathy and cooperation between groups. One such bridge that can be used to display and explore ideas, cultures, and behavior while promoting learning is the learning model for managers (TLMFM). It can facilitate appropriate variations in training to fit specific circumstances and sensibilities, preventing the Sims and Sims training corollary to "one size fits all: One Learning Style doesn't fit — at all" (1993, p. 88).

The place is the southeastern United States; the company, a leading international telecommunications organization; the purpose, structured organizational learning to improve company performance. Over 200 senior executives gathered for a six-day off-site meeting. Participants were from over 50 different countries, representing age, sex, race, and ethnic diversity on a global scale. The exercise started with all participants taking TLMFM, an instrument that introduces four domains of learning based on a person's preference for cognitive or affective learning, and the person's preference for concrete or abstract experiences (see Figure 11.1). The results indicated a roughly even distribution in all four quadrants of the model, which in the hundreds of applications of the model had never been seen before. Participants were introduced to their individual learning style, as described by TLMFM, and the learning styles of their colleagues. They were asked to consider their TLMFM learning style during the exercise. The experiences and events that followed were tailored to appeal to each of the model's four learning types.

The "OrgSim, A Simulated Global Organization" exercise was next on the agenda. The OrgSim is a learning-based simulation; that is, it is designed to simulate the experiences of individuals in any organization. What the participants learn from their involvement in the simulation can be applied to all kinds of organizations. The OrgSim exercise itself focuses participants on Quadrant IV of TLMFM, concrete/affective skills, and requires them to become actively involved in the process of the exercise. The debrief or processing of it moves the discussion to cover the other three quadrants and an exploration of what else was learned.

In the OrgSim Global (Murrell & Charkis, 1992), participants are expected to try to realize their professional goals, whatever those may be. As they work with others in the group who have similar goals, they discover some of the possibilities and limits to their own behavior.

Every group that creates its own organization makes something unique, because the nature of this organization will depend on the individual goals of all the participants and how they interact with one another. Participants can experiment with new behaviors, learn from exhibited behavior patterns, and learn to change those patterns if they find them inappropriate. Thus, each participant has an opportunity to teach him or herself and to see first hand the effects of working together at an organizational level.

The participants were divided into five world regions, a corporate headquarters staff, and six customers. It was the responsibility of the organizational teams to develop listings of the challenges and opportunities facing MCI in all the countries of the world. These were then to

FIGURE 11.1
Learning Model for Managers

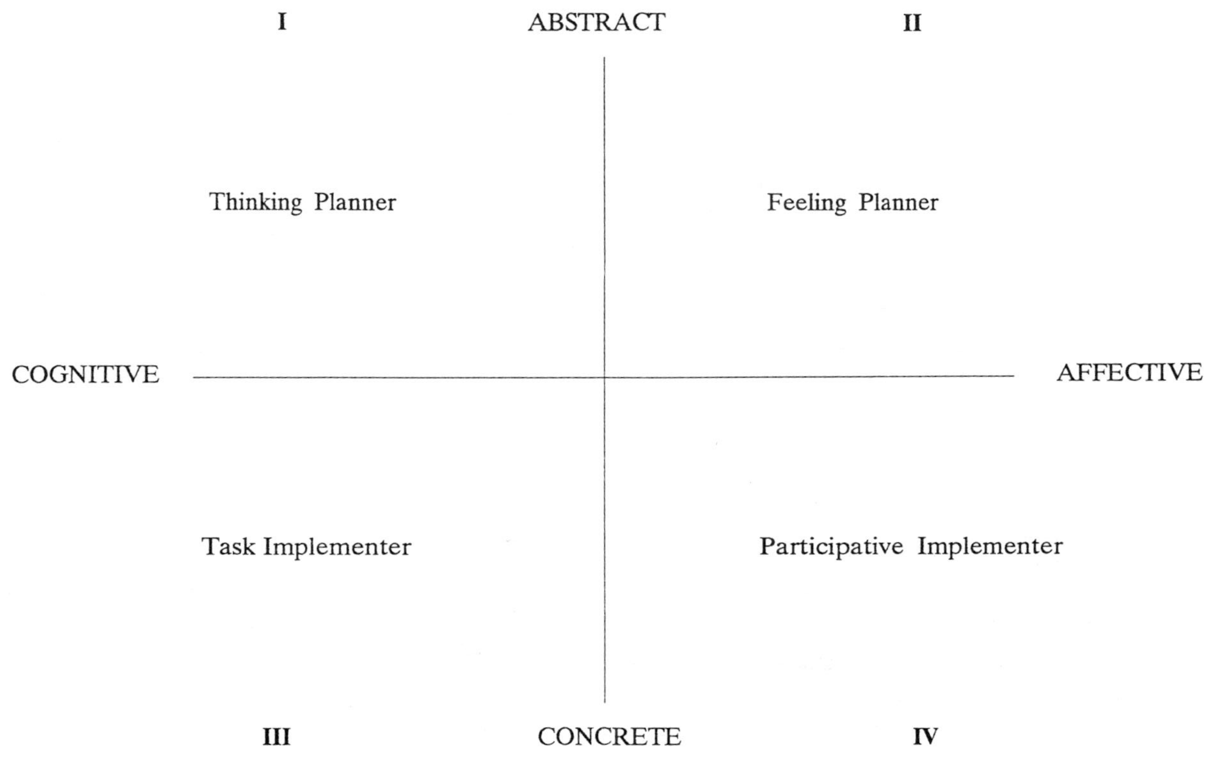

be sold as products to the customer group, and the process was managed by the headquarters group.

The simulation ran for three hours. During this time professional roles were drawn; regional teams and work groups were organized; and products were designed, produced, and sold to customers.

Excitement and emotions ran high, urgency was dominate, tempers flared, and participants worked at a feverish pitch to accomplish personal and collective goals. Required interactions cut across every possible demographic group and human interaction style. The environment created by chaotic, fast changing circumstances demanded considerable coordination and cooperation across all regions of the world.

When the simulation ended, participants were divided into teams of six, including one member from each of the global regions or work groups, to identify lessons learned through a brainstorming and sharing process. In this phase participants were required to use cognitive/abstract analysis learning skills from TLMFM Quadrant I, and affective/abstract learning skills from Quadrant II. Once brainstorming was complete, participants were required to develop an action plan for change using TLMFM Quadrant III cognitive/concrete learning skills and then present their recorded results back to the corporate human relations team sponsoring the workshop.

The process of the Global OrgSim exercise purposely focused participants into each of the four quadrants of the TLMFM. Each participant experienced his or her learning comfort zone and personal areas of learning discomfort, one of the primary items of personal realization that can stem from TLMFM. This aspect of the process overpowered traditional barriers to interaction and learning. New attitudes, pathways, and relationships were forged for enhanced learning of the lessons that can really make a difference in personal and professional life. The senior executives attending the retreat declared victory as an organization and a commitment to similar future training. In their words, the environment created looked much like the chaotic and fast changing world they live in every day.

What is TLMFM that helped make this exercise so productive? TLMFM introduces four domains of learning based on a person's preference for cognitive or affective learning and the person's preference for concrete or abstract experiences. Because it is important for managers who deal directly with people to learn how to use a variety of learning styles, the manager will be given special attention as the model and instrument are discussed. The following goals were important in developing this learning model:

Create a model that will help explain cognitive and affective learning styles in such a way that managers and trainers can gain an appreciation for and understanding of the various ways in which learning takes place.

Clarify conceptually what a learning environment is so that participants in a learning program can gain an understanding of how experiential learning methods differ from other learning methods.

Create an instrument, based on the model's assumptions, that will provide immediate self-awareness feedback to help individuals know more about how they and others learn best.

Develop an instrument that will help individuals to connect their awareness of their own learning preferences to the nature of what and how a manager learns and to understand why experiential learning and employee and management development must differ from traditional classroom learning.

Develop an instrument that will generate thought and discussion about the process of learning, so that program content will be seen as only a part of the total learning experience.

Learning comes not only through thinking or cognition but also from experience and affect or feeling. Although some people have realized this for a long time, it is still good news for many when they discover that it is acceptable to be emotional and have feelings and that they can take pride in being able to learn from emotions and feelings. Although everyone probably has a mixture of learning preferences, a way was needed to identify a person's preferred position on a continuum from the cognitive to the affective, integrated with a personality preference ranging from concrete to abstract.

TLMFM assumes that the difference in a preference on the affective-cognitive dimension of learning is a key factor in how a person learns. This assumption is based on the idea that the affective and cognitive end points can be defined so that they correlate with a people versus task orientation (Blake & Mouton, 1984). The cognitive and affective bipolar dimension is also substantiated as separate learning modes by Piaget (1954). Although empirical research may not show a strong correlation between a preference for the cognitive style of learning and task orientation, they seem to be closely related because of the similarity in their definitions.

This task-person and cognitive-affective correlation provides an opportunity to use this learning model for stressing the relationship of learning style and personality type to the behavior of an employee or a manager. Although managers, like other people, likely prefer learning in a particular way (left and right brain preferences), it is important for them to develop the ability to learn by both thinking and feeling because they have responsibility for the performance of other employees. The model can illustrate this importance. In training managers, the trainer should thoroughly discuss this issue and show how the model correlates with the career changes and challenges managers may expect to face.

The model's second dimension (the vertical axis) uses, as did Kolb, a concrete-abstract continuum. However, this model reverses the positions of the end points in order to place concrete (the down-to-earth point) on the bottom and abstract (the in-the-air point) on top. A preference for the concrete reflects a person's desire to come into contact with the real object, to touch it, or even to physically manipulate it. The abstract end of the continuum reflects a preference for dealing with the world in terms of thinking about it and for manipulating ideas or thoughts. The vertical axis represents the way people tend to experience life and is loosely associated with the psychology of Jung (1924). The preference for experiencing life in the concrete indicates a desire to perceive objects and experiences through the direct sensual contact.

TLMFM, therefore, contains two primary axes, ranging from cognitive to affective in the horizontal dimension and from concrete to abstract in the vertical dimension. The axes divide the model into the following four domains: I, thinking planner; II, feeling planner; III, task implementer; and IV, participative implementer.

TYPES OF LEARNING

Cognitive

A person who shows a marked preference for learning through thought or other mental activity is a cognitive learner. People who grasp intellectually very quickly what they are trying to learn or who simply prefer to use controlled thought and logic will be found on the cognitive axis. Rationality appeals to these individuals, as do logic and other thinking skills that are necessary for this type of learning. Although this statement is not based on hard research, it appears that a high cognitive orientation correlates with a high task orientation rather than with a people orientation. The research about possible left versus right brain functioning correlates a cognitive orientation to individuals who are left-brain dominant. Therefore, the left side of the axis was deliberately assigned to the cognitive orientation to serve as an easy reminder.

Affective

Affective learners are more comfortable with and seek learning from their emotions and feelings. These individuals desire personal interaction and seek to learn about people by experiencing them in emotional or feeling ways. This type of learner would potentially be highly people oriented. A manager with this orientation would probably seek out social interaction rather than focus exclusively on the task components of the job. In right-brain research, affective learners are said to be more intuitive, more spontaneous, and less linear. They seek out feelings and emotions rather than logic.

TYPES OF LIFE EXPERIENCING

Concrete

People with a preference for the concrete enjoy jumping in and getting their hands dirty. Hands-on experiences are important to them. As managers, these people want to keep busy, become directly involved, and physically approach or touch whatever they are working with. If they work with machines, they will get greasy; if they work with people, they will become involved.

Abstract

Individuals preferring this style have no special desire to touch, but they want to keep active by thinking about the situation and relating it to similar situations. Their preferred interaction style is internal — inside their own heads. Language, symbols, and figures have great attraction for these learners.

THE FOUR LEARNING DOMAINS

A person is unlikely to be on the extreme end of either axis, and no one type of learning is best. Any mixture of preferences simply represents a person's uniqueness. The model is useful in helping people differentiate themselves, and it offers a method for looking at the way different styles can fit together. This section describes the four domains that are represented in the model.

The descriptions of these domains could be of special interest for managers, because they will help the manager understand the relationship between managerial action and learning style. A manager should be capable of learning and functioning well in all four domains, especially if he or she expects to face a variety of situations and challenges. The successful manager is likely to be the one who can operate in both a task and people environment, with the ability to see and become involved with the concrete and use the thought processes to understand what is needed. The normative assumption of the model is that a manager should open him or herself to learn in each of the four domains. In doing this, the manager may well build on his or her primary strengths, but the versatility and flexibility demanded in a managerial career make clear the importance of all four domains. In addition, a manager who understands the learning styles of his or her colleagues, supervisors, peers, or subordinates can most effectively help them learn. Facilitating learning in supervisors, peers, and subordinates can expedite team building, employee development, and multicultural understanding. TLMFM can provide a bridge to a new rapport and empathy between work team members that can help them accomplish organizational goals more effectively.

Domain I: The Thinking Planner

A combination of cognitive and abstract preferences constitutes domain I, where the thinking planner is located. This domain might well be termed the place for the planner whose job is task oriented and whose environment contains primarily symbols, numbers, and printouts. The bias in formal education is often toward this learning domain, and Mintzberg (1976) was critical of this bias. In this domain, things are treated abstractly and often their socio-emotional elements are denied. In addition, some criticism can be directed at exclusively case-based teaching, because it is also contained in the more abstract realm (Murrell & Blanchard, 1992).

The domain I learner should do well in school, should have a talent for planning, and is likely to be successful as a staff person or manager in a department that deals with symbolic or untouchable realities. This domain represents an important area for management learning. Of the four domains, it seems to receive the heaviest emphasis in traditional university programs and management development seminars, particularly financial management seminars.

Domain II: The Feeling Planner

A combination of affective and abstract preferences constitutes domain II, where the feeling planner is located. The managerial style associated with this domain is that of the thinker who can learn and who enjoys working with people but has limited opportunity to get close to them. This domain is important for the personnel executive or a manager with too much responsibility to interact closely with other employees. Socio-emotional analysis skills are represented in this area. Managers in this domain should be able to think through and understand the social and emotional factors affecting a large organization. The world of organizational development theory that many academics live in is represented here, while organizational development consultants or practitioners only fall back in this orientation occasionally.

Difficulties in this area sometimes arise when good first-line supervisors who have a natural style with people are promoted into positions that prevent them from having direct contact with others and are expected to determine without concrete experience the nature of and solutions to personnel problems.

Domain III: The Task Implementer

A combination of cognitive and concrete preferences constitutes domain III, where the task implementer is located. This domain contains decision makers who primarily want to understand the task and who can focus on the details and specifics of the concrete in a thoughtful manner. If these people are allowed to think about a situation, they can see the concrete issues and, after close examination, can make a well thought out decision. A person in this domain is often a task-focused doer. If the interpersonal skill demands are low and if the emotional climate is not a problem, this person is likely to do well.

Domain IV: The Participative Implementer

A combination of affective and concrete preferences constitutes domain IV, where the participative implementer is located. The manager with people skills who has the opportunity to work closely with people is found in this category. This is the place where implementers and highly skilled organization development consultants reside. This domain is for those who like to become involved and who have the ability and interest in working with the emotional needs and demands of the people in an organization. This is the domain that is emphasized by most of the practical management programs, and it can be used to complement the traditional educational programs of domain I. This is the realm of the simulation or role play or, as the authors prefer, the world of the Live Case teaching design. It is an active, hands-on learning environment where practicing one's skills and understanding produces real and immediate feedback about performance and learning needs.

VALUE OF THE LEARNING MODEL FOR MANAGERS

The strength of TLMFM is that it can reveal invisible differences in people. People have a natural and traditional tendency to divide themselves into groups for the purpose of resource and power distribution. For millennia, people have been very concerned with visible differences (for example, sex, age, and race) and using visible differences for the basis of these group division decisions. However, visible differences are often trivial; they are only the tip of the iceberg. The significant differences between people are invisible. Examples of some of these invisible differences are religion and sexual orientation (Figure 11.2). Deeper and more significant are management style, communication style, learning style, and thinking style. Various instruments have been devised to measure these constructs[1] and produce consistent results. Establishing validity and reliability of any model and instrument of this type is difficult or impossible. However, if the face validity is positive

FIGURE 11.2
Visible and Invisible Differences

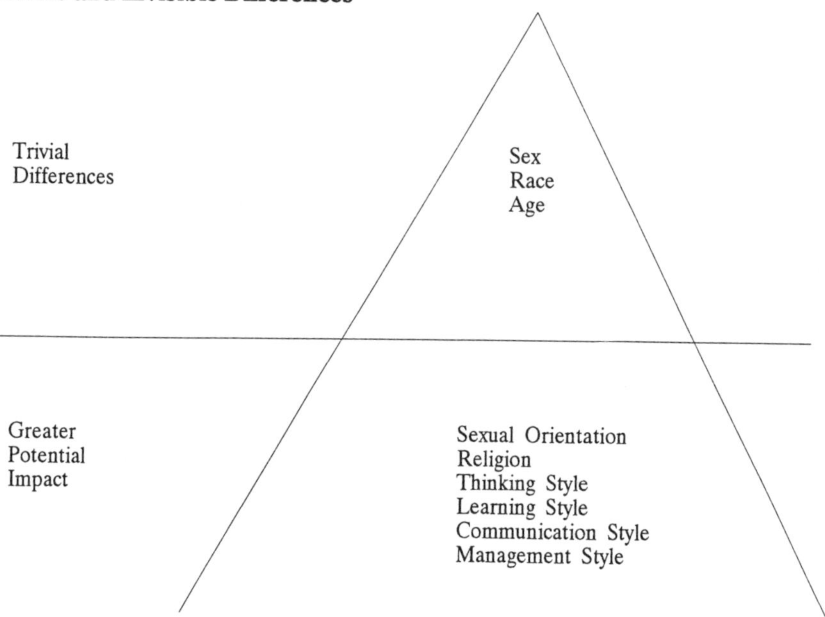

and if the learning value is apparent, then the material should be useful when it fits the training and learning goals. The results of these instruments are not intended to label respondents, but simply to give them feedback on their preferred styles of learning, communicating, or thinking.

TLMFM is particularly valuable when used as a prelude for other training. Team building, university classrooms, employee development, multicultural understanding, and training program design can benefit participants significantly by helping them understand more about their own and others' learning preferences.

TLMFM is used at Motorola University, the training and development institution for Motorola, Inc. employees. In one team building exercise, participants take TLMFM, score it, and consider their own position on the model. Then without discussing the results with others, they think about where their colleagues might fall on the learning style model. They consider their experiences in working with others on teams, or in the course of daily business interactions. Then they build a mental picture of themselves in relation to their coworkers. Once the mental picture is complete, all participants share their results, comparing actual learning model positions with anticipated learning model positions. Next, they conduct a short version of the OrgSim, and, finally, in the debrief, they discuss how knowledge of learning styles influenced interactions between coworkers, and the outcome of the simulation.

The value contributed to this exercise by TLMFM is an insight into its different learning domains that help participants personalize their lessons learned. The OrgSim clearly helps each participant surface self-imposed restrictions that reduce his or her effectiveness during the exercise. In turn, TLMFM helps participants to see their self-imposed restrictions from a variety of perspectives, assisting them to break through defensive barriers to learning. In this respect, TLMFM can help overcome a significant detriment to learning described by Chris Argyris in his 1991 *Harvard Business Review* article "Teaching Smart People to Learn." Put simply, because many professionals are almost always successful at what they do, they rarely experience failure. And because they have rarely failed, they have never learned how to learn from failure. So whenever their single-loop learning strategies go wrong, they become defensive, screen out criticism, and put the "blame" on anyone and everyone but themselves. In short, their ability to learn shuts down precisely at the moment they need it the most (p. 100).[2]

In the increasingly competitive global economy, managers must take advantage of every possible competitive edge, including improving their own performance. To exempt any aspect of their learning as off limits because it may be embarrassing, threatening, or leave participants feeling vulnerable or incompetent is unsatisfactory. Exercises like this one used at Motorola University can help participants break through barriers to learning, expand their learning comfort zones, and examine what Argyris calls their "master programs" and "theories-in-use," the rules by which they actually behave (1991, p. 103). It is theorized that properly facilitated learning experiences, with the support of objective verification from coworkers, in the safe environment of the simulation, and the analytical framework of TLMFM can have a positive impact on what Benjamin Bloom calls the affective outcomes of learning. Although Bloom's (1982) work was focused on school learning, the relationship between a person's learning experiences and his or her willingness to engage in future learning seems correct. Success or lack of success in learning, particularly in the affective aspects of learning, will have a direct bearing on a participant's desire for similar future experiences (p. 160) and can either close a person into a limited box or open them into a risky but exciting new world.

One key to this learning process is trust. Jack Gibb (1991) says trust is the foundation of effective team building. Trust in self and others leads to valid information sharing, mutual goals and plans, and appropriate controls and structures. TLMFM can facilitate this process by helping to reveal valid information about group members. It can provide accurate predictions about how people actually behave with each other during learning experiences. This prediction is particularly important for a beginning team with diverse group members. Learning style similarities can easily transcend cross-cultural differences and provide the data necessary to begin meaningful dialogue. Another trust enhancing aspect of TLMFM use is the immediate nature of its feedback that can be used to avoid the unconscious narrowing of methods and experiences, discussed by Argyris, in the beginning of a team experience. For example, B. J. Chakiris, as president of a major organization development consulting firm, has used TLMFM results to arrange mentoring relationships between managers. Her experience indicates that change depends upon content, a common language, and similar values that can be identified through use of TLMFM. Data-based team experience depends on information to make it work and should not be restricted by unconscious or conscious habits and preferences that restrict diversity. In *Change Management, A Model For Effective Organizational Performance* B. J. Chakiris is joined by Patricia Felkins and Kenneth Chakiris in saying, "group learning and team work in change management demands an understanding of some basic concepts: diversity and commonality, communication and coordination, and confirmation and renewal" (Felkins, Chakiris, & Chakiris, 1993, p. 191). TLMFM can be used to facilitate the required understanding.

CONCLUSION

Most managers do not have much time to delve into how or what they learn. Even so, their continued learning is critical to their managerial success. Managers who are open and receptive to more information and broadening experiences learn more of what they need to know to make the best decisions in carrying out their responsibilities. Managers developing a better understanding of their own and their coworkers' learning styles can gain an appreciation for and understanding of the various ways in which learning takes place. An increased understanding of learning better ensures managers are exposed and receptive to more information and experiences interpreted through several different frameworks. Accordingly, experiential learning and management development for enhancing professional life must differ from traditional classroom learning. TLMFM is a tool that can deliver a significant portion of the needed information and build more efficiently on experience. Its value lies in its ability to provide communication bridges across a variety of differences including management layers, cultures, races, sex, and age groups.

NOTES

1. Additional instruments used in the writing of this chapter include: *Mindex*, Your Thinking Style Profile (Albrecht, 1983); *Communications Profile Questionnaire* (Michalak Training Associates, Inc., 1989); and *Learning Style Inventory* (Kolb, 1976).

2. Argyris defines "single-loop" learning with an analogy of a thermostat: "A thermostat that automatically turns on the heat whenever the temperature in a room drops below 68 degrees is a good example of 'single-loop' learning. A thermostat that could ask, 'Why am I set at 68 degrees?' and then explore whether or not some other temperature might more economically achieve the goal of heating the room would be engaging in 'double-loop' learning."

REFERENCES

Argyris, G. 1991. Teaching smart people to learn. *Harvard Business Review*, *69*(3), 99–109.

Blake, R. R., & Mouton, J. S. 1984. *Managerial Grid III* (3rd ed.). Houston, TX: Gulf.

Bloom, B. S. 1982. *Human characteristics and school learning*. New York: McGraw-Hill Book Company.

Felkins, P. K., Chakiris, B. J., & Chakiris, K. N. 1993. *Change management, a model for effective organizational performance*. White Plains, NY: Quality Resources.

Gibb, J. 1991. *Trust: A new vision of human relationships*. Hollywood, CA.: Newcastle Publishing (original work published 1978 by the Guild of Tutors Press, International College).

Jung, C. G. 1924. *Second impression*. H. Godwin (Trans.). New York: Harcourt Brace.

Mintzberg, H. 1976, July/August. Planning on the left side and managing on the right. *Harvard Business Review*, pp. 49–58.

Murrell, K. L., & Chakiris, B. J. 1992. *OrgSim: A simulated global organization*. Chicago, IL: BJ Chakiris Corporation.

Murrell, K. L., & Blanchard, K. 1992. OrgSim: Using an organizational simulation to create a "live" case. *The Journal of Management Development*, *2*(7).

Piaget, J. 1954. *The construction of reality in the child*. M. Cook (Trans.). New York: Ballantine.

Sims, S. J., & Sims, R. R. 1993. Diversity and difference training in the United States. In R. R. Sims and R. F. Dennehy (Eds.), *Diversity and differences in organizations: An agenda for answers and questions* (pp. 73–92). Westport, CT: Quorum Books.

12

Learning and Learning Styles: A Review and Look to the Future

Serbrenia J. Sims and Ronald R. Sims

This book has emphasized, among other things, the extreme importance of understanding individual differences, learning principles, factors that affect motivation of students and trainees in learning situations, and the variety of individual learning style models that instructors and trainers can consider in their efforts. It should be evident to those responsible for teaching and training that an increased understanding and use of learning style data can provide them with important information. Most importantly, each teaching or training endeavor will have learners with disparate learning style preferences and a variety of learning strengths and weaknesses that have been developed through earlier learning experiences, analytical abilities, and a host of other experiences they bring with them.

To enhance learning, instructors and trainers must recognize that individuals learn and teach differently, and what may be an optimal learning or training method for one may discourage another. Indeed, instructors and trainers should make sure that a variety of training or learning opportunities are presented to students and trainees to increase the likelihood of advancing learning.

This chapter is intended to provide a brief review of key points discussed in this book and to highlight other ideas that will increase effectiveness in understanding, assessing, and using learning styles to enhance learning.

ASSESSING LEARNING AND TEACHING STYLES

Campbell (1991) has recently noted that there are at least 32 commercially published instruments being used by researchers and educators to assess the different dimensions of learning style. The instruments vary in length, format, and complexity. Some require special training to administer and interpret, whereas others can be given by following a few simple directions. Some instruments measure just one dimension of style, whereas others measure two or three.

Although the different instruments have many similarities and basically attempt to measure learning style preferences, the terminology used to label the learning styles varies widely, as suggested by Curry (1987) and in Chapter 2 of this book. As can be seen in the discussion throughout this book, there are many ways of describing and assessing learning styles — that is, the typical ways a person behaves, feels, and processes information in learning situations. The essence of the models briefly mentioned thus far described similar phenomena observed from different vantage points — much like the blind men who were explaining an elephant by reporting only certain parts of its body. Thus, learning style is demonstrated in that pattern of behavior and performance by which an individual approaches educational experiences. It is the way in which each person absorbs and retains information and skills; regardless of how that process is described, it is dramatically different for each person.

As highlighted throughout this book (and particularly in Chapters 2 and 3), over the years many diagnostic instruments have been developed, each with its specific intent and measuring specific types of factors. The instrument selected should generally be based on the level of instruction.

As a means of summarizing some of the discussion throughout this book on learning style instruments, this chapter provides some additional discussion on several ways of describing and assessing learning styles that can be used by the instructor in his or her learning initiatives.

Honey and Mumford: Four Learning Styles

Honey and Mumford (1986a and b) have produced four basic styles of learning found in managers, with fairly full descriptions of each style. In addition, they produced an 80-item questionnaire called the Learning Styles Questionnaire (LSQ) (respondents are asked to agree or disagree), which may be used as a more objective way of determining which style an individual falls into. The vast majority of these items are behavioral, that is, they describe an action that someone might or might not take. Occasionally an item probes a preference or belief rather than a manifest behavior. The LSQ is scored by awarding one point for each ticked item. The LSQ is designed to probe the relative strengths of four different learning styles (activist, reflector, theorist, and pragmatist).

Activists prefer to learn from immediate experiences and new challenges. They are bored with implementation and longer-term consolidation and are the life and soul of the managerial party. Reflectors prefer to observe data before making conclusions. They like to consider possible angles and implications before making a move, so they tend to be cautious. They enjoy observing other people in action and often take a back seat at meetings. Theorists adapt and integrate information in an objective manner. They prize rationality and logic, tend to be detached and analytical, and are unhappy with subjective or ambiguous experiences. They assemble disparate facts into coherent theories. They like to make things tidy and fit them into rational schemes. Pragmatists prefer to test ideas and theories in practice. They respond to problems and opportunities as a challenge (the activists probably would not recognize them as problems and opportunities).

Grasha-Reichmann: Three Styles of Learning

Reichmann (1974) classifies three learning styles (dependent, collaborative, and independent) with the Grasha-Reichmann Learning Styles Questionnaire (Reichmann, 1974). The Grasha-Reichmann Learning Styles Questionnaire consists of 90 items and has a self-report scale. A person who scores high as a dependent learner generally prefers a teacher-directed, highly structured course with explicit reading assignments, explicit class assignments, and a predetermined number of tests. The dependent learner would most likely prefer a straightforward lecture without term papers, but if a term paper is to be assigned, the dependent learner would want the topic to be assigned by the teacher, with fairly detailed instructions. A person who scores high as a collaborative learner prefers a discussion class with as much interaction as possible. The collaborative learner prefers group projects and collective assignments, such as case studies. The person who scores high as an independent learner likes to have some influence on the content and structure of the course. This type of student would like some role in the determination of the material covered, the number of tests given, and so forth. Independent learners would prefer that the teacher serve as a resource person rather than as a formal lecturer. If a paper is to be assigned, independent learners would prefer to choose their own topic instead of having the teacher assign a specific topic.

Dunn and Dunn: The Five Elements of Learning Style

Dunn and Dunn (1978) suggest that learning style is based on an individual's response to five categories of elements: environmental, emotional, sociological, physical, and psychological. An individual's needs or preferences in each category add up to his or her learning style.

The Dunns' model is a complex, comprehensive picture of the needs and preferences that influence how — or whether — we learn something. It acknowledges that learners differ in their reliance on auditory, visual, tactile, and kinesthetic perception processes; in their orientations of self, peers, and authorities; in the power of their motivation to learn; and in the strength of their sense of responsibility for the results of the process.

It admits that individuals differ in their needs for mobility; in their daytime and nighttime energy levels; in their intake needs — do they need to smoke, chew gum, or drink something when they are concentrating? The Dunns' model is unique among the models discussed here in its coverage of various environmental and physical elements of learning style and its recognition that people respond differently to their surroundings in a learning situation, especially if what they are learning is complex or difficult. The Dunns' emphasis upon various environmental and physical elements of learning is important for those responsible for training to understand in the design of training programs and training environments most conducive to efficient and effective training.

Price, Dunn and Dunn: Productivity Environmental Preference Survey

Responses to 100 items on this Likert-type scale (Price, Dunn, & Dunn, 1982) produce a profile clustered around 21 different elements. The Productivity Environmental Preference Survey is designed to identify and analyze the conditions that encourage an individual's best performance in such things as solving problems, making decisions, and learning. It is concerned with how a person prefers to learn, not why, and reveals the pattern of needs and preferences that is his or her learning style.

Murrell: Four Learning Models for Managers

Murrell's (1987) model (see Chapter 11 for a more detailed discussion of the model) was designed exclusively for managers and introduces four domains of learning based on a person's preference for cognitive or affective learning and the person's preference for concrete or abstract experiences. Responses to a 20-item questionnaire (Learning Model Instrument) result in four learning domains (feeling planner, participative implementer, task implementer, and thinking planner). The feeling planners enjoy learning situations that allow them to learn with people in concrete situations but give limited opportunity to get close to them. Participative implementers prefer learning situations that allow them to interact with people and still get their hands dirty. They prefer hands-on experiences and prefer to keep busy. Task implementers prefer learning situations that are task-focused where they can focus on details and specifics in a thoughtful manner. Thinking planners show a preference for learning through task oriented experiences in an environment that contains primarily abstract things, numbers, or printouts.

Other Learning Style Instruments

There are several other commonly used instruments, and their application to the adult learner is not discussed in other chapters. These instruments are the Guglielmino Learning Style Inventory, the Jacobs-Fuhrman Learning Inventory, and the Trainer Type Inventory.

Guglielmino Learning Style Inventory

This instrument is a self-scoring form geared to the young adult and adult learner. It consists of 58 statements, to which the individual responds on a five-point scale. The instrument measures problem solving, creativity, and change. The results are plotted on a grid, and the score measures the readiness of the individual for self-directed or self-paced instruction.

In training, for example, the score would probably indicate the feasibility of deciding between a classroom approach or investing in computer-assisted instruction, contract learning, or independent projects. If, for example, the scores of the majority of the population fell below the norm, it would be a wiser decision to use methods that were group-referenced rather than individualized.

The Jacobs-Fuhrmann Learning Inventory

This particular inventory is of special interest to training and development practitioners because it assesses both the trainer and the trainee style.

This inventory is generally based on Blanchard's theory of managerial style as it relates to maturity levels of the learner and diagnoses three styles: dependent, collaborative, and independent. The dependent learner is essentially one whose learning style is less mature — he or she needs structure, direction, external motivation, reinforcement, and encouragement. The interaction collaborative learner is one who wants interaction and essentially wishes to be partners with the instructor in the process. The independent learner is self-directed, intrinsically motivated, and needs the trainer only as a facilitator or consultant.

The role of the trainer in each of the situations varies in accordance with the dependence of the learner. The expert, director, or authority role, which generally involves the use of passive methods of instruction such as lecturing, demonstrating, assigning, encouraging, testing, reinforcing, and transmitting, is best used with more dependent learners.

In the collaborative role, interaction, questioning, modeling, coordinating, evaluating, and managing are required on the part of the trainer. It becomes a partnership, and the process is interactive.

The facilitator or consultant role of the trainer involves a process of coaching, providing resources, listening, and negotiating and is a minimally directive approach best used with independent learners.

The factor of aging is not relevant to learning style and is not a gauge (Ament, 1990). One can most definitely have a 60-year-old dependent style or an 11-year-old independent. Generally, it would appear that learning maturity is a factor of self-esteem and self-confidence, not chronological factors. This particular inventory is one of the few that measures both learning and training style. It follows current managerial thinking and is consistent in its approach (Ament, 1990).

Trainer Type Inventory

The Trainer Type Inventory (TTI) (Wheeler and Marshall, 1986) is designed to help trainers to identify their preferred training methods in order to:

identify the areas in which they have the greatest skill and expertise, which they can share with other trainers and

identify the areas in which they can attempt to increase their skills, thereby increasing their ability to address all aspects of the adult learning cycle (Kolb & Fry, 1981).

The title "Trainer Type Inventory" reflects an attempt to avoid confusion with Brostrom's (1979) "Training Style Inventory," published in *The 1979 Annual Handbook for Group Facilitation*. The TTI was originally designed in the belief that trainers train others most comfortably using or emphasizing their own preferred learning styles. Wheeler and Marshall hypothesized that, for example, trainers who are abstract conceptualizers probably would feel very comfortable integrating theories with events, making generalizations, and interpreting — and would be most effective in training other abstract conceptualizers as described in Kolb's (1984) model. With this approach, trainers could grow and develop most by expanding their skills to include methods that would appeal to the active experimenters and concrete experiencers in training programs, thus addressing the preferred learning styles of a greater number of trainees. However, Wheeler and Marshall discovered that there was no significant relationship between a trainer's own learning-style and training-style preferences. Nonetheless, the usefulness of the instrument becomes apparent when respondents identify their preferred or typical training styles. Such recognition has proved to be an exciting and valuable experience for many trainers. Further value is found when the respondents share insights, training techniques, and advice with other trainers who want to build skills in areas outside their current repertoires or comfort ranges.

The TTI describes four training approaches, categorized as listener, director, interpreter, or coach. The listener trains the concrete experiencer most effectively and is very comfortable in the activity and publishing steps of the experiential learning cycle. The director obtains the best results from the reflective observer and usually is very comfortable during step 3, processing (particularly in helping trainees to make the transition from "How do I feel about this?" to "Now what?"). The interpreter trains in the style favored by the abstract conceptualizer (step 4, generalizing), and the coach trains in the style favored by the active experimenter (step 5, applying).

Wheeler and Marshall (1986) report that respondents have found the TTI to be valid and useful, particularly as a tool for identifying specific trainer development needs. In addition, some revisions have been made to the instrument to reflect the contributions of respondents. Wheeler and Marshall (1986) emphasize that the TTI is intended for use in professional development work and is not intended to be used as a psychological test.

There is no question that there are other learning and teaching style instruments available in the marketplace. The factors to examine when selecting an instrument are: the age and level of the learner, the ease of implementation, the ease of scoring, the validity of the instrument, and the reliability of measurement.

Such data and sample tests are generally available through the publishers of psychological testing materials. In most cases, sample kits are available that contain the actual instrument, a guidebook, applications, and other such data.

LEARNING STYLE ANALYSIS — HOW GOOD IS THE INSTRUMENTATION TO IDENTIFY LEARNING STYLES?

The purpose of learning style analysis is to identify student strategies for learning and to wed them with instructional or training materials, experiences, instruction, and methods that foster a high rate of return — efficient, lasting achievement within a logical amount of time (Corbett & Smith, 1984). A fundamental prerequisite for use of any analytical device in learning style analysis for teaching or training (or research) is the demonstration of a significant level of reliability and validity for the instruments. The Ohio State University's National Center for Research in Vocational Educational Education published the results of its two-year study of instruments that purportedly identified learning and cognitive styles (Kirby, 1979). Selected instruments were appraised as having "impressive reliability and face and construct validity" (p. 72). Certainly instruments like those would be the ones most appropriate for instructors and trainers to use in choosing learning style instruments.

Selected learning style instruments have been well-researched and reported extensively in the literature; others are the products of interviews by their developers, clinical applications, or other research studies. Instruments that have been validated through experimental investigations represent a more solid foundation. St. John's University's Center for the Study of Learning and Teaching Styles released a report summarizing the known reliability and validity data of many of the better known learning style instruments (Center for the Study of Learning and Teaching Styles, 1983). In addition, interested instructors and trainers should see Ferrell (1983); Curry (1983, 1987, 1990); Veres, Sims, and Shake (1987); Sims, Veres, and Shake (1989); and Sims, Veres, and Locklear (1991) for more recent research on learning style instruments.

THE USE OF LEARNING STYLES AND LEARNING STYLES RESEARCH

Researchers (McCauley & Natter, 1980; Miller, Alway , & McKinley, 1987; Tobias, 1982) indicate that persons with certain styles of learning do better in school than individuals with other styles. One reason for this difference in performance is that instruction, counseling, and other personnel services usually match the learning styles of those groups who find success (Palmer, 1987; Schmeck, 1983). Roberts (1977) reports that there are striking mismatches between students and instructors when learning and teaching styles are compared. While mismatching is appropriate for developmental reasons, students have more positive attitudes toward school and achieve more knowledge and skills when taught, counseled, or advised through their natural or primary style rather than through a style that is secondary or undeveloped, particularly when adjusting to a new situation that creates stress (Charkins, O'Toole, & Wetzel, 1985; Dunn, 1988; Matthews, 1991; Vallerand, 1988), such as beginning experiences in higher education.

According to Kolb (1981, 1984), learning style develops as a consequence of heredity factors, previous learning experiences, and the demands of the present environment. Although learning style is relatively stable, qualitative changes result from maturation and environmental stimuli (Cornett, 1983). Sternberg (1990) argues that styles of thinking and learning, which differ widely among individuals, are as important as levels of ability, and institutions should reward all styles equally through their organizational delivery systems.

With a variety of models, the literature denotes advantages of adjusting services to the learning styles of students. Marshall (1985) found that communication between counselor and client was enhanced when both had similar cognitive styles. Griggs (1985) indicated that students with a high need for structure responded better to the use of formal contracts in counseling that specified desired behavior, expected outcomes, and rewards for meeting specifications of the contract, whereas students with a low need for structure responded well to more open-ended and less well-defined activities and outcomes. When student development staff taught high-risk students about their learning preferences so that they could select instructors with teaching styles that more nearly matched their learning styles, students in the experimental group had better grades after two semesters in school than their counterparts had in the control group (Jenkins, 1981).

Matthews (1991) notes that in some institutions administrators use learning and teaching style information to transfer students to other sections when a problem arises regarding a mismatch of style in a particular class (Claxton, Adams, & Williams, 1982). Because research shows that individuals are inclined to enter academic and vocational fields that are consistent with their own learning styles (Biberman & Buchanan, 1986; Canfield, 1988; Kolb, 1976; Myers & McCauley, 1985; Torbit, 1981), another use for learning style information is career guidance. Also, Claxton and Murrell (1987) reported that administrators used learning style data to successfully change teaching strategies of faculty in departments that had high dropout rates.

Learning style research also suggests that we should recognize the responsibility of the student or trainee in the enhancement of learning as suggested in a recent article (*The Teaching Professor*, 1993): "The most realistic approach to the accommodation of learning styles in teaching programs should involve empowering students through knowledge of their own learning styles" (p. 138). So write Fleming and Mills (1992) in a recent article on the implications of learning style research. Many experts propose that teachers should accommodate learning style differences. Fleming and Mills do not absolve teachers of responsibility, but they shift the primary responsibility to students themselves (*The Teaching Professor*, 1993).

In our view it is the analysis and subsequent discussion of learning styles that is the most useful part of the process, rather than the acquisition of a particular label. Most individuals do not fall entirely into one category. We hope a better understanding of the components of the basic approach to learning as possessed by individuals, rather than black and white and arbitrary definitions will be obtained from this discussion. The learning style can be used in the following ways:

1. It can help an individual to understand her or his own likely approach to learning opportunities, and perhaps how to use that basic approach better. It may be important to note on this point that we take the view that increased self-knowledge is enabling rather than disabling.

2. We feel that it may help the individual increase his or her range of learning; a desirable goal will be that each individual shall have a fully integrated range of learning styles. We suspect that by the time instructors or trainers actually get students or trainees, it may be too late to aim realistically at this goal.

3. It certainly should help instructors, trainers, or advisers to suggest learning opportunities that are congruent with learning style instead of antagonistic to it.

4. The authors believe that instructors should be able to construct learning groups more effectively in the sense of more consciously choosing which students to put with which other students in learning groups or on a work activity. We are clearer about the questions that are opened up here than we are about the answers. Should abstract conceptualizers and concrete experiencers be put together?

5. Perhaps part of the answer to the last question is derived from the view that we can help people understand what they might learn about each other. It may be that with a group that has devoted some attention to analyzing learning styles and their individual differences, individuals within the group, and perhaps the whole group, will be better able to make use of the skills available in it. For example, instead of seeing the reflective observer as a non-contributor, he or she may be capable of contributing in a particular way. Perhaps, more importantly, we should be able to assess better potential relationships of learning style between students and instructors. It is easy to see that a reflective observer will have significant difficulties in working with and learning from a concrete experiencer. Again reality obtrudes; it is likely that the learning styles reflect basic individual patterns and the discomfort is likely to arise in many areas other than that of learning.

6. Students and instructors can refine and improve their understanding of learning and learning skills. This seems to be an area that is in need of continued study. Clearly we should be doing more to help students to improve their skills. We should be capable of relating skills to particular learning styles and particular learning opportunities. Examples of learning skills are: the ability to establish effectiveness criteria for one's self, the ability to measure one's effectiveness in different situations, the ability to identify one's own learning needs, the ability to take advantage of learning opportunities, the ability to review one's learning processes, the ability to listen to others, the capacity to accept help, the ability to face unwelcome information, the ability to take risks and tolerate anxieties, the ability to analyze what other successful learners do, the ability to know one's self, the ability to share information with others, the ability to review what has been learned, and the ability to help others learn.

Clearly instructors should help students improve their skills and should be capable of relating skills to particular learning styles and learning or training opportunities. In our view, learning style information can be crucial to an instructor's credibility and ability to place a student in relevant learning or training experiences. Instructors and trainers must continually find a response to the question of how learning styles and the associated learning skills relate to learning or training opportunities.

It is not our attempt to argue that learning styles are more important than methods of determining learning needs or that they are more important than alternative processes for learning. We are certainly saying that, unless learning and teaching styles and methods are assessed together, the likelihood of enhancing learning is much diminished and owes more to luck than those in higher education and training should allow.

Whatever instrument is used to assess learning styles and whatever labels are given to those learning styles, students and instructors need to be aware of their own preferred learning styles and the particular characteristics inherent with each of those styles. With this knowledge, students will understand the learning process better, and instructors will understand the teaching process better.

Because many studies (Campbell, 1991) have indicated that the most successful students in a classroom happen to have the learning preferences that match the learning preferences of the instructor, effective instructors must attempt to devise strategies other than those that they prefer to use. Instructors must reach those students who are mismatched with their own learning and teaching style. Many instructors have been adding instructional techniques to their repertoire for years just for the sake of variety; now there is a better reason for doing so. Not only has some research shown that many students' grades are higher when their learning preferences are matched with the instructor's but also, in most cases, students report higher scores on instructor effectiveness and course evaluations (Campbell, 1991).

KEY FACTORS OF LEARNING STYLE

Unquestionably, all of us, by the time we reach adulthood, have developed our own unique learning patterns, mental processes that follow an individualized path leading to mastery of material. When all of the research is dissected, three facts about learning style become evident.

1. By the time we reach adulthood, each of us has developed our own methods of learning. That is, adult learners each have a unique and well-established style.
2. Higher education instructors as well as trainers have developed methods of delivering materials, putting together sessions, and transferring content

to their participants. That is, instructors and trainers also have a fairly well-established teaching or training style.

3. The more compatible the style of learning is with the style of instructing or training, the more likely it is that there will be a positive learning or teaching experience.

Interestingly enough, colleges and universities often develop dominant teaching styles through their organizational culture, as do training departments. It is perhaps for this reason, among many others, that learners will, if given the option, select one institution over another, one instructor or trainer over another, or one approach to a program over another. For example, an individual who is primarily a visual learner may elect correspondence courses over classroom participation simply because he or she feels more at ease with self-paced, self-administered learning experiences.

As another example, institutions will at times adapt their style to the predominant style of their learners, as was the case cited by Ament (1990) with the licensed practical nurse training program at one community college. Understanding individual differences in pace of learning, the community college spent many hours of time and invested many thousands of dollars adapting components of its Nursing Refresher program to self-paced instructional modules. This not merely allowed them to be more flexible in their admissions to the program, but also freed instructional time for coaching and mentoring students. The majority of students responded exceptionally well to the adaptation, and those who did not were given the option of doing programming through the regular classroom system of instruction. In the final analysis, the majority of students were accommodated in relation to their individual style and were successful in completing the refresher program. Ament (1990) notes that, because of the shortages in the profession, this meant more nurses could return to work, and a significant improvement in the critical shortage was evidenced in the long run.

DIAGNOSING LEARNING, TEACHING, AND TRAINING STYLE

Instructors and trainers must recognize that there are a few considerations that should be made as a precursor to using instrumentation of any kind. Any instrument is merely an indicator — it develops a database from which decisions can then be made in a more objective manner. There is no correct style. Instruments merely give a picture of the range of individual styles and may give an indication of the dominant style of a given population. Style is a component of many factors such as personality, brain-dominance, prior learning, aptitudes, abilities, and other factors and is as individual as a fingerprint. Testing can only give patterns of individuals and provide norms. The intent is to provide data to make decisions and not to provide labels from which judgments can be made.

Instruments are limited in the data they provide. In spite of the accuracy of the particular instrument, each instrument in itself is designed to diagnose only a limited facet of the entire process. In order to utilize the instrument effectively, one must realize the strengths and limitations of the tool and recognize that it can provide only the specific data it was intended to measure.

There is no right or wrong teaching or training style. Again, each instrument is intended merely to measure data and give facts — nothing more. The application may illustrate that one style is completely compatible with 10 percent, 50 percent, or 100 percent of the class. That simply means that there is a match within a specific range.

Style can be varied in accordance with methodology — we can, for example, deal with a learning situation through lecture, case study, games, or other methods. Varying from lecture to film or from lecture to case approach may broaden the factor of compatibility and enhance learning simply because we are utilizing other factors that may be a component of learner style.

Even when style is diagnosed accurately for both learner and trainer, learning outcomes can differ because of pacing. Regardless of instruments and accuracy, the results of any tool must be taken within a broad context and used merely as normative data. Individual differences will occur, and it is very unlikely that there will ever be 100 percent compatibility in learning and teaching style within any group. What we aim for, therefore, is to diagnose the norm and adapt to a group norm while taking individual differences into account.

BEGINNING A LEARNING STYLE APPROACH

Many steps can be taken to begin a learning style approach to teaching, depending upon the course or subject being taught. The following is a list of strategies that can be successful in most classes:

Allow students to select their own seats — front or back, near the windows or door or near friends.

Make some short-term assignments (due the next class meeting) and some long-term assignments (due in two, three, or four weeks).

Combine individual assignments with some group assignments.

Give step-by-step instructions when they are needed, but encourage students to experiment on their own when that is appropriate.

Vary written feedback on papers with verbal comments to individual students.

Allow students to help each other learn and work together when possible.

Give at least one major oral assignment.

Allow students to talk to each other while they are working at their individual assignments when it is appropriate to do so.

Allow extra credit for special creative endeavors.

Give additional chances to earn grade points other than written tests.

Give some directions orally, some in writing.

Provide constant encouragement for students who are slow in understanding or performing or who have trouble expressing themselves in writing.

Allow students to complete some assignments outside of class.

Make class assignments as relevant as possible. Show how readings and projects fit into real-life situations.

In some cases, mismatches between the instructor's learning style and the student's learning style can be valuable because this mismatch forces students to stretch or "style-flex" as they use their nonpreferred learning modes. By the time students have reached higher education, most are skilled at this adapting. Nevertheless, many college or university students still need encouragement as well as assistance in adjusting their learning style to the teaching style of their instructors.

Successfully dealing with the challenge of matched or mismatched learning styles can be rewarding to instructors. They need to be aware of the learning styles of their students, knowledgeable about the characteristics of different styles, and willing to accommodate student learning preferences when appropriate. When instructors know that they have students who have a strong preference for social involvement, they can give them an opportunity for group assignments, give those students positive feedback about their accomplishments, and provide a warm, personal learning environment. For students who strive for independence, instructors can use a more personal approach. They can plan lectures and problem-solving activities, allow students to set their own goals, and give students descriptive feedback.

Instructors who want to implement the use of learning styles into their courses need to understand that doing so is not a complicated endeavor. As highlighted throughout this book, many commercial instruments are available, or instructors can construct their own. Once instructors can identify the different learning style preferences of their students, the next step is to try to use some different approaches to teaching that might appeal to those students who are mismatched. Instructors need to make sure that all students are exposed to a variety of instructional strategies that foster academic success and lead to more positive self-concepts.

In conclusion, learning styles can be used by instructors and trainers in the following ways:

to give feedback to trainees on their own preferred styles of learning and domains of strength;

to help a new group of human resource management specialists or trainees to learn more about one another in order to work together more effectively; and

to provide an overall explanation of the training environment so that participants will receive a conceptual understanding of the experiential approach to learning as suggested by adult learning theorists (Kolb, 1984; Knowles, 1984).

SUMMARY

It is urgent that those responsible for teaching and training in higher education and other organizations recognize, accept, and understand diversity in regard to learning styles. Acceptance of style as a fundamental strength of each person contributes to the development of self-esteem and, ultimately, to achievement. When students have feelings of accomplishment and satisfaction, the retention rate is higher than when students feel frustration and cognitive dissonance (Charkins, O'Toole, & Wetzel, 1985).

It is also important that instructors and trainers first know and care and then teach about learning style, thus helping students and trainees understand their own strengths and weaknesses. Orientation sessions before the beginning of school and orientation classes during the first semester appear to be a practical starting point in colleges and universities. Derry and Murphy (1986) indicated that one major educational objective is to teach students how to learn and how to manage and monitor their selection and use of various learning styles and strategies. Therefore, instructors have a responsibility to help students develop primary and secondary styles of learning, as well as adjusting instructional delivery and assignments to strengths of students. As students adjust to the college or university environment and mature beyond the learning style restrictions of their first year, the development of a repertoire of learning styles becomes important to the student expecting to obtain a degree.

It is emphatically necessary that instructors and trainers use a variety of teaching and training techniques. The traditional lecture and independent project fit the learning style of only some learners. It may be advisable for instructors to give a variety of work assignments and to have several bases for assigning grades.

Administrators should hire faculty and other support staff with diverse learning styles because such styles guide teaching, counseling, and communication practices. Many instructors tend to be introverts and to think abstractly or intuitively (Hanson, Silver, & Strong, 1984). Thus, there may be little match of teacher and learner. To serve themselves better, therefore, learners need choice in the selection of instructors and other personnel who work with them, so they can select persons who more nearly match their own styles. Advisors are able to assist in the selection process, helping students enhance their learning and find academic success in colleges and universities.

Institutions of higher education should encourage faculty to do research in the area of learning style and teaching strategies. Information on styles, when linked with other data on students, holds great promise for helping instructors to improve their teaching and enhance student learning.

REFERENCES

Ament, L. 1990. Learning and training: A matter of style. *Industrial and Commercial Training*, *22*(3), 13–16.

Biberman, G., & Buchanan, J. 1986. Learning style and study skills differences across business and other academic majors. *Journal of Education for Business*, *61*(7), 303–307.

Brostrom, R. 1979. Training style inventory (TSI). In J. E. Jones and J. W. Pfeiffer (Eds.), *The 1979 annual handbook for group facilitation*. San Diego, CA: University Associates.

Campbell, B. J. 1991, July/August. Planning for a student learning style. *Journal of Education for Business*, pp. 356–358.

Canfield, A. A. 1988. *Learning styles inventory manual*. Los Angeles, CA: Western Psychological Services.

Center for the Study of Teaching and Learning Styles. 1983. *Learning styles network instrument assessment analysis*. Jamaica, NY: St. John's University.

Charkins, R. J., O'Toole, D. M., & Wetzel, J. N. 1985. Linking teacher and learning styles with student achievement and attitude. *Journal of Economic Education*, *16*, 111–120.

Claxton, C., Adams, D., & Williams, D. 1982. Using student learning styles in teaching. *AAHE Bulletin*, *34*, 7–10.

Claxton, C. S., & Murrell, P. H. 1987. *Learning styles: Implications for improving educational practices*. ASHE-ERIC Higher Education Report No. 4. Washington, DC: Association for the Study of Higher Education.

Corbett, S. S., & Smith, W. H. 1984, Autumn. Identifying student learning styles: Proceed with caution! *The Modern Language Journal*, *68*(3), 212–221.

Cornett, C. W. 1983. *What should you know about teaching and learning styles*. Bloomington, IN: Phi Delta Kappa Foundation.

Curry, L. 1990, October. A critique of the research on learning styles. *Educational Leadership*, pp. 51–52.

Curry, L. 1987. *Integrating concepts of cognitive or learning style: A review with attention to psychometric standards*. Ottawa: Canadian College of Health Service Executives.

Curry, L. 1983. Individualized CME: The potential and the problem. *The Royal College of Physicians and Surgeons of Canada Annals*, *16*(6), 512–526.

Derry, J. J., & Murphy, D. A. 1986. Designing systems that train ability: From theory to practice. *Review of Educational Research*, *56*, 1–39.

Dunn, R. 1988. Teaching students through their perceptual strengths or preferences. *Journal of Reading*, *31*, 304–309.

Dunn, R., & Dunn, K. 1978. *Teaching students through their individual learning styles: A practical approach*. Reston, VA: Prentice-Hall.

Ferrell, B. G. 1983, February. A factor analytic comparison of four learning styles instruments. *Journal of Educational Psychology*, *75*(1), 33–39.

Fleming, N. D., & Mills, C. 1992. Not another inventory, rather a catalyst for reflections. *To Improve the Academy*, *11*, 137–155.

Griggs, S. A. 1985. Counseling for individual learning styles. *Journal of Counseling and Development*, *64*, 202–205.

Hanson, J. R., Silver, H. F., & Strong, R. 1984. Research on the roles of intuition and feeling. *Roeper Review*, *6*(3), 4–7.

Helping students understand how they learn. 1993, April. *The Teaching Professor*, pp. 3–4.

Honey, P., & Mumford, A. 1986a. *The manual of learning styles*. Maidenhead, Berkshire: Peter Honey.

Honey, P., & Mumford, A. 1986b. *The learning styles questionnaire*. Maidenhead, Berkshire: Peter Honey.

Jenkins, J. 1981. *Promising persistence through cognitive style analysis and self-management techniques*. ERIC Document Reproduction Service No. ED 22 142. Carbondale, IL: Southern Illinois University.

Kirby, P. 1979. *Cognitive style, learning style and transfer skill acquisition*. Columbus, OH: National Center for Vocational Education.

Knowles, M. S. 1984. *The adult learner: A neglected species* (3rd ed.). Houston, TX: Gulf.

Kolb, D. A. 1984. *Experiential learning: Experience as the source of learning and development*. Englewood Cliffs, NJ: Prentice Hall.

Kolb, D. A. 1981. Learning styles and disciplinary differences. In A. W. Chickering and Associates (Eds.), *The modern American college* (pp. 232–253). San Francisco: Jossey-Bass.

Kolb, D. A. 1976. *Learning style inventory technical manual*. Boston: McBer & Company.

Kolb, D. A., & Fry, R. 1981. Experiential learning theory and learning experiences in liberal arts education. *New Directions for Experiential Learning*. San Francisco: Jossey-Bass.

Marshall, E. A. 1985. Relationship between client learning style and preference for counselor approach. *Counselor Education and Supervision*, *24*(4), 358–359.

Matthews, D. B. 1991. The effects of learning style on grades of first-year college students. *Research in Higher Education*, *32*(3), 253–266.

McCauley, M. H., & Natter, F. L. 1980. *(Myers-Briggs) Psychological type differences in education*. Gainesville, FL: Center for Application of Psychological Type.

Miller, C. D., Alway, M., & McKinley, D. L. 1987. Effects of learning styles and strategies on academic success. *Journal of College Student Personnel*, *28*(5), 400–404.

Murrell, K. L. 1987. The learning-model instrument: An instrument based on the learning model for managers. *The 1987 annual: Developing human resources* (pp. 109–119). San Diego, CA: University Associates.

Myers, I. B., & McCauley, M. H. 1985. *A guide to the development and use of the Myers-Briggs type indicators*. Palo Alto, CA: Consulting Psychologists Press.

Palmer, P. J. 1987. Community, conflict, and ways of knowing. *Change*, *19*, 20–25.

Price, G. E., Dunn, R., & Dunn, K. 1982. *PEPS (Productivity environmental preference survey manual)* (rev. ed.). Lawrence, KS: Price Systems.

Reichmann, S. 1974. *The refinement and construct validation of the Grasha-Reichmann student learning styles scales*. Unpublished master's thesis, University of Cincinnati.

Roberts, D. V. 1977. Personalized learning processes. *Revista Review Inter-Americana*, *7*, 139–143.

Schmeck, R. R. 1983. Learning styles of college students. In R. F. Dillon and R. R. Schmeck (Eds.), *Individual differences in cognition* (pp. 223–279). New York:

Academic Press.

Sims, R. R., & Veres, J. G. 1985, Summer. A practical program for training job analysts. *Public Personnel Management, 14*(2), 131–137.

Sims, R. R., Veres, J. G., & Locklear, T. 1991. An investigation of a modified version of Kolb's Revised Learning Style Inventory. *Educational and Psychological Measurement, 5*(1), 143–150.

Sims, R. R., Veres, J. G., & Shake, L. G. 1989. An exploratory examination of the convergence between the learning styles questionnaire and the learning style inventory II. *Educational and Psychological Measurement, 49*(1), 227–233.

Sternberg, R. J. 1990. Thinking styles: Keys to understanding student performance. *Phi Delta Kappan, 71*(5), 366–371.

Tobias, G. 1982. When do instructional methods make a difference? *Educational Record, 11*, 4–9.

Torbit, G. 1981. Counselor learning style: A variable in career choice. *Canadian Counsellor, 15*, 193–197.

Vallerand, A. H. 1988. Differences in test performance and learner satisfaction among nurses with varying autonomy levels. *Journal of Continuing Education in Nursing, 19*(5), 216–222.

Veres, J. G., Sims, R. R., & Shake, L. G. 1987. The reliability and classification stability of the learning styles inventory in corporate settings. *Educational and Psychological Measurement, 47*(4), 1127–1133.

Wheeler, M., & Marshall, J. 1986. The Trainer Type Inventory: Identifying training style preferences. In J. W. Pfeiffer and L. D. Goodstein (Eds.), *The 1986 annual: Developing human resources*, pp. 87–97.

Index

About the Contributors

James A. Anderson is the Dean for the Division of Undergraduate Studies and directs the Teaching Excellence Initiative for faculty at North Carolina State University. He has recently published one of the few handbooks for the formal assessment of diversity in higher education.

Richard W. Bishop is a Senior Consultant in the Applied Sciences Group of Booz-Allen & Hamilton, Inc. and a graduate student at the University of West Florida. His academic interest is culture and its influence on learning.

William T. Geary is Associate Professor of Business Administration at the College of William and Mary. His research interests include accounting education, behavioral accounting, and health care.

Robert L. Hewitt is Associate Professor of Social Work and Field Practicum Coordinator at Shippensburg University. He has published and presented a number of articles and papers on issues concerning adolescence, family models, family policy issues, and direct social work practice.

Leslie K. Hickcox is an Associate Faculty in the departments of Communication, Human Studies, and Learning Assessment at Marylhurst College. She has designed and implemented programs in higher and adult education since 1975 and has presented learning style workshops throughout the United States, Australia, and New Zealand.

David A. Kolb is the E. Mandell de Windt Professor in Leadership and Enterprise Development in the Department of Organizational Behavior at the Weatherhead School of Management, Case Western Reserve University. Dr. Kolb's book, *Experiential Learning: Experience as the Source of Learning and Development*, is an integrative statement of 15 years of research on learning styles and the learning process.

Kenneth L. Murrell is a Professor of Management at the University of West Florida and president of Empowerment Leadership Systems. He is also coauthor of *Empowerment in Organizations: How to Spark Exceptional Performance* and has written over 100 articles, technical papers, chapters, book reviews, and research reports.

William Purkiss is a Professor of Communication Studies at Chaffey College.

Mary Ann Rainey is an independent Organization Development Consultant and on the faculty of the Gestalt Institute of Cleveland.

J. E. Romero-Simpson is an Associate Professor in the Department of Management, University of Miami. Dr. Romero is the author of many total quality management and learning-related articles in both English and Spanish.

Ronald R. Sims is Director of the Masters in Business Administration Program and the Floyd Dewey Gottwald, Jr., Professor of Business at the College of William and Mary. He is the author or coauthor of more than 60 articles and 11 books. Among his books are *Ethics in Organizations: A Call for Renewal*; *Training Enhancement in Government Organizations*; *Diversity and Differences: An Agenda for Answers and Questions* (with Robert Dennehy); and *Changes and Challenges for Human Resource Professionals* and *Total Quality Management in Higher Education: Is It working? Why or Why Not?* (both with Serbrenia J. Sims).

Serbrenia J. Sims is an independent researcher and consultant. She has published a number of articles and books on a variety of training and higher education topics. Her most recent books are: *Diversifying Historically Black Colleges and Universities: A New Higher Education Paradigm*; *Student Outcomes Assessment*, and *Managing Institutions of Higher Education into the 21st Century* (with Ronald R. Sims).

Blue Wooldridge is an Associate Professor in the Department of Political Science and Public Administration, Virginia Commonwealth University.

ISBN 0-313-29278-7
90000>
EAN
9 780313 292781
HARDCOVER BAR CODE